Winners Don't Quit
Today They Call Me Doctor

by

Dr. Pamela McCauley-Bell

**Infinite Possibilities Publishing Group, Inc.
Florida**

This book is available at special quantity discounts for bulk purchases for sales promotions, premiums, fundraising, or educational use.

For details, write:
Special Markets, IP Publishing Group
P.O. Box 150823
Altamonte Springs, Florida 32715-0823
e-mail: info@ippublishingonline.com

IP Books
Published by Infinite Possibilities Publishing Group, Inc.
P.O. Box 150823
Altamonte Springs, Florida 32715-0823
email: info@ippublishingonline.com
Website: www.ippublishingponline.com

Copyright © 2003 by Dr. Pamela McCauley-Bell

All rights reserved. No part of this publication may be produced, stored in a retrieval system or transmitted in any form or by any means electronic, mechanical, photocopying, recording or otherwise, without the prior written permission of the publisher or except in the case of brief quotations embodied in critical articles and reviews.

Cover Photographs by:
Michael Cairns
Wet Orange Studios
www.michaelcairnes.com

Cover Design and text layout by:
Designs By Rachelle, Rachelle Harris
www.designsbyrachelle.com

Library of Congress Control Number: 2003113551

ISBN: 0-9729912-2-0

Printed in the United States of America

10 9 8 7 6 5 4 3 2

"In a society that finds scores of people whining about their circumstance, or status in life, it is refreshing to read a book that reaffirms fortitude and will power. In her personal story, Dr. McCauley-Bell, has brought clear focus to the ingredients needed to realize one's full potential"

- Howard. G. Adams, Ph.D. (Doc)
President, H.G. Adams & Associates, Inc.

"A truly inspiring story about how challenges in life can be overcome with faith, determination, and perserverance; A book that will motivate and empower you. It will have you exclaiming, "I TOO can do it!!!"

-Kim and Kitty Elshot
Central Florida, Process Engineers

TABLE OF CONTENTS

Dedication

Acknowledgements

Foreword

Introduction

What Do You Mean.....I'm Pregnant!?   16

She's Depending On Me   65

Make Me Wanna Holla!!   103

Never Can Say Goodbye   118

The 48 Hour Day   128

I Got Work To Do   160

A Dawning In Dallas   204

A Way Out Of No Way   225

This book is dedicated to my parents, Maurice McCauley, Sr. and LaFrance McCauley. Thank you for believing in me. I love you both, more than words can ever say.

With all my love,

Pamela

ACKNOWLEDGEMENTS

The completion of Winners Don't Quit...Today They Call Me Doctor" is the result of immense support from countless loving, giving and thoughtful individuals who sowed generously into my life for over twenty-five years. I thank God for His guidance and wisdom in leading me to the fulfillment of my dream to publish this book.

Most recently, I must thank my publisher, Ms. Shelley Parris for being a wonderful woman of vision and excellence. Shelley, you are lighting a candle for the world. I must also thank IP Publishing Director of Public Relations, Ms. Renee' Crooks, editor Ms. Tremene Triplett of ISL, Inc. and Ms. Diane Sears for your support in creating the Winners Don't Quit Movement. To my Soror Vanessa Echols, I extend my heartfelt thanks for your eagerness to support me in the preparation of the forward and serving as "Quality Control" in the production of this book.

For supporting me in my early years, I wish to thank Mrs. Sandi Bennet, Ms. LaMonia Parker, Revered W.B. Parker, Ms. Angel Carr, Ms. Patrice Miles, Ms. Karen Self, and Dr. Nancy Knox. Mrs. Bennett, thank you for seeing the potential in me even when I didn't see it. As for my loving family I would like to thank Mrs. Camille McCauley, Lewis and Annie Stokes and various other Carr and McCauley family members.

During my undergraduate time at the University of Oklahoma when I needed so much support, I wish to thank the office of the Minority Engineering Program, Dr. Adedeji Badiru, Dr. Jerry Purswell, Dr. Laguros, Dr. Bob Foote, Joe Marshall, Manuel Bustos, Karla Greene-Bonzie, Jaquine Littel and Sandy Kay Welch. Your support and faith in me made the difference at one of the most challenging times of my life. Dr. Howard G. Adams and the GEM Program thank you from the bottom of my heart for believing in me and planting the seed of a graduate degree in engineering. Doc, you changed my life. I also want to thank the National Science Foundation for the innovativeness in developing the NSF Creativity Fellowship.

As my journey continues and the efforts to produce this book became difficult, I would not have completed this without the support of an incredible network of friends including Ms. Marsha Reeves-Jews, Ms. Dixie Garr and Ms. Leisa Smith. I also want to thank my dear friends Ms. Mercedes Hutchinson-Mapp and Mr. Jimmy Walker for your friendship through the years. My sincerest appreciation goes to my Soror and Little Sis, Dr. Lesia Crumpton-Young for encouraging and focusing me in some of the most challenging moments of completing this manuscript. To my wonderful Prayer Partner, Sandra Jeter, thank you for always praying for me, teaching me the importance of tithing and making me laugh no matter what was happening in my life. To "First Prayer Partner" and best friend Evelyn Robinson, your undying faith in me, heartfelt prayers, generous spirit and constant ear to listen have been a consistent source of strength to me. My dear friend and business partner, Karen Waltensperger your faith and support of this book and my other inspirational efforts has been a gift from heaven.

Mrs. Jill DeNucci, I would like to say thank you from the bottom of my heart for your support in so many areas including editing the details of the manuscript, keeping me on schedule and making sure I had lunch and your famous coffee. To Mrs. Juanita Taylor thank you for your prayers, organizational skills and excellence in all that you do. As for my business partner and lifelong friend, Dr. Mark Waltensperger, I don't know how I will ever be able to thank you for your unwavering faith in me and your commitment to helping me achieve this and many of my other visions.

To my sisters Mrs. LaWanna Porter, Ms. Pipina Figaro-Smith and Ms. Princess Hill, thank you for loving me and still going on our annual trip even when I am difficult! I love you all so much. To My Sister Marcella, whose memory I will always cherish, thank you for encouraging me early in life to go for my dreams. My dear Big Brother Mr. Maurice McCauley, Jr., you are my unspoken hero. Thank you for always loving me, supporting me and believing in me.

To my parents, Mr. & Mrs. Maurice McCauley, Sr. I say thank you for the inspiration, love and faith in me. You have shown me the meaning of unconditional love. I want to thank my beautiful daughter, Annette Cherice for being a source of energy, enthusiasm and encouragement every step of my life - Bitty Doll, I love you. To my in-laws, Mr. & Mrs. Eureal Bell, thank you for raising such a wonderful son and finally, my dear husband, Michael Bell, thank you for loving me, believing in me and sharing your life with me.

Foreword

Before you read Winners Don't Quit, you should know it was written for a specific group of people: those who have achieved their life goals, those who are still working on their goals and those who have given up. In other words, it was written with you and your situation in mind. But this is not just a book. It's a life plan for every living, breathing soul.

I heard Pamela McCauley-Bell's story in the mid-90s, before we ever met face-to-face. A friend who attended a girl's empowerment workshop in Orlando, returned from the event, excitedly telling me about the accomplishments of a sharp young woman who was pregnant and unwed at 15, on welfare, a survivor of domestic violence and went on to become the first African-American woman in Oklahoma to earn a PhD in Engineering. I will admit it; I was skeptical. As a television journalist by trade, I'm trained to question everything and everyone. It sounded like a movie of the week drama. The next time I heard about Dr. McCauley-Bell, one of my colleagues at WFTV in Orlando was reporting on a story about a local woman who was named a finalist in NASA's astronaut program. It was the same Dr. Pamela McCauley-Bell. We finally met a few months later when I served as MC for an event where she was the guest speaker. My skepticism was over. This woman is for real.

As you read her life story, perhaps like me, you'll find that Pamela's story is also yours. I was not a pregnant teen. I am not an engineer. But I know what it is to set life goals that some will laugh at and others think are unrealistic. Try explaining that you want to be a television news anchor while growing up in an area where most people in your neighborhood and your family didn't even dare to dream of going to college.

Anyone who has had to overcome adversities and setbacks in life or move ahead despite the naysayers will identify with Dr. McCauley-Bell's life journey. She is dispelling the myth that success requires a personal cheerleading section encouraging you every step of the way. Instead, she is issuing a challenge for you to encourage yourself. This is a life plan that you can put into action right now, today. She is not offering the same old keys to success that you've heard since you could read. This is a real story of determination and vision that can be used by anyone as guidance to set goals and identify what they need to do to achieve their dreams. Dr. Pamela McCauley-Bell is proof that this plan of action works.

So if you are serious about making a positive change in your life, if you are ready to commit yourself to moving forward, then I challenge you to read about a woman who could have been just another statistic, someone who could have given in and given up, but, instead, she is someone who forged ahead when everything logical said she should have given up.

If you are ready to make that commitment, turn the page. Find out why WINNERS DON'T QUIT!

Vanessa Echols
Morning Anchor WFTV

INTRODUCTION

As soon as the applause died down, I walked away from the front of the cafeteria and settled back into my seat. As Mrs. Bennett, my former biology teacher at Emerson Alternative School, spoke to the young ladies, she further emphasized the points that I had made. I looked around the room. I noticed all of the hopeful smiles, warm looks, and nods of approval that I received from the faces of the many young women to whom I had just spoken, with whom I had just shared some of my life. I was thrilled to feel like I had genuinely connected with them. But I wanted more. I didn't want to leave them just being impressed with me. No, that would not do it. That would not be enough to keep them, to empower them, to inspire them. If they didn't know before, I wanted them to know today that they had the ability and the power to make an exciting and incredible life for themselves, and for their children. I wanted to walk over to each of them and say: today, make up your mind to do it... yes, you can and should choose to have a great life. I wanted so much for each of them to truly believe that they had the power to make this decision, and I hoped and prayed that they would make this decision-- today. Despite all of the statistics about how they, as teen mothers, would end up on welfare and without hope, I wanted them to know that I was living proof that they didn't have to succumb to that statistic. Yes, it would be challenging but there was a way for them to overcome difficulties such as teen pregnancy, poverty, domestic violence, and other difficulties to make their dreams a reality. This message of hope was for them, and I desperately wanted to make sure that they knew the story of triumph didn't begin or end with me.

After my talk, I was approached by a group of young women, each of them asking if they could call me, or e-mail me, and if there was any way they could stay in touch so that they could be encouraged. I am always eager to encourage young people, and I quickly gave them my e-mail address and office phone numbers. After these exchanges and warm sisterly hugs, I wished them well and asked them to stay in touch. However, as they walked away, my excitement began to diminish. The feeling was oddly replaced by a sense of despair that slowly came over me. I knew that, with me speaking to an average of 8,000 people a year, it would be nearly impossible to offer these young women continual encouragement and support. But I genuinely wanted to be there for them, to encourage them to be all that they could be, and experience the joy of watching them discover their inner strength. I hoped to give them something to hold on to in moments of doubt and a reason to never quit, something to keep them motivated and determined deep down inside. I knew that the only thing that I could give them that would accomplish this tremendous goal was knowledge of their own inner strength and power. Before I could finish this thought, a beautiful young lady approached me. With tears in her eyes, she shared that she was the mother of two young children. The tears began to roll down her face, and all she could say, was "Thank you . . .I'm so proud of you. . . I mean it's really cool what you've done." As she continued to smile and to try to talk through her tears, she hugged me and again said thank you. I felt my face get warm and salty tears filled my eyes. As I fought them back, I realized that she wasn't just saying that she was proud of me. She was also feeling "hope." Hope that she, too, could make a great life for herself and her two children. I swallowed hard and looked in her face. I told her that she had a great future, and that she just needed to choose it. I also told her to work hard, to believe in herself, to create a positive life, and to never quit. She hugged me again, and walked into the hall to return to her class.

At that moment I was totally convinced that I had to do more to reach young women. Though I had been toying with the idea of writing a book, at that moment, I was committed to making this book a reality. I felt a need to write something that would generate hope; that could reach many young people, especially young women, all over the world. I wanted to tell them how much they could do; I wanted to reveal their inner strength to them; I longed to tell them how great their lives could be and how they were in charge of making this decision. I wanted to give them hope and energy to fly with eagles and to reach their dreams. I prayed that something I would say, something I could do, or something I could write would accomplish this goal

Through the pages of this book, my desire is to encourage, motivate, and help all those who I encounter to be all that they can be in attaining and reaching for the their true purpose and goals.

To my dear reader: I'm encouraging you to make that decision today. Choose to have the life you want and deserve. I trust that you want a fulfilling, prosperous, and loving life. I'm here to say that no matter what your current situation, whether you're a welfare recipient, abused wife, drug user, neglected child, overweight teen suffering from food disorders, sexually abused, incarcerated, the most unpopular person in your school, or a person that never received the family support or love that you should have received – whatever your situation -- you, YES YOU, can have a great and successful life. Whatever failures you've experienced are not final. Today, you can turn your life around. Even if no one that you know has succeeded, if no one in your family, no one on your street, no one who looks like you – has accomplished the things that you dream about – YOU can do it. You are in a position to make YOUR dreams come true. The choice is up to you. These techniques are for all of us. If you have not ever experienced any of the previously mentioned issues, but rather have had a good and solid upbringing, full of love, this book can still be a source to encourage and empower you to achieve all that you desire.

How can I speak with so much confidence about something such as your success? How can I so positively talk to you about overcoming obstacles and making your dreams come true?

Because I have seen numerous successful people and they have an important characteristic in common. I call that characteristic "positive living" Positive living simply means having a purpose, believing in yourself - against all odds, understanding the mistakes that you've made and correcting them, so that you can move toward your goals.

I am confident that you can have a life of success and I speak from my own experiences. I have had to deal with the negativity, low expectations, and the consequences of my own poor choices in many instances. Applying the principles of positive living and never quitting was essential for me to rise above my doubts and fears. Positive living also is being willing to believe in yourself despite your shortcomings, having the courage to dream big, believing you can make your dreams come true, even when you fail, learning to love yourself, demonstrating active faith in your dreams, goals and vision and never, ever giving up on yourself.

One of the most inspiring things I did as a teenager was to read Dr. Maya Angelou's *"I Know Why the Caged Bird Sings."* This is a beautifully written and moving account of her early years. Reading a book written by an African American woman moved me and warmed my soul. Each of the beautifully and eloquently composed phrases by Dr. Angelou gave me a kind of inspiration that still gives me chills twenty-five years later. She became one of my greatest "sheros." When I learned that she had overcome so many challenges in her life it became a source of hope for me. Hope that inspired me to dream greater dreams than others thought I should dream and to believe that I could make them come true. It is my desire that you will find that hope and I pray that this book or something you encounter will give you that empowerment to make your dreams come true and that nothing can ever take it away from you.

In addition to empowering you to accomplish your goals, I also hope that this book will help you to feel good about who you are **today** and to encourage you to accept yourself *just as* *you are!* That does not mean that you can't or shouldn't want to make changes, but recognize today that you are a special and unique gift to this earth. Acknowledgement of this means that you know you deserve love, appreciation, and happiness. Of course, as children, our parents are primarily responsible for providing these things. But, with maturity, we must all take responsibility for our lives, our actions, and ourselves. Simply put, we are responsible for our happiness, the people that we allow into our lives and the pursuit of our goals. This again, allows us to see that we really are the ones who will make the decisions about how we will spend our lives. I hope knowing that you have immense control over your future gives you energy, enthusiasm and a path to positive living.

    I look forward to helping you discover the joys of positive living as you move toward making your dreams come true! Yes, it will be challenging, but the rewards are there. I promise you they are real. Always remember: winners don't quit, and you, my friend, are a winner!

CHAPTER 1

WHAT DO YOU MEAN.....I'M PREGNANT!?

I was trying so hard to get comfortable on the patient's bed in the doctor's office. As I lay there with the paper strip crinkling at my every move to position myself, I thought, it couldn't be much longer. Surely it's a waste of time for all of us —my Mom, my brother, and myself — to be here at the doctor's office today. All I needed were a few Rolaids, and maybe a little more Alka-Seltzer, and I'd be just fine. But, no, Mom had to go make a big deal of this.

As the urinalysis and the blood work were completed, I was asked a thousand questions, which I really didn't feel like answering. I was only thinking about how much I'd rather be at home lying on the couch watching *General Hospital*. I thought the action is sure getting hot on *General Hospital!* God, I would love to have their lives: great clothes, gorgeous men, and families with lots of money. Well, that's certainly the way to live, I thought. I can't wait 'til I'm grown and can get me some serious clothes and a baaaad car! At fifteen years old, I was sure I knew just what I wanted. Just as I started to think about all of the details of my future car, I was interrupted as the door slowly opened, and the doctor walked in. I quickly sat up on the edge of the examination table.

He was a young doctor, with dark wavy hair, and an olive complexion. He kind of reminded me of Rocky (the prize fighting character Sylvester Stallone made famous in the 1980's), except a lot nicer. As he walked over to me, he had a concerned look on his face. As I placed my cold hands under my thighs to warm them, he sat at the end of the office, just staring at me with a puzzled look on his face.

He said, "Well, you're not sick."

"I told you I wasn't sick when you were in here before," I said, "and I also told my Mom I wasn't sick," I continued.

"No, you're not sick," he said, turning to write something in the file. "You're not sick, but you are pregnant."

I could not believe what I was hearing. Immediately my heart started pounding so hard that I could feel it in my throat. How could this be happening to me? How was I going to tell Mom? How can I make all this go away?

"Are you okay?" he asked, starting to walk over to me. I wanted to nod my head to say yes, but I couldn't move.

"Pam," he said, "are you okay?"

"Are you sure?" I asked quietly. "Are you sure I'm... can your test be wrong?" Inside I was praying like I'd never prayed before that some type of error, some horrible error, had been made in the lab.

"There's always a chance that a test is wrong, but we're reasonably certain that you are pregnant, Pam." He looked at me with so much concern. "If you'd like to get another test, I can schedule another appointment for you tomorrow, but today we really must share this information with your mother."

"Oh, please no! I don't want her to know," I appealed.

"I am required to share this information with your mother. Do you want to tell your Mom yourself?" I shook my head without looking up at him. "We need to get your Mom from the waiting area."

"No, no," I whispered through my tears.

He walked over to me and touched my shoulder. "Do you want me to tell her?"

I couldn't even make out the words. I just nodded my head, yes.

As Mom came into the room, she looked at me with concern. "Is everything okay?" she asked the doctor with worry added to her usual assertive tone.

The doctor was standing on one side of me and my mother was on the other, as he said, "Well, I'm not sure if it's good news or bad news, but your daughter's pregnant."

"Pregnant?!" Mom gasped. She lost her balance as she said it a second time. "Pregnant?" She kept from falling completely only by grabbing onto the table. I could see her standing beside me, but I could not bear to look up into her face.

"Pamela?" she spoke my name like a question, as if to ask, "Why, how – how could you?"

I raised my eyes to look at her and tears were rolling down my face. She didn't say another word. She just looked at me, and I looked back towards the floor.

Seeing the hurt in her face told me that this was even more horrible than I had ever imagined. As I gathered my things and prepared to leave the doctor's office, I still couldn't stand to look my mother in the face. I could hear her talking to me, though.

"Pamela, why did you do this? Why did this happen?" I could say nothing.

All I could manage to say was, "I'm sorry, Mom. I didn't mean to."

"You didn't mean to?" she asked. "Were you raped?" she continued in a very sarcastic tone. "I don't think Eddie raped you," she retorted.

"No, Mom, no, he didn't," I said. Of course she knew that was not much of a possibility. I was so in love with Eddie Stokes. She knew it, and absolutely hated it. I suspected I could be pregnant when I was late with my period. Eddie and I had gotten an early pregnancy test from the store. When the test read positive, he said that I shouldn't even worry about it. Maybe it was wrong, but I cried so hard! Later my period started so I assumed that the test had been wrong. Now, it seemed maybe the test wasn't wrong after all!

As we exited the exam room, Mom went to pay at the reception window. My brother, Maurice, walked over to her, and I read her lips as she told him that I was pregnant. I waited near the door, as far away as I could, and still be in the building. As they both walked toward me, I put my head down until they got closer, and then turned to walk out to the car. Mom stepped up and passed me. Maurice walked next to me, not saying a word but somehow comforting me. Of my three siblings, Maurice was always the only one whom I felt I could really count on when I was at odds with Mom. We were not extremely close, but I always felt like he liked me — which was more than I could say for my sisters, LaWanna, the baby of the family, and my older sister, Marcella. They weren't completely at fault. I didn't like them most of the time either, but Maurice was different.

I remember when I was five years old and Maurice was six. We were walking to school in Spencer, Oklahoma. Spencer was the rural area of Oklahoma City, where many black families had lived for decades. Mom had moved all of us into my grandmother's two-bedroom house because Daddy went to Europe for a year with the military and she didn't want to take us so far away from home. Although the walk to school was probably less than a mile, it seemed to go on forever, especially when we had to walk by the fence where a big, mean, black and brown dog was chained up! As we approached the fence, my hands clenched my books. I hated, hated dogs. I was so afraid of them. Unfortunately, I was walking on the side near the dog because Maurice didn't want me to walk too close to the street. He always took the street side of the walk. I thought, "If we walk fast, we could pass this fence really quickly." I didn't even look at the dog, but, out of the corner of my eye, I saw something approaching. Suddenly the dog was right up on the fence with the deepest, meanest barking I had ever heard! I dropped my books, and ran into the street. Maurice grabbed my hand to keep me from running in front of the moving traffic. We ran back the way we had come. I was crying and shaking all over and looking back at my books that were way up by the fence, with red dirt all over them.

Maurice was still holding my hand. I felt his hand shaking too. I knew he was scared, but he couldn't let me know.

In his strongest little voice he said, "He can't get out, Pam. He's not on his chain, but he's still inside the fence."

"I want Momma!" I said. "I wanna go home!"

"Pam, we gotta go to school," he said. "Momma ain't gonna let you stay home."

I kept crying.

"Stay here," said Maurice. "I'll go get your books, and then we'll cross the street."

"NO!" I yelled, still holding tight to his hand. "That big ol' dog will get you!"

"No he won't; wait right here. I told you, I'll go get your books, and then we'll cross the street and finish walking on the other side."

"But Momma said to walk on this side of the street so we don't get runned over by cars," I said.

"She won't get mad if we go on the other side for one day," he replied as he pulled his hand from mine. I saw him walk as tall as any six-year old I'd ever seen. My "big brother" walked right up to that fence, and picked up my books with the dog barking only six inches from his shaking, little brown hands. He quickly hurried back to me, and handed me my books.

"Okay, let's cross the street," he said.

"I wanna go home," I was still crying.

"It'll be okay... come on." He took my hand and held it as we stood looking both ways on the street. Although there wasn't much traffic at all, we looked both ways several times. "Let's go," he said, pulling me with a little tug as we ran across the street.

When we got to the other side, he made sure I walked on the side away from the traffic, like he always did, and far, far away from that mean old dog. I don't think Maurice ever knew how much that meant to me, but from that day forward, I adored my brother.

Some ten years later, there we were walking to the car outside of the doctor's office, and Maurice was walking beside me, and as always, comforting me without even knowing it. I thought, "I wish he could do something to save me this time too." But no, being pregnant was more than being afraid of a dog, and my brother couldn't do anything to help me now.

When we arrived at the car, our burgundy Chevy

Caprice, Mom quickly opened the car door. She reached over to the passenger side and lifted the lock. Maurice opened the other door, and pulled the front seat forward, so I could get in the back. We would usually have exchanged at least a few words about who was going to sit up front, but the back seat was the only place I dared to sit at this point. In fact, I would have preferred the trunk!

On the drive home there was complete silence. I heard an occasional sniffle from Mom. As she sat up front driving, I saw tears flowing from beneath her very large, dark sunglasses as she turned to look over her shoulder while trying to change lanes. She cried all the way home.

I just lay down in the back seat. I was half praying and half thinking. I thought, "God, if I could just press myself between the spaces in the seats and never come out, I would be so happy." "Maybe this isn't really happening," I thought. It can't be really happening. This couldn't be happening, and at any moment I'm going to wake up from this dream, this terrible nightmare.

My half-hearted prayers were abruptly ended when the car slowly pulled into our parking spot. Mom and Maurice got out of the car without saying a word. I walked slowly up the stairs. We had just moved back to Oklahoma City because Daddy decided to retire from the Army after 20 years of service. We were all so proud of him, especially Mom. While they were looking for a house, we moved into an apartment on the North West Expressway, an area Mom thought would be convenient and would have good schools for us to attend. LaWanna ran to meet us on the steps. She and Mom stopped halfway. I started moving faster to get by them. I knew Mom was going to tell her.

Before I could get into the apartment, I heard LaWanna say, "Pregnant! She's pregnant?" I heard her cry before I reached the top of the stairs. I knew she'd be shocked and disappointed, but I never expected LaWanna to cry about this. It seemed like I couldn't possibly hurt anymore. I didn't even acknowledge her. I just turned and walked inside.

LaWanna asked, "Momma, what are you gonna do?" Though I should have waited to hear the reply, I quickly closed the door to the room that LaWanna and I shared. The still sound of their shocked responses penetrated the door and the walls.

"Pregnant at fifteen, my God," I heard Mom say. LaWanna asked again, "Momma, what are you gonna do?" Mom still didn't respond. And although it seemed strange for LaWanna to ask Mom what she was going to do, this was the correct question. Virtually nothing in our family was said or done openly without Mom's approval or support.

I buried my face in the pillow, and the tears began again. All I could think was, "All of my dreams, all of my hopes, they're gone, they're all gone — I don't want to have a baby! When I do have one, I don't want it to be like this. How can this be happening? How *can* it be happening?"

I started thinking back to the first time I met Eddie Stokes. He was tall, flamboyant, and the most beautiful ebony color I had ever seen in my life. He was so confident, too — no, not just confident, Eddie was arrogant! And he didn't make any apologies for it. But I liked it - his arrogant confidence. He never seemed to worry too much what people thought about him, and simply did whatever he wanted to do... including skipping some classes, drinking, and smoking. But he took good care of himself. He was a hard worker, and invested most of it in his Volkswagen Beetle and his clothes. He thought there was no finer man in the state — and I agreed. I fell in love with him almost immediately. When we were together, it was like nothing mattered, especially none of my problems. He understood me too. It didn't matter to him that I wasn't the prettiest girl in the school or the smartest. The only thing that mattered to Eddie was that we had so much fun together, and I adored him. I used to love to see him laugh. He'd get this really big smile with his teeth still clenched together. Then he'd open his mouth, and let out the funniest laugh. Then he'd say a sound like "hee-hee." I loved that laugh, and the man that it came from. Well, I thought he was a man. I was thirteen, and he was sixteen. I felt so important having an older boyfriend. He had friends who were seniors, and they always made me feel special because whenever they saw me, they'd ask about Eddie. That seemed so long ago now. As crazy as it seems, I didn't even expect us to be in this position after we met. I mean we had sex, unprotected sex, so why in the world would I think I wouldn't get pregnant?

An hour seemed to pass before my door was opened. Yet, when I barely opened my eyes to look at the clock, only ten minutes had gone by since I last looked at it. Mom came in. I didn't want to talk to her. I didn't even want to look at her, so I closed my eyes and rolled over pretending to be asleep. As she sat there on the bed, I peeked out of one eye, and could see tears rolling down her cheeks, her lips tight, and her eyes staring straight ahead. There's no way I could bear to talk to her at this point. Soon, she got up and left the room. When she left, I began to sob. This was the hardest, most desperate, saddest cry I think I've ever experienced in my life. I cried so hard that the whole bed was shaking. I must have exhausted myself because I eventually cried myself to sleep.

The next morning we were set to go to another doctor's office because I just knew it couldn't be true, and Mom wanted to get me in to see our own doctor. Well, when we got there, she told them we'd been to a clinic the day before because I'd had standard cramps and nausea, and they said I was pregnant. Unfortunately for me, the test and our doctor came up with the same conclusion.

"Yes, Mrs. McCauley, your daughter is pregnant." Knowing my age and the concern on our faces, he then shifted the point of his conversation. "Now, she appears to be about ten weeks along." As he said that, he sat down in his chair with the nurse in the room as well.

He said, "I'm not sure if this is good news or bad news,

Mrs. McCauley."

My mother snapped, "Well, it certainly isn't good news. She's only fifteen!"

"Well, yes, ma'am, I understand. But, if you want to continue the pregnancy, I'd be glad to serve as your daughter's doctor, but if you'd like to consider alternatives, I have some information I can offer you."

My mother looked over at me. I slowly nodded my head, yes. I knew exactly which alternatives he was talking about. I immediately looked away after I nodded yes. He proceeded to discuss the details of the alternative while I looked at the wall. My mother sat completely motionless, and stared at the doctor. No, she stared through him. She seemed to be in total disbelief that she would even consider this "alternative" for her daughter. He finished his monologue by handing my mother a couple of pamphlets and assuring her that he'd seen situations like this before, and our family would be just fine. After collecting this information about the "alternatives," as he so put it, we got in the car and drove home. We rode in complete silence. As my brother drove, I sank deep into the back seat. I could hear my mom crying. Each time I heard her sniffle, I sank deeper into the seat wishing I could hide underneath it.

When I got home, I went straight to my room. It seemed to be the only place I could feel comfortable after all this began to happen. As I lay in the bed and tried to pray, I thought, "God, surely, You understand." But I was so ashamed to talk to God. I thought, "He must be so mad at me." God is getting back at me for being so terrible, for talking about people, lying to my Mom, skipping class, and most of all for having sex. He's really mad at me. "You understand that I don't want a baby. God, I don't think you'll be madder at me if I have an abortion. Lord, You know how much I want a good future; I want a good life. But, Lord, I can't have this baby and have that good life. It wouldn't be fair to have a baby and not have anything to give this child. I know I can't, Lord. Please, Lord, understand. Please, Lord, help me through this. I'll be so good if you help me through this."

While I was praying, I decided maybe if I got on my knees, He might hear me better. So I knelt by my twin bed. As the tears fell from my cheeks onto my folded hands, I prayed. "Lord, You know I didn't mean to get pregnant. I know I was stupid. I know this wasn't what I was supposed to do. Lord, I lied to you, Mom, my best friend and cousin, Angel, and to myself. I said I wouldn't do it, but I knew I wanted to, and then I even looked forward to it. But, Lord, I can't have this baby! It'll be a terrible life for the baby, a terrible life for me. Everybody'll think I'm a terrible person; they'll think I'm a tramp. Please understand, Lord, I just can't have this baby. Lord, I'm sure you don't want to hear anymore of this foolishness from me. You're mad, and I deserve it. But please, Lord, hear my prayer and answer. Amen." I got up and lay back in my bed, too tired to sleep, too hurt and too frustrated to even cry anymore.

After lying in my bed for a little while, I got up and went into the kitchen. I thought I'd get some Pepsi and watch a little television in the living room. As I entered, I heard my Mom on the phone.

"Annie?" she said.

"Oh, my God," I thought. She's calling Eddie's parents. I had been too afraid to even mention Eddie's name — let alone call him. After all, Mom and Dad never liked him from day one. And now they had a complete reason to hate his guts, to despise him. I leaned toward the living room to hear Mom on the phone. Mom could not see me yet.

"Annie, this is LaFrance," Mom said. "Well, Annie, I have some bad news... Pam is pregnant." I heard a long pause on my Mom's end.

"Yes, I've taken her to two doctors. I'm certain she's pregnant. Where's Eddie?" said Mom. "Pamela! Come here." I waited a few seconds so she wouldn't know I was eavesdropping. Then I walked into the living room. She handed me the phone and got off the couch in one motion.

"Hi Annie," I whispered barely able to speak in front of my mother.

"It's me," I heard Eddie's voice on the other end of the phone.

"You're pregnant." Eddie said in a soft voice, not as a question, but as a matter of fact. He didn't sound at all surprised because, before we moved from Virginia six weeks prior, I was late with my period. Then after praying really hard, I'd started my menstrual cycle about a week later. Obviously it wasn't the cycle I was looking for, because I was pregnant after all! Being ten weeks at that time meant that I would have had to been pregnant when we took the pregnancy test back in Virginia.

"Yes," I said, "I am."

"Well, you're pregnant," he said as if it was his way of accepting it.

"Yes, Eddie... you already said that. I'm pregnant."

"Well, what are you gonna do, Rochelle? What do you want to do?"

He always called me Rochelle. I loved being called by my middle name. It seemed like it helped me escape the boring, somewhat mundane, middle-child syndrome that I had been born into. Being Rochelle was a lot more fun, and just hearing him say my name brought back so many great memories of all the wonderful times we'd had at the basketball games, at the football games, and just hanging out together. I never expected those great times to lead to all the hurt, frustration, and disappointment that I felt at this moment.

"Eddie, I don't want to have this baby."

"Well, okay, Rochelle," he said. "Whatever you want to do, just let me know. You know I love you." The thoughts raced through my head...I muttered, "I love you too." All I could think of was that I wished we'd love each other more, more than this – enough love to give us the strength to make better choices and not end up here.

All of a sudden, his mother got back on the phone. "Rochelle?" Annie was always so sweet and cheerful. But now, though she spoke in her normal high-pitched voice, she was not her usual bubbly self. "Rochelle? This is Annie. What do you want us to do, baby doll?"

"Annie, I don't want to have this baby. I just don't think I can give it a good life. I don't think I can offer it the things I want my baby to have."

"Well, Rochelle, sweetie, we'll be by you, whatever you want to do;" she paused for a moment, "I just really hate that you and Eddie did this."

"I know, Annie. I'm sorry." My Mom reached for the phone. I handed it to her, and she and Annie continued to talk. She looked at me sharply with a unique blend of anguish, concern, disappointment, and love.

"Annie? I've worked out some details with the doctor, and we're planning to go to the clinic tomorrow morning. They said if we wanted to terminate the pregnancy, we've got to do it quickly. I'll give you and Lewis a call tomorrow evening, okay?" I heard her say a few other things about money and the move to end the conversation. "Take care, Annie. Bye-bye."

I went to my room. Later I found out that Lewis and Annie had agreed to pay for half the cost. Mom came into the room and reported the financial plan to me, and explained that Eddie and I needed to pay them back. This was our doing and our decision, not theirs, and we needed to pay for it.

Just before I went to bed that night, Mom came into my room. She sat on the bed that my sister slept in. She didn't even look at me. She handed me a list of instructions.

"These are the instructions you need to follow before we go to the abortion clinic in the morning." Abortion? That was the first time I'd heard her say that word since we'd decided to go through with this "alternative." I knew how terribly difficult this was for my God fearing, Christian Mother.

"Yes, Mom. Okay."

I looked at the list. They needed my first morning's urine, and there were a few other instructions. I put the list next to my bed and dozed off to sleep.

I must have woken up at 4:00 or 5:00 in the morning; it was still dark outside. I just lay there for a while, praying to God again that this wasn't really happening... that I'd wake up and all of this would have been a bad nightmare. But then as I rolled out of bed to go to the restroom, I stepped on a piece of paper, and looked down. It was there, the paper with the instructions for the abortion clinic. "It's real. This whole awful, terrible nightmare, it's real and it's happening to me!" is all I could rationalize.

I lay back down, and started to cry again. I heard LaWanna turning in her twin bed. I didn't want her to hear me. "Little Miss Perfect," she is ... and I don't want her to see just how imperfect I'm realizing that I am. This was one of those times when I wished I could be like LaWanna.

LaWanna and I had an interesting relationship. She was Mom's pet and always agreed with everything Mom said. I, on the other hand, was stubborn and difficult. We were sisters and sometimes friends, but we just didn't have that closeness. I always wished we did. Now, I wished I could wake her up and tell her how sad I was, but that would just make me feel stupid. Maybe she'd understand, but I wasn't about to take a chance that she wouldn't, and end up feeling even more stupid.

As the sun rose, I got dressed, preparing to go to the clinic. I heard Mom and Dad up; they always managed to rise early. I could smell coffee brewing. Daddy hadn't said a single word to me about the pregnancy, the abortion, and certainly not Eddie.

"Pamela? We need to get there early." My mother always looked beautiful. She had on a beautiful black jumpsuit this day. Even with all the frustration and pain, she managed to smile and reach for me, giving me a hug. We hadn't talked much and certainly hadn't hugged since this whole ordeal began.

"Pamela, all this is gonna work out," she said. "I'm not

sure why you would do this. You had me to talk to and you had your older sister, Marcella, to talk to. You didn't have to do this to yourself. If you wanted to have sex, you shouldn't have gotten pregnant. Unless, of course, you and Eddie planned this," she said, releasing me from her embrace and looking into my eyes.

"No, Mom! There's no way in the world I'd want this right now. I did not plan to get pregnant." How could she think this?

"Well, as I said, it'll all work out," Mom said.

I was still in shock that she'd think I planned to get pregnant at fifteen. But I suppose she didn't really know what to think at this point.

We headed down the steps, and got into the car to leave. On the way to the clinic, I thought, in just a few hours all of this will be behind me. I can start leading my normal life again. I can try out for cheerleading at my new school. I can be popular. I can go out on dates. Who knows? Maybe I'll even find a new boyfriend, and leave all of this bad stuff with Eddie behind me.

We arrived at the clinic. There were several people there before us. I had put my urine sample in a paper bag. I was surprised to see some girls with theirs right there in their hands. I was so embarrassed; I had put mine in a plastic bag and two paper bags. Actually, they weren't all girls; they were women of all ages, colors, and nationalities. In fact, I think I had seen one earlier that week when we had a class field trip to the Oklahoma State Capitol. She looked like a state representative. So we covered all branches of life, and appeared to cover all socioeconomic and ethnic backgrounds.

As we made our way to the front of the line, I gave the urine sample to the nurse, and they hurried us all into a room for instructions. We sat in a small room with chairs lined up in rows of about five chairs per row. We paid close attention to the explanation of the procedure. The first nurse, who was very cavalier about the process, explained that she'd had two abortions and there was nothing to worry about. This was a very easy process. A second nurse spoke with more sensitivity, as if she wanted us to know that if we changed our minds at this point, it would be okay. I looked around the room... None of us looked directly at each other. We just looked around, and if our eyes happened to meet, we looked away. As they talked about the procedure and all that would take place, I looked around. I couldn't concentrate much, couldn't focus much on what was going on. But I did manage to hear them say that the procedure would be painless, and at this stage, the baby wasn't even going to know what was going on. I fought back the tears; I never expected to be in this situation. I faced the facts, "But I am, so I need to just shut this internal whining and deal with it." Then they moved each of us to our separate rooms.

Soon a nurse and the doctors came into the room. My Mom came in too. She reached for my hand.

She said, "Pamela, after all this is over, we're going to take a nice vacation, honey. I don't want you to worry about anything. We're going to go on a vacation, and we're going to enjoy it." I looked at her face, her beautiful Egyptian brown complexion, with all the love and concerned worry clearly discernible through her smile and gentle touch to my forehead. She even had Egyptian features. My Mom really was beautiful. I was sure she was a direct descendant of Egyptian royalty. One time when I was in elementary school, I remembered bringing home a book with sculptures of Egyptian Queens. I showed Mom how much her nose resembled the nose on one of the Egyptian sculptures. She thought it was so funny that I saw a resemblance between her and a thousand year old statue; nonetheless, I think she was very flattered that her 1,000-year-old likeness was royalty.

She rubbed my hand. "God," I thought, "how can she be so nice with what I've done?" I felt so much worse. I pressed my lips tightly, and fought back my tears.

"Okay, Mom," I said, "I can't wait."

Mom reached down and kissed my forehead and softly said, "I love you baby."

"I love you too, Mom."

Mom seemed nervous as she turned to leave the room. This was strange to see her this way because nothing ever made my Mom nervous or afraid. But she struggled fast and hard to try to recover from the irregularity in her emotions. As soon as she left, the nurse said, "The procedure won't take very long, but the doctor needs to check you first." She told me to scoot down on the table and put my foot in the stirrups, and then she draped me with a cold paper sheet.

Another doctor came in; he was a huge man. Nothing like the two doctors I'd previously met. He had a rough voice and was broad and heavy with a gray and black beard.

With my feet in the stirrups, he told me to slide toward the end of the table. After I slid down, he checked me. "God, I hate being here," I thought. Things couldn't be any worse ...or so I thought.

All of a sudden, I heard him say, "Nope! This one won't work. Nope!"

I thought, "What is he talking about?" As he exited the room, the nurse came over with a concerned look on her face.

She said, "The doctor says you're too far along in your pregnancy to complete the abortion. It looks like you're further along than we thought. You're beyond your first trimester; that means you're beyond twelve weeks of pregnancy. And here in the state of Oklahoma, we cannot perform an abortion if you're more than twelve weeks. The closest place for this procedure is Denver, Colorado." It was 1978, and that may have been the law at that time, but it did not make me understand my situation any better.

"You mean I'm not going to have the abortion?" I asked. My mind was racing. "How can this be? I want this problem to be over. How can this be happening to me?"

"No, honey. We can't do it here; you're too far along.

Here are your clothes; get dressed. I'll go get your Mom, and tell her."

As I put on my clothes, I prayed, "Lord, I asked you to help me. You know I just made a mistake; I didn't mean for this to happen. Now I'm going to have to go to Denver. We don't have the money for that. Lord you know we barely had enough money to get here today. Oh, my God, now what's going to happen? What's going to happen to me?"

They moved me out to the lobby quickly after I had gotten dressed. I saw my Mom with a very frustrated look on her face, once again. There was another lady standing there in the lobby with her.

"Well, Pamela, they said that you're too far along. You can't have the abortion."

"Mom, I don't want to have this baby! I want to go to Denver!!!"

"Hold on, let's just get the information."

As we headed out, the lady with whom my Mom had been talking said, "You know what? Don't worry about it, honey. My daughter's here, and I know it's gonna work out for her and for you too." She seemed sincere as she continued, "And you know what? I'm gonna pray for you."

"Thank you," I said.

But inside all I could think was, "You're gonna pray for me? Well, my prayers sure don't get much; maybe yours will get more. But right now if you want to do something for me, save the prayer, and give me a ticket to Denver." That's exactly what I wanted to say to her. But of course, my good upbringing and my mother's backhand kept me from saying something like that.

As we walked to the car, I said, "Mom, I don't want to have this baby."

She snapped, "Denver's too far to go! I do not want to go to Denver. In fact, I've been thinking. This is my grandchild. This is an abortion; this is killing a baby."

"Mom, I don't want to have the baby!" I said.

"Pamela, if you didn't want to have a baby, then you should not have been screwing with Eddie!"

"Mom, I don't want to have a baby!" And the tears began to flow. "I don't want to have a baby!" And before I knew it, I was sitting down on the ground in the parking lot, crying.

"Get up, Pamela!" she said, walking very quickly toward me. "Get up! Let's go home." And she grabbed me by my arm, put me in the car, and we drove home once again, as we had done many times in these past few days--in silence, except this time I couldn't wait to get home to cry. The tears flowed from my eyes like a river. I didn't even have the strength to wipe my eyes. By the time we got home, the front of my shirt was soaked with my tears.

When we got home, I went to my refuge, straight to my bedroom, to sleep. As I did, I heard Mom pick up the phone. With the door barely open to my room, I heard her calling one of her sisters, my Aunt Camille. She and Aunt Camille had always been close.

And I heard her say, "Camille, you know what? Pam's pregnant."

Now I knew that going to Denver was out of the question. If she was calling her sisters to tell them, then I knew the pregnancy was going to go through; it was not going to be terminated. She would not bear the scrutiny of an aborted grandchild with her seven sisters. So I came out of the bedroom, and sat on the couch. Maybe one last time I could talk to her about it and explain to her that this would be hurting the baby. It would be hurting me; it would not be any good for me to have this child. As I sat on the couch, she continued her conversation with my Aunt Camille, telling her that they had talked to Eddie, and we just decided that it would probably be best for me to have the baby instead of trying to have an abortion at this stage. As I sat there, she sensed that I wanted to talk to her. Inside I was screaming, "How can they decide this for me?" It's not fair, God please help me. I just put my head down and dropped on the couch.

"Camille," she said, "let me call you back," and she got off the phone. She came over, and sat next to me on the couch. "Pamela, Daddy and I will help you. We'll help you take care of the baby," while placing her arm around my shoulder.

"But, Mom, this is not your responsibility. This is not your baby. You shouldn't do this. I don't want to have a baby," I said. "I don't want to be a Mom, not now."

"Well, Pamela, you did this, and I don't want to kill my grandchild. When we were there in that abortion clinic, and I was sitting there waiting, my heart was racing the whole time. I thought, "Oh, my God, this is my grandbaby!" She put her hand to her chest as if it was actually paining her heart to do such a thing.

"Mom, you're not doing this; it's my decision."

"I know, Pamela, I know it's your decision. But you'll be okay. You'll be a good little mother; you help a lot with MaRisha. And it'll work out." MaRisha was the first grandchild in our family born in 1976 to my sister, Marcella. She was now 2 _ years old. She was so precious, and I absolutely adored her.

"Mom, how can it work out? How can I give a child anything? MaRisha's my niece. I don't have to take care of her all the time. This baby will be with me all the time."

"It'll work out, honey." Then she gave me a hug. "When I was just talking to your Aunt Camille, she said we should get you in the Alternative School in downtown Oklahoma City. You remember? It used to be called the Adult Day School, and now they call it Emerson Alternative. She said Sylvia went to school there when she was pregnant."

Goldie and Sylvia were two of my cousins, my Aunt Camille's daughters. They were about five years older than me, and they both had gotten pregnant before they had gotten married. My older sister, Marcella, had gotten pregnant, too, out of wedlock. Then she had gotten married after graduating high school. That just seemed to be the way things were going in my family, but I really, really had not expected for it to happen to me. And not only was it happening to me, my situation seemed to be worse than anyone's. I was only fifteen! I don't know if anyone in the family had been as young as me when they had a baby. Leave it to me, I thought, to really, really do it the wrong way.

Mom continued, "We'll enroll you in Emerson Alternative School on Monday. Just rest up this weekend. We'll go tomorrow and withdraw you from Putnam City, and get you enrolled in the new school on Monday. It's a little bit of a drive from the house, but I'll drop you off every morning. Aunt Camille said you could come over to her house after school every day; she's near downtown so the bus can drop you off there. Then I'll come pick you up."

Mom stood up and went toward the kitchen. I knew she was trying to help and figure out a way to make this work out, but I couldn't even begin to think that everything would be ok. I saw that all I had planned for my entire life was crumbling before me. But what could I do? I felt totally helpless for the first time in my life.

"Okay, Mom," I said. I didn't even have the strength to say anything else.

"All right, sugar. It's gonna work out."

I made my way to my room, and I called Eddie. He sounded like he was just waking up. "Eddie," I said, "I can't have an abortion. I'm too far into the pregnancy." He didn't respond for a second. "Eddie?" I said.

"Yeah, I'm here," he replied. "Well, Rochelle, what are you going to do?"

"I have to have the baby." I started to cry. "I guess I have to be a Mom," I said through my tears. "I'm not ready for this."

"Rochelle, don't worry. I'll do my part, and we can even get married," Eddie assured as he tried to comfort me.

"Eddie, I need to go, I don't feel good. I'll call you later." We said our good-byes, and I went to my room to finish my crying, and to try to figure out what in the world was going on. My whole life was a wreck.

Since Mom had made her calls and told my aunts, now I was sure my cousins knew. So I decided at this point it was my turn to call and let them know. So, I picked up the phone and called my cousin, Angel. Angel and I had always been very close.

"Hi, Angel."

"Hi, hon. How ya doin'?"

"Well, I've been better. Angel, I'm pregnant."

"You're what?"

"I'm pregnant."

"Pam! But I thought you said you didn't have sex yet. You'd not even had sex with Eddie."

"Well, I did. I mean; I lied. Angel, I'm sorry I lied to you. I didn't want you to think badly about me."

"You're pregnant, Pam? Oh, girl, I'm so sorry. What are you gonna do?"

"I can't have an abortion. I'm too far along for that. So I guess I'm just gonna have this baby."

"Really?" Angel asked.

"Yeah."

"Gosh, um.... Well, hon, what did Eddie say?"

"Well, he was surprised. He said he'd do his part, and send money to help. But, you know, he's not gonna be much good to me all the way in Virginia. I'm here all by myself."

"Well, I'm here. We can still go places and do stuff sometimes."

"Well, thanks, Angel, but I don't think I'm gonna feel like doing much. I just can't believe I'm pregnant."

"So you had sex with Eddie?"

"Yes," I confirmed.

"Well, what was sex like?" Her mood immediately switched to show her schoolgirl interest – I know she didn't mean any harm, but sex was just about the last thing in the world that I wanted to discuss.

"Angel, I don't really want to talk about it now."

"What was it like, Pam? Come on tell me." Of course Angel was a virgin – like I wished I were right then.

"It was okay. It got me pregnant. I just wanted to call, and tell you this, Angel. I'll call you back later."

"Okay, hon. Take care."

"Bye."

My sister, LaWanna, came into the living room

"Rochelle, want to watch some TV?"

"No, I don't feel good. I'm just going to bed."

"Okay. Well, Mom says you're going to have the baby."

"Yeah, I'm gonna have it."

"Well, everything's probably gonna work out. But you know, you guys shouldn't have been having sex."

"I know, LaWanna. I know we shouldn't have been having sex."

My brother, Maurice, turned around on the couch.

"Come over here and sit down." He looked at me, and then he glanced at LaWanna. "Leave her alone," Maurice said, coming to my rescue again. I always knew I could count on him, no matter what difficulties I encountered.

My brother never said much, but when he did, I paid attention. He was kind of quiet, very much to himself, and never had many friends. But for the few friends he had, they were the lucky ones. He was so loyal and giving, but reserved. I was the most outgoing person in the family. I always had lots of friends and a full social schedule, from cheerleading to basketball and everything in between.

My sister, LaWanna, loved being home and loved being Mama's pet. It also seemed like she was never far away when Mom was disciplining my brother or me. She'd quickly speak up to reinforce just how wrong the action was that got us in trouble, and stand next to Mom verbally seconding everything she said to us. She really was Mom's pet! Boy, she did a good job of that.

I remember one time, my brother and I, who always managed to get into continuous mischief, got into some raisins after we were supposed to go to bed. Mom had a rule about no snacking after bedtime, and we were to go to sleep early enough to be ready and alert for school. We thought we'd run downstairs, grab a few raisins, and go back up to our room. Well, lo and behold, before we could even get the cabinet open, LaWanna was knocking on Mom and Dad's bedroom door.

"Mom! Dad! They're in them raisins!" Boy, did we get it for breaking that rule! We used to always tease LaWanna about being a tattletale all the time.

Mom was furious. "Didn't I tell you guys to go to bed?"

When LaFrance McCauley told you to do something, and you didn't do it, you could plan on catching it. So LaWanna was the Cindy Brady, or the tattletale in our family. Not only was she a tattletale, but she was also Miss Know-It-All. And always, whatever Mom said, whatever Mom thought she wanted to say, LaWanna agreed with her. That was my baby sister. But as annoying as she was, somehow, we still managed to love her. She had her very sweet ways and she always seemed to be proud to tell people I was her big sister. I'm sure she loved me and I loved her too. That's just the way she was.

My older sister, Marcella, was already in Oklahoma when we moved back from Virginia two months prior. She was really more like a second mother to me. Somehow, I felt like I never met the expectations that Marcella had for me or maybe I was just envious of her. I envied the close relationship she and my Mom had. I always wanted to be that close to my Mom. I wanted to be the one she talked to, the one that she laughed with, and told stories — grown-up stories — to, but it was always Marcella, and boy, did I envy that!

Marcella came to the house later that day. I was sitting in the living room on the floor leaning on the couch. She sat on the couch.

"Mom says you're gonna have a baby."

"Yeah, I am."

"Do I have to go through this again?" I thought. "Why can't everybody just come in one room, tell 'em all Pam's pregnant, she's stupid, she's gonna have a baby, she messed up. Yes, she's only fifteen, why don't we just put a "Stupid" label on her head and leave it alone?" But, I just answered her question.

"What were you thinking about? Why were you having sex with Eddie?"

Oh, boy, here goes the mother part of her.

"Marcella, I don't know. I just don't know." I turned to focus more on the television.

"Didn't you know you could talk to me? I would have taken you to get some birth control pills."

"Yeah, Marcella," I said. "Right!" I thought. As soon as I'd asked her to do it, as soon as I'd gotten it out of my mouth, she'd have been telling Mom and the whole family would have known. No stinking way was I gonna ask her to get some birth control pills! But there was no need to tell her that now.

"Yeah, I just didn't think I'd get pregnant. I really didn't think I'd get pregnant."

"Well, you were wrong. I wish you would've talked to me," she said, and she got up and left the room.

This was on Saturday evening, and it seemed to be the slowest weekend of my life; dragging by as everyone heard the bad news that I was pregnant. Not only that, we were going to church the next day. Well, Mom could tell Mother-Dear (my grandma), but I was not going to go through that Baptist ritual of apologizing to the church. Well, of course, I didn't want to, but if LaFrance insisted, I'd be up there. Instead, she was supportive and said I didn't have to apologize to the church. Mom said she didn't agree with that tradition, and she thought it was unfair to the girls.

It was time for dinner. I smelled the wonderful scent of fried chicken, collard greens, mashed potatoes, and gravy. Well I was glad to know I hadn't completely stopped sensing good things. Mom was in the kitchen. I asked her if she'd told Reverend Parker. "We won't even tell anybody at the church," she said. "It's really no one's business. You've just moved back here, and they really don't know who you are, so I really don't see a need for you to get up in front of the church and apologize." She looked over at me and said, "But you do need to apologize to God." Looking back at the stove she continued stirring the gravy and added, "He's the only one you need to get to forgive you." I turned to leave the kitchen, but then quickly turned back around to plant a quick kiss on Mom's cheek. I moved quickly to head back to my room.

All I could say was, "Thank God! Thank God I don't have to stand in front of all those accusing eyes. After all, how does a Baptist church get off having young people get up and humiliate themselves? If I get up, how come Eddie wouldn't have to get up, too? Why do all the young women have to get up and apologize to the church? They sure didn't get in this condition alone." Since I managed to escape this ritual, I decided not to let it trouble me too terribly much. I had so many other things to try to figure out.

Finally, it was Sunday evening, and I was going to bed. I thought, hopefully, tomorrow when I wake up, some of this nightmare can begin to be over. Just before I dozed off to sleep, my sister knocked on the door.

"Rochelle, telephone! It's Eddie."

Boy was I glad for this call! I practically ran to the telephone.

"Hi!"

"Hi, Rochelle. How are you doing?"

"I'm fine."

"What are you doing?"

"Oh, nothing."

"I just called to tell you, I'm going to join the Air Force."

"You're going to do what?"

"I'm going to join the Air Force."

"But Eddie, I thought you were going to go to college?"

"Well, now that we're gonna have a baby, I think we're gonna need some money."

"Well, but I want you to go to college. Can't you just work? You know, and still go to college? I can get a part-time job." I was almost pleading. I desperately wanted us both to fulfill our dreams, despite our future of becoming teen parents.

"No, Rochelle. One of us needs to have a job, a full-time job, so we can take care of this child. After that, we can get married." Eddie spoke with firmness. I knew this was not open for discussion.

Okay, I thought. Marriage really wasn't at the forefront of my mind, but seeing as how I was going to have a kid, it just came with the package.

"Okay, Rochelle. I just wanted to tell you that. LaWanna said you were about to go to sleep, so go on back to sleep. You need your rest."

"Okay, but...um...I want to talk, Eddie." I said, "How could you just drop this news on me and go?"

"No, I need to go. Some friends are waiting for me. I'm going out tonight." I could tell he was eager to get off the phone.

"Whom are you going out with?" I couldn't believe this! Drop this news on me, and now you have to go?

"You don't know 'em," he quickly added.

"Okay. Well, um...Eddie, I mailed you a letter yesterday."

"Okay. I'll call you when I get it, Rochelle. I need to go. Bye-bye."

"Bye, Eddie." I just hung up the phone, and the tears started to flow.

How is this happening to me? Not only am I pregnant, my boyfriend is hundreds of miles away. I feel like a slut because everyone is looking down on me, and now he won't even make time to talk to me!!! I have really messed up my life. God, I know I don't deserve your help, but I sure wish you'd make an exception, and help me out of this horrible situation that I've created. I fell off to a night of restless sleep.

I was so happy to see the morning sunshine that I got dressed in my favorite pants and a pretty red shirt with ruffles. I put on my lip-gloss, and started looking for my red socks. I thought, "If I couldn't be cute in my sassy sandals and boots, I could at least match in these old goofy tennis shoes." No one could really tell I was pregnant yet. Mom kept telling me I needed to wear comfortable shoes – comfort minus fashion. I didn't have the strength to argue or disagree today.

Mom and I headed down the highway to Emerson Alternative School, my new school, the school for pregnant teens. I thought about all the terrible things my cousins had told me about this place.

"You're going there? That's Adult Day," they said it with emphasis to stress the toughness of the environment. "Oooh, there's some rough girls down there!" they told me. "You gonna have some crazy girls in your classes!"

"Really?" I asked.

"Girl, yeah! You say something crazy to them, they're gonna beat your behind!"

"What are you talking about? I'm just going down there to go to school."

"You just watch!" my cousin added, "And watch yourself too!"

As I rode down to the school, not only was I concerned about changing to a new school, but also a big part of me was scared. Scared to death. What if they wanted to fight me? What if they thought I was strange? What if they thought that they just didn't like me? Well, I've dealt with all these thoughts before. But this was the first time I had to deal with them thinking not only about myself, but also about somebody else. Someone I was completely responsible for — a baby.

We entered the parking lot at Emerson. As we went inside,

I noticed it was an old building. Some of the pipes in the ceiling and the paint on the walls looked very old. The bell rang as we walked through the halls, and I saw my new classmates. All of them seemed to be moving slowly, nothing like "regular" high school students. Of course, large, round bellies slowed some down. We walked up the stairs, and went to enroll.

As we sat down to select the courses that I wanted, I tried to take as many courses as I thought were possible. "The more classes I take, the more work I can have to do each night, the faster I can be done, and the faster I can be out of here. After all, I don't have anything else to do while I'm sitting around here getting big and pregnant. There is nothing at all for me to do. Nothing to do but write Eddie letters every day and hope he eventually writes me back." These were my thoughts about Emerson, pregnancy, and Eddie. I knew Eddie loved me, but he was just busy, I thought. He'll write soon, and I'll study, that was the game plan. So I decided to just do that.

My first day at Emerson seemed like the second longest day of my life – right after the day we found out I was pregnant. The teachers were nice; Mr. Law, Mrs. Webb, and Mrs. Bennett all seemed to be especially concerned about helping the new "pregnant teen from Virginia" get settled into school at Adult Day. I really didn't expect to make any friends at Emerson Alternative School, but much to my surprise, I managed to make a couple of good friends. One in particular was Cynthia Cunningham. Cynthia was from a small town in Oklahoma. In fact, I'd never even heard of the town. She was soft-spoken, shorter than me (about 5'2") and had the prettiest smile. She was immediately warm and friendly to me, maybe because we were the only two girls that had not transferred to Adult Day from Oklahoma City public schools.

I soon learned that Cynthia was one of the sweetest people that I had ever met. In fact, not only was she sweet and thoughtful, but we also had a lot of similar experiences. She, too, had been a cheerleader before her pregnancy. She was in love with her baby's daddy, and he was hardly acting the way she expected him to act after she got pregnant. Sometimes he'd call, sometimes he wouldn't. Sometimes he'd write, sometimes he wouldn't. And just like me, she was writing and calling every day, feeling like she was playing the fool.

It was so nice to have somebody like Cynthia, who understood. Because as much as I loved my sister, my cousin, and my Mom, there really wasn't much understanding that they had for my situation at this point. I felt so inferior when I was around them. Maybe it was just me.

The most hurtful part of this whole mess was that I never expected Eddie to act like this if I got pregnant. Oh, we had talked about what if I got pregnant even though we never expected it to happen. What would we do? I never expected him not to respond to my letters, to have two or three of them on his desk at a time, to hear that he hadn't even gotten around to opening them yet. Oh, yes, I'd call him, and we would talk, but of course he was always in a hurry. I sat in class thinking about the awful conversation with Eddie the night before.

"Eddie, did you get my letter yet?" I asked.

"Oh, yeah."

"Did you read it?"

"I... I haven't had time yet. But I'm gonna read that one and the one you sent a couple days ago, later today." As always, he had to run because he had friends he was going out with, work he had to do, or his best excuse was that he had to go somewhere for his parents.

I finally got the name of some of those friends he said I didn't know. One of his friends he seemed to be going out with an awful lot was Sabrina.

"Oh, Sabrina's just a good friend of my sister's. You know, Sabrina and Felicia have been friends for years," Eddie would say.

Right! His sister, Felicia, who I knew very well, never, to my knowledge, had a good buddy named Sabrina. Nonetheless, they all seemed to be going out together all the time. And of course, he always said it was three of them going out together. This bothered me so much, but I just tried to trust Eddie. I didn't dare tell my Mom and Dad what was going on with Eddie.

Cynthia and I talked incessantly about all of these things that seemed to be going on in both of our lives. In fact, we talked so much, most of the time we'd get in trouble. Actually, I think I was the one doing most of the talking, and our sweet, but tough, biology teacher, Mrs. Bennett, would always catch me with my mouth open.

"Pam? Are you getting your work done back there?" Mrs. Bennett would ask.

"Yes, Mrs. Bennett, I'm getting my work done. I'll be done in just a few minutes." Mrs. Bennett was always pleasant and would look over her glasses with a half smile the first time she made an inquiry. She was a slender woman, with curly brown shoulder-length hair and green eyes.

It was interesting that most of the students were black women but we seemed to be able to relate to a white teacher who obviously had a very different life than we had. But I suspect it was because Mrs. Bennett believed in us.

Somehow, Mrs. Bennett always managed to catch me just as I was about to get to the best part of the story. I would have to shut up, start writing, and almost without exception, forget where I was in my story when I had a chance to get back to it at break. But anyway, I managed to get my work done. Mrs. Bennett was not having any slacking in her class. Even though she kept me from my stories, I appreciated the normalcy of her expectations, consistent with my previous classroom experiences before Emerson. In an effort to show understanding to their pregnant girls, it seemed that some of the teachers allowed the students at Emerson to get away with too much. That wasn't the case with Mrs. Bennett; she was understanding but she expected us to work, do things correctly and get things turned in on time. It was a challenge sometimes to meet her expectations but I was glad to do it.

One day, I was moseying along, getting my stuff together, and trying to get out of the class, as I always planned to do — early. But, I never managed to get out of there early. Mrs. Bennett was cleaning up her desk. All the other students had left, and as I exited the room, Mrs. Bennett said, "Pam!" "Oh Lord, what did I do today?" I thought.

"Yes, Mrs. Bennett?"

"What do you plan to be when you get out of school?"

I almost dropped my books. Was this someone asking me what I planned to be? What I planned to do with my future? This was the first time since I had gotten pregnant that anyone had asked me what *I wanted* to do. I felt a rush of emotions: joy, excitement, fear, and even a bit of confusion. I had to fight back the tears. Up to this point, my friends, cousins, and society were telling me what was going to happen to me — that I was going to be on Welfare, that I was going to be in poverty for the rest of my life, that I was going to raise a bunch of thugs, that I'd have a do-nothing kind of child, and of course, I was told that I had no future. But this person, this tough biology teacher, Mrs. Bennett, was the only person, other than my parents and my immediate family, who expressed any belief in me and my future dreams. Could she even begin to imagine how much asking me this question meant to me?

"Well, Mrs. Bennett, I used to want to be a doctor." I couldn't even make eye contact with her as I said those words. God, I hope she doesn't start laughing at my answer.

Well, she looked up, looked over her glasses, and said, "Pam! You can still be a doctor."

At this point, my eyes filled with tears. I could no longer fight back the tears. All the hurtful things I had heard, all my cousins saying, "We thought you were going to be a doctor. We thought you were going to go to college and be somebody. How are you going to do anything now?" It seemed that her one positive comment washed away all the hurt and pain that I had experienced in recent months from people telling me, deciding for me, forecasting for me, that I would be nothing. At this point, Mrs. Bennett said I could still be a doctor! I walked into the restroom next to Mrs. Bennett's classroom and hurried into the stall. Before I could even close the door, tears were rolling down my face. But these were not tears of pain or sadness. These tears were flowing because of an overwhelming feeling of joy, hope, and freedom from the life that I thought being a teen mother had sentenced me to. "I can still have a good life," I thought. "Mrs. Bennett says I can. I can still be a doctor!"

From that day forward, I loved Mrs. Bennett. She'd always been a teacher I really liked, and someone whom I respected. I enjoyed being in her class. I mean I really loved her after showing concern for my future and her belief in me. I admired her and appreciated her taking the time to care and to express her concern for me and so many other students. Even though I didn't completely stop talking in her class, I made sure that when I did my homework for her, it was absolutely perfect. I made sure when I went to talk to her that I had everything ready and just so-- in the kind of format that she wanted. Not only that, but I wanted to share some of my other goals, dreams, and feelings with Mrs. Bennett, so I started to tell her about Eddie and how some of these things were bothering me. She always listened closely, with interest, and without judgment.

One day I was so upset about Eddie, and I was feeling like my Mom was angry with me, and I felt completely confused. I had to talk to someone so I sat down next to Mrs. Bennett's desk when everyone else went to lunch. I started telling her how hurt I was about how Eddie was acting and how I felt like such a disappointment to my family. Mrs. Bennett looked very concerned. Of course, she let me finish my entire story. Then she gently spoke. "Well, Pam," she said, "you know we have a school counselor here, LeMonia Parker. LeMonia is right here on campus if you ever need to talk to someone, someone who's a professional to help you understand these feelings. I'm sure

LeMonia would be more than happy to talk to you." She paused, "I'm always happy to listen, but LeMonia is a professional, and she may be able to help you with some of these feelings." We talked a few more minutes and Mrs. Bennett offered her usual encouragement. Soon, I was starting to feel better.

"Thanks, Mrs. Bennett, for listening and for helping me feel better. I'll call LeMonia to schedule an appointment," I said.

So later that week I made an appointment to visit with LeMonia. She was an African-American woman in her late thirties, with an afro and a very warm and friendly smile. I went into her office. As I walked into her office I thought, "Why am I going in there? I'm not crazy! I don't need a counselor. All I need to do is get out of school, make a little money, so I don't have to depend on anyone, and convince Eddie that he's wrong for tripping with me. Yeah and if I pray to God and stop being a sinner, I know everything will be okay, then I won't need to talk to a counselor." But, something kept me moving toward her office. Before I knew it, I was sitting in front of Ms. LeMonia Parker's desk.

She said, with a warm smile, "Mrs. Bennett says you want to talk to me."

"Yes, Ms. Parker. I guess I'm not really sure why I'm here. I mean I don't really know if I need counseling, but I'm just... I'm just not happy right now."

"Well, Pam," LeMonia said, "that's okay." She was so nice; she seemed like she could be a friend. It seemed natural to think of her as "LeMonia," but I wouldn't dare call her by her first name to her face. She had to be Ms. Parker.

"Sometimes we all have days like that where we're not really sure what's bothering us, but we just feel like something is bothering us. Why don't you tell me what's going on in your life? I mean, other than the fact that we know you're pregnant; we know you have a baby on the way. Tell me about the baby's father."

"Well, his name's Eddie. He joined the Air Force, and

after he gets settled, we're going to get married."

"Oh, okay. Well, did you all plan to have the baby?"

"Oh, no. No, it was an accident. Well, I guess... see, Eddie didn't like to use condoms, and he said if I didn't let him go without them, other girls would. I'm sorry, he said, if I made him use condoms, he could have sex with other girls instead, who wouldn't make him use condoms. He didn't like them because they weren't natural."

"Oh," said LeMonia, leaning forward as is if to hear me and focus on every word.

"And I, well, you know, Ms. Parker... I mean I love Eddie. I was a virgin. I didn't think I was going to get pregnant. We didn't have sex that many times, not that many times at all. I didn't expect to get pregnant."

"Well, Pam, unfortunately, one time is all it takes."

"I guess so. Actually, we had sex more than one time."

She laughed and reached for her coffee cup. "Well, Pam, okay. Whatever it was, you know it was enough to get you pregnant. You're not the first young mother to experience pregnancy after a "little sex." Tell me about your family."

"Well, my Dad's retired from the U.S. Army." It always made me so proud to tell people that Daddy was retired from the U.S. Army. It seemed like there were so many girls at this school whose Dads didn't even live in the house with them, much less have a job and be retired military. I was so proud of my Daddy.

"Yes, my Daddy retired from the military, and then we moved back here to Oklahoma. See, all my family on my Mom and Dad's side live here. That's why I have a lot of cousins."

"Okay. And your Mom?"

"Well, she works. She's a secretary, and she works at the Health Science Center."

I was proud of my Mom, too. Mom had dropped out of high school so she and Daddy could get married, after she had my oldest sister, Marcella. It was years later when she went back to get her GED and got a trade so that she could enter the workplace. In fact, I remember when she received her GED, and got the letter in the mail. She was screaming and jumping up and down when she got it. It was a great celebration.

As usual, she checked the mail about mid-day. It was a beautiful, warm Virginia spring Saturday. On this day I saw her walk quickly back into the house. She threw all the mail, except for one letter, on the dining room table. Then she quickly opened the envelope in her hand. As she read the letter, she started yelling, "I passed! I got my GED! I passed the test!!"

And the tears rolled down her face, and she ran for my sister, Marcella. They embraced, hugged, and jumped up and down. That was such a happy day. Even though I envied the warmth that she and Marcella expressed, I was so proud of my Mom and Marcella. You see, Marcella had encouraged Mom to go back and get her GED, and to get some secretarial training so she could go to work. Mom did the secretarial course, and started looking for a job. It did so much for Mom's confidence to be qualified to be a secretary.

"Yes, Ms. Parker. My Mom's a secretary," as I got back to my story. "My family, we're going to be buying a house soon, my Mom said.... In fact, Mom and Dad are going to try to get enough room so I can have a place for the baby, even though I don't plan to stay with them for very long. You know, this is my and Eddie's baby, and we're going to take care of it. We're not going to put this responsibility on anybody but us." I had to let her know that I was not just a slut or an irresponsible person with no plan or goal to take care of this child that I was going to have.

"Oh? It sounds like you have a plan."

"Yes, ma'am, I do. But some days I just wonder."

"What do you wonder about?"

"Well, you know, I wanted to do so much. I wanted a great life. Mrs. Bennett says I can still be a doctor, but Ms. Parker, I just wonder. Everybody says it's going to be hard. Everybody says I'm not even going to be able to go to school. They say that the baby's going to cry all the time, and I'm going to be tired. I'm not going to be able to do anything like study, and I'll be too tired to finish school. My Mom, she says she's going to help me, but this is my baby. Maybe I should.... I know I can't have an abortion.

But Ms. Parker, do you think it's wrong to do adoption? Eddie and I may not stay together. Neither of us have much money. I mean, if I can't give a baby anything, the baby's going to be unhappy, and I'm going to be unhappy with it. Would it be better for the baby to be adopted by some people who'd love it, and have a lot to give it?"

"Oh, there's nothing wrong with adoption, Pam. In fact, it can be a great thing for everyone in the right environment," Ms. Parker said.

"Well, I know. But...It's not that I'm selfish or that I don't love this baby, I just want what's best for everybody. Actually, I should have been thinking about that sooner. My Mom says that adoption is not a good choice; I'd regret it some day. I think she's right, I would regret it some day. But won't I also regret having a child that I can't give anything to, that I can't make a good home for? I'm basically going to be depriving the child. Right?" My tone begged for her approval.

"Well, Pam, that's your choice, and only you can make that choice."

"Well, all right, but I don't know what to choose. I don't know yet, so I guess that's what's bothering me," I smiled at Ms. Parker, as she said nothing. She just smiled back. I reached for my books, and thanked her. "I'm sure I'll figure something out," I replied.

Somehow, talking to Ms. Parker had helped me feel better. I sat there and I thought: I wouldn't dare share with Mom that I had spoken about personal family business, with an outsider. She wouldn't like it that I had talked to anyone about our family. Only good reports and shows of confidence are allowed outside the house. Mom didn't approve of divulging family business. Family business is family business only, but, right now, I just couldn't talk to her about those things or to anyone else in the family either. I need someone to talk to. I couldn't figure this out by myself, and sometimes I felt like I was going crazy. Anyway, LeMonia was a counselor. Wasn't I supposed to talk to somebody like that? She helped me feel so much better, so it couldn't have been all bad.

I grew close to Ms. Parker in the coming weeks, and we talked about many things. I trusted her, and felt so comfortable sharing my fears, ambitions, and problems with her. I remember talking to her about the names we were considering for the baby. Of course, if it were a boy, he would be named – Lewis Edward Stokes, III – if I had a boy.

"Eddie Stokes better marry me!" I thought. I don't think many other men would want to raise somebody else's child that was third generation – the third! I wanted a simple, but elegant, name for my baby if it were a little girl.

I went through so many name books and decided on Annette Sherice. I wrote her name several times and even talked to Ms. Parker about it. The name Annette had part of Annie's name in it and I certainly loved Annie (Eddie's mother). She had been so sweet to me during my pregnancy, so I loved the thought of the baby having part of her name. My Mom's name had already been taken with the family's only other grandchild, my sweet niece, "MaRisha LaFrance Washington," so that was out. I knew Mom wouldn't mind the baby having part of Annie's name.

One day when I was talking to LeMonia, I wrote out the name "Annette Sherice Stokes." She looked at the paper and said, "Pam, that's a very pretty name, but you may want to reconsider the spelling of her middle name." She was still looking at the paper. I wasn't sure what she was talking about, but then she continued, "Pam, her initials will be ASS." As soon as she said this, we both burst into loud laughter. At that moment, the spelling for Sherice became Cherice.

By now I was about seven months along, moving right along through this pregnancy. God, did I have a big belly! Some days I just could not believe it was all mine standing out there in front of me, this huge stomach! I remember the first time I noticed my stomach starting to stick out. I went home and cried. Then I eventually thought, "Hey, this just comes with the territory." I was way beyond the point of crying. I didn't try to use the cream on my stomach to keep the stretch marks from coming; it was just all there, right there in front of me. I deserved this big belly and all the stretch marks, I reasoned.

I still wrote Eddie letters every day, and still got about one a week from him. Then along my seven and a half month, his letters stopped coming even once a week. One day I called him, and told him I needed to talk to him.

"Well, Rochelle, I'm really busy, but I need to talk to you, too." His tone was serious.

Boy, I didn't like the sound of his voice.

"What's wrong, Eddie?" I quizzed.

"Tell me what you need to talk about first."

"Well, I'll talk to you later." He was having second thoughts about talking to me.

"No! Talk to me now! What is wrong?"

"Well, you know I've been going out with Felicia and her friend, Sabrina?"

"Yes," I said. "Go on, Eddie."

"Well, there's something about Sabrina." Oh, my God, I thought. Is Sabrina pregnant, too? He's sleeping with her? What is going on here?

"Eddie, what are you talking about?"

"Well, I'm starting to have feelings for Sabrina. I mean, I think I'm in love with Sabrina. Rochelle, I think I'm in love with Sabrina."

"Oh, my God! You what? Eddie, how could you do this to me?" I was screaming and tears were streaming. I was hot and dizzy, and it hurt so much. "Eddie how can you do this to me? I'm pregnant with our baby, and you're sleeping with someone else?!"

"No, Rochelle, I haven't had sex with her. I haven't even kissed her. But I think I'm in love with her," he said.

"How the hell are you in love with her?!" I was yelling and crying hard, with a pain in my chest that was painful, so painful.

Isn't that just great, I thought. Here I am carryin' that nigga's baby, and here he is in love with a woman that he hasn't even touched. This is so unfair but who said life was fair? I couldn't even make myself say anything past my tears. I slammed the phone down, and went to my room and just cried and cried and cried.

Whom could I tell this to? This horrible, embarrassing, and crazy situation!

I certainly couldn't tell my mom. As nice as she was trying to be about all this, she was still very frustrated, very hurt, very angry, and there wasn't a single a day where I didn't feel like I had betrayed and embarrassed my parents. I couldn't tell my sisters either, they'd both tell Mom. My brother probably just wouldn't understand. Then could I tell my cousins or friends? I don't even think I could tell Cynthia this. No, even her boyfriend wasn't doing this. So I lay there and I thought, "I can tell LeMonia." This thought brought some relief to my aching heart. As I drifted off to sleep, I thought, "I'll talk to LeMonia; she'll help me."

The next day, as soon as I went to school, I didn't even go to my class. I went straight to the trailers where the counselors were.

"Ms. Parker, can I talk to you?" I asked. I was choking back the tears.

"Sure, Pam, come on in." She was her usual pleasant and thoughtful self.

Before I could even get a word out, the tears started to flow.

"I talked to Eddie yesterday, and he's in love with someone else," I said through tears, ashamed to look her in the face. "My God," I thought, "she's really going to think I'm stupid. Stupid and weak to love a man that would do this to me."

LeMonia sat up in her chair. "He's in love with someone else? When did this happen? Back up, tell me the whole story," she said while handing me a box of tissues. Her face was concerned and serious with that "Black women don't play that" look. She was fully focused on every word I said and I knew by the look on her face that she was eager to help me.

"She's a friend of his sister, Felicia, and they've been hanging out. They both joined the Air Force at the same time, and went to the same basic training and school together. They hang out together all the time. Well, he's in love with her and the worst part of it is he hasn't even kissed her. She hasn't even had sex with him, and I'm having his child, and he's in *love with her!* How can this be to happening to me? Why is this happening? It's so unfair! I am so stupid to even love him when he's done this to me!" I clenched my fists and hit them on her desk, just needing something to hit to release my anger.

"Pamela, nobody said that life was fair, honey. Nobody said it was going to be fair, or easy, but you can handle this. If Eddie's in love with somebody else, I know it hurts and hurts a lot, but that's something that you can learn to deal with in time. The main thing you need to do now, Pam, as much as this hurts and as frustrating as it is, is take good care of yourself and your baby. You don't need to get too upset about this."

"How can I not be upset? He's in love with somebody else!" I yelled.

"I understand that's frustrating. Believe me, I understand. I've had challenges too in my life, I understand. But you have to take care of yourself and this baby. Did you talk to your parents about this?"

"Are you kidding? Do you know, if I told them this.... First off, they already hate him; they'd probably go scalp him.

Then on top of that, they'd think I was so stupid to still be in love with Eddie. I'm the black sheep of the family; I betrayed them. I'm a nobody; I'm the stinking middle child. I don't know why they even still want me." I was crying, getting louder, and more breathless with every statement.

"Pamela! You're really upset about this. Hold on, Pam; let's not go overboard. You're upset with Eddie now. You don't have to make everything bad. It's just Eddie right now. Your life can be great with or without Eddie." Her tone was serious now. "Don't let him have this type of control in your world."

"I know the problem now is Eddie, but I do feel like I've disappointed and embarrassed my family all because I was so in love with him, and this is how he shows me love? All I've done for him?"

"Well, I'm sure there are some frustrations with this, but right now let's deal with this situation with Eddie."

"All right, Ms. Parker." As I calmed down, she handed me more tissues.

"Would you like some water?"

"Yes, I would." Once again, she showed that award-winning, warm smile, and I began to calm down. We talked everything out to the degree that I could, between tears, one itty-bitty, little teeny-tiny step at a time figure things out.

By the time I got up to leave her office, I was still weak, but I felt like I had renewed strength and renewed confidence. Despite Eddie being in love with Sabrina or anybody else, I was going make it. I didn't know how, but I knew I would. I had to! One thing I realized was, if I'm going have this baby, if I'm going to carry on with this and raise this child, I had better be strong. I had better be independent, and I had better be able to provide a good life for this child. This child did not ask to be born and did not ask to be born to a fifteen-year-old mother. There was no reason in the world this baby should have to live a life of poverty and frustration. But it was totally up to me to make this happen. Now, Lord, if You will help me, I promise to do my part.

Eddie and I talked about once a week after the "Sabrina call." He tried to be warm, but I was so hurt I just didn't have much to say to him.

I was really moving along with my pregnancy now. I was about eight months, eight and a half, and then I had about three more weeks to go. I wanted to take the breathing classes. I thought it might be better if I had my baby without having any drugs. You know, the natural way. I never really thought much about how I'd do childbirth, but I remember in health class about natural childbirth being better for the child, so I talked to Mrs. Bennett about it.

"Sure," she said. "You can have natural childbirth. You might want to enroll in the Lamaze classes."

"Yeah, those are the breathing classes I saw on TV." I said

"Well, maybe you can enroll in those," she said. I immediately thought about the childbirth classes Mrs. Bennett had given us. Each mother would go through the breathing exercises and have their labor coach going through each step with them. I realized that if I was going to do this I needed a labor coach.

"But I don't have a coach. Eddie isn't here. You know, Mrs. Bennett, he's joined the Air Force so he's not available, and I really don't want to ask my Mom or Dad to do it." I thought I probably wouldn't want him to coach me now even if he were here.

"Well, Pam, I'll be your coach."

"Will you, Mrs. Bennett?" I was shocked and delighted at her offer.

"Sure, I'll be your coach, Pam. In fact, I have some information here. You give them a call and see what time they want to meet. I can't do it on Wednesday nights, I have to take my kids to soccer practice, and I can't do it on Thursday. But if there's a Monday or Tuesday class, then we can go to that one together, and I'll be glad to be your coach."

"Thank you, Mrs. Bennett! Thank you so much!" I reached across her desk and gave her a hug. I went to the principal's office and called the place where the Lamaze classes were held. I wanted to hurry and call before Mrs. Bennett had time to change her mind. Sure enough, they had a class on Tuesday night. I came back and told Mrs. Bennett, and there we were, a team in the Lamaze class on Tuesday night. Mrs. Bennett had already taught a lot of details and relaxation techniques for childbirth. So I was so glad she was coming to the class with me.

I got some brochures and information on the class. It looked like most of the stuff Mrs. Bennett had covered in class at Emerson Day School as she helped us to prepare for our deliveries, and to help remove some of the fears that most of us had. I think every one of us girls were terrified about the thought of delivering a baby. But, Mrs. Bennett had done a fairly good job of preparing us.

At the Lamaze class, Mrs. Bennett sat behind me, and lifted my shoulders when they told us to practice pushing, panting, and breathing. I thought it was kind of funny, and everyone else seemed to laugh too. I couldn't help but envy the other people in this class; I was sure I was the only single mother there. I was certainly the youngest mother there, and almost all of the women were there with their husbands. I looked at each and every one of their left hands; they had a beautiful gold wedding band or a diamond ring on their finger. God, this sure isn't the way I expected to have a baby. But just the same, here we are, here we go. "Pant, Choo," started the instructor.

"Come on, Pam, you need to make these noises. "Choo, Choo, Choo," said Mrs. Bennett.

"Like a Choo - Choo train?"

"Yeah, Choo, Choo, Choo." Boy, that brought back memories--memories of cheerleading days long behind me, now. Choo, Choo, instead of being a cheer, now meant getting ready to deliver a baby! Mrs. Bennett and I grew ever closer over the next four weeks as we went through the Lamaze class together. She had such a thoughtful, loving personality. I also found out that she had three children – two boys and a daughter. Her daughter had been adopted and was Korean. The boys were named Reginald, Jr. and Brooks, and her little girl was Tara. She talked so much about her "beautiful Tara." She and her husband decided to adopt a little girl after they'd had the two boys. She saw no reason to wait for a "white" baby girl when a beautiful, sweet Korean little girl was available and in need of their love. So, they didn't wait and that's how they wound up with Tara.

The next few weeks went by very quickly. As I was watching the news one night, I felt water running down my leg. No! It's my water breaking! Mrs. Bennett said it could feel like this.

"Mom!" I said. "My water's breaking. Let's go. We need to go to the hospital. Call Mrs. Bennett, she's going to meet me there."

"Pamela, are you sure?"

"Yes, Mom. My water's breaking. Let's go to the hospital. I know I'm not using the bathroom on myself – this has to be my water breaking."

"All right. Maurice!" she yelled to my Dad. "Pam thinks she's about ready to have this baby. I'm going to take her to the hospital." Daddy ran downstairs to help us get everything in the car.

We got in the car and hurried along to the hospital.

"Pam, you think you're really having this baby?"

"Well, I don't feel any contractions, Mom. But they said if the water breaks, then I have to go to the hospital 'cause that means the baby's about to come."

"Well, we'll get on over there and see. You know, the doctor's probably going to send us back home. I don't think you're going to have this baby; you haven't had any complaints of any pain or anything."

"I know, Mom, but let's just go. I think.... I still have this water running down my leg. I really think I'm going to be having this baby tonight." I was starting to feel really nervous.

"All right," she said, as she sped up and drove a little faster to the hospital.

By the time we got to the hospital and got me signed in, Mrs. Bennett was there. The nurse rushed me back and started to check me out as soon as I was positioned on the table.

"Yep, your water broke," she said.

"See, Mom? I told you." I had to inform my Mom I knew something, since she had come back to the exam area with me by that time.

As the nurse said, "Sounds like you're going to be having a baby here soon." Mom and Mrs. Bennett were going to coach me through my labor and, as afraid as I was now, I was so thankful to have both of them with me.

Mom stepped out of the room to call Daddy, Eddie, and his parents to let them know I really was in labor. Mrs. Bennett stood next to me, and held my hand with an excited smile.

"Pam, you're going to have the baby in a few hours, and you're going to do great. Your Mom and I will be right here to help get you through it. Just remember all that we covered in the Lamaze class. You're going to be fine."

And soon I did. But it wasn't soon enough! All the panting and chooing with Mrs. Bennett and my Mom taking turns coming in and out of the room, breathing with me, and telling me to relax and breathe moved the labor along. But God, those labor pains hurt!!

"Choo, Choo!"

"Don't push. You can't push yet." Some of those labor pains hurt so bad I tried to focus on anything but the pain. I think I counted every eyelash on Mrs. Bennett's eye as I focused on her face discussing my choo choo and my effort to block the pain out.

"Come on, Pam! Choo, Choo, Choo." As she Choo'd and panted with me, I knew she was in a hurry to leave the room and go and get herself a cigarette! Yep. Unfortunately, Mrs. Bennett smoked. It never bothered me or any of the other girls. I think it affected her more than any of us because she was always talking to about being healthy and having positive habits. It really didn't matter to me now, as long as she could Choo and pant with me through this major contraction! Then Mom came in. Mom held my hand really tight.

"Choo, Choo, Choo, Choo! Oh, Mom, this contraction really hurts!" Mom began to choo and pant harder than I had ever choo chooed with a cheer. But we somehow made it through that contraction. Mom was really holding my hand tightly and chooing with all her might.

"Mom, you better cover your face and your mouth. You're going to hyperventilate if you don't." When I said that, a look of so much concern and compassion came over her face because I was worrying about her at that moment.

"Don't worry about me, sweetie," she said. "You just keep breathing. I'll be okay." Soon after that, the doctor came in with a nurse.

"Let's see if we can deliver a baby before 7:00 a.m.," the doctor said.

"Well, let me check you one more time. Well, it looks like you're going to have a baby in just a few minutes." Down went the stirrups. "Let's go! This is the time that you can push," Mrs. Bennett said.

The nurse asked, "Who's going to delivery with her?" Mom and Mrs. Bennett had agreed that it was best for Mrs. Bennett to go in to the delivery room with me. When the doctor said it was "delivery time," Mrs. Bennett grabbed her hospital scrubs and ran to the restroom to put the scrubs on over her clothes. She put her curly hair in the paper head cover.

Mrs. Bennett and the nurse took me into the Delivery room.

"Choo!" Mrs. Bennett lifted me up. "Push, Pam! Push!"

"Aaaagghhh!" I pushed and pushed and pushed.

"Here comes a baby," said the doctor.

"You have a little girl!" said the doctor.

"Oh, thank goodness! You did it, Pam! You did great!" I could hear Mrs. Bennett laughing. I thought I felt a tear roll off of her face and onto my forehead. But of course I was sweating so much, it could have just been perspiration.

"Pam, you had a little girl! You did so good! I'll go get your Mom." Mrs. Bennett ran out of the delivery room, and soon my Mom came into the room in her scrubs.

"You have a daughter! Ohhh, well, honey, you got through it," Mom said, reaching down to kiss my cheek.

"Thanks, Mom. Thanks, Mrs. Bennett."

"The nurse said you made it before 7:00 a.m." She came in just under our goal at 6:59 a.m." That was such a bittersweet moment for me, seeing my beautiful daughter born to me, a fifteen-year-old mother at 6:59 a.m. on May 3, 1979. She was so beautiful, so small, so much in need of a Mother and Father to meet her needs. While all these thoughts ran through my head, the nurse laid a warm blanket over me.

I must have immediately dozed off to sleep after that because the next thing I remember is waking up several hours later in my hospital room. It was a rainy, overcast day. I remember the nurse coming into the room and telling me they wanted to bring me my brand-new little daughter.

Mom called while the nurse was in the room to tell me that she and Daddy were on the way to the hospital, and she'd picked up a cute little outfit for her new granddaughter. She said that she and Mrs. Bennett had a cup of coffee after I fell asleep that morning. She also said Mrs. Bennett had to go directly to Emerson to teach, and didn't even have time to go home to change clothes. Mom seemed so grateful to Mrs. Bennett for being there and coaching me through labor. She said she had talked to Eddie and he was excited about the baby being born and was going to give me a call as soon as she called him with my room number.

The nurse brought my sweet baby in the room and handed her to me, I held her close. When the nurse closed the door, I started to cry. All I could think of was, "I want so much for you, my precious little daughter, Annette. And I have so little to give to you today." I kissed her on her forehead, and prayed for strength and guidance. I promised her, and promised God, that I would do the very best that I could. No matter what it took, I would see to it that she had a good life.

CHAPTER 2

SHE'S DEPENDING ON ME

I only stayed in the hospital for a couple of days after Annette was born. Going home was so exciting. It would be the first time that I had been back in Oklahoma City with my friends and my cousins without the restrictions of being pregnant. This was significant to me because I had learned that I was pregnant when we moved back to Oklahoma City from Virginia. So, I was looking forward to going home, to starting to try to live my life normally again. Although I knew I wasn't going to be like my cousins, foot loose and fancy free with no responsibilities, I still knew I was going to have a good time. Not being pregnant, being fifteen years old, I figured there still had to be some fun for me to have, even though I had to take care of my baby first. I went back to school just for a couple of hours each day when Annette was one week old. I was moving a little slowly, but I was so glad to be back in school. Mom and Dad helped with Annette. Mom took me to school then stayed with Annette for a couple of hours. Some days we'd get a lady from church to help out for a few hours. This was necessary because the school year was ending in a few weeks, and I wanted to be ready for my final exams.

As I recovered from having Annette, Mom took off work for a few days, teaching me all the finer points of caring for her: how to hold her, when to change her, how to know when she's hungry, wet or just fussy. It was so much, I felt so overwhelmed. Lord, will I ever understand all this? How will I ever understand all this? Somehow I have to learn to manage, manage as a Mom, as a teenager, and then figure out how to do well in school.

Mrs. Bennett stayed after class to make sure I was ready for my Biology final, and I talked to all of my other teachers to make sure I was ready for each exam. I was so glad to be finishing my school year on time. In fact, Emerson finished even earlier (one week) than the school my brother and sister were attending.

Unfortunately, things weren't going any better with Eddie. I was still so concerned; I was afraid Eddie was still in love with Sabrina. Yes, he told me he didn't really love her, and he'd still be there for our brand new baby daughter, and me, but somehow I still didn't believe it. He'd sent flowers while I was in the hospital, but I didn't expect much else. Even though Eddie joined the Air Force, and was preparing to set up child support for Annette, I wasn't even looking forward to seeing him any time in the near future. My hopes were very dim for a future with Mr. Eddie Stokes.

Lewis and Annie sent me flowers, and started talking to Mom about when they could come to Oklahoma City to meet their new and only grandchild. They decided they would come to Oklahoma City sometime in June or July. I was so thankful for their loving response – especially because things were so shaky with Eddie and me.

Annette was born on May 3rd, 1979, and, since the day she was born; she seemed to become more and more beautiful. She was so precious and sweet; I loved her so much. Every time I got up to hold her and to get her a warm bottle, she was such a delight – even when I was tired. While I still had a burning desire to give her everything, this feeling was enriched with the love that I felt for her every time I held her. This was my baby, and I loved her so much. As sweet as she was, it was still difficult getting up every four hours to feed and change her. Sometimes when I had to get up in the middle of the night, I felt guilty for being so grumpy. She was such a sweet baby, how could I be irritated? "Lord, help me through this," is all I could say in the really tired moments. One beautiful May morning, I got up to feed Annette. As I prepared her bottle, I heard a knock at the door. "It's awfully early. "Who's at the house at 8:30?" I wondered. My brother and sister had gone to school, and my mom and dad were already gone to work. It was just Annette and me in the house. So, I looked through the peephole in the front door. "My God! Could this be who I think I'm seeing?" It was Eddie. "But how did he get here? Why didn't he call? Furthermore, what does he want?" I opened the door. I couldn't say a word; I just looked at him. He reached out, and hugged me.

"Aren't you going to say hello to your daughter's father?" he asked while releasing his embrace just enough to look into my eyes. He had the most beautiful brown eyes. I felt a rush of adrenaline to my head and my heart. Eddie grabbed me again and hugged me so tight – snapping me out of my trance-like state.

"Hi! How'd you get here?" I asked. He pointed to a shiny new motorcycle in my parents' driveway.

"Rode every bit of the way, just to see my new beautiful daughter." He smiled, "And her beautiful Mother."

"You rode all the way from Colorado?" I asked, still too nervous to smile.

"You better believe it!" Eddie said, straightening his back and slapping his leather gloves into one hand. Always cool – that was Eddie Stokes.

He still had that unbelievable charm. One look from him, one movement of his hand, his head, and I was all his. I reached for him, and this time I embraced him. All of a sudden, I heard the whistle from the teakettle with the water boiling in the kitchen.

"Come in. I'm making Annette's bottles." He came in, closed the door, and followed me.

"Where's my daughter?" Eddie asked, looking around the room.

"She's upstairs. Hold on just a minute." As I turned the teapot off on the stove, I zipped around the corner, and went upstairs to get Annette.

I was so nervous; when I got upstairs, my hands were shaking. My God, this is real: Annette, Eddie, and me! We have a child together. It seemed so hard to grasp the concept that I, only fifteen years old, had a baby with Eddie and he was only eighteen. Eddies was someone who I only wanted to go to the prom with and admire how great he looked in his jeans. Oh! I loved it to see him in his jeans, but God knows admiring him in jeans was a far cry from having a child with him. This was the real deal. As I took Annette downstairs to him, I cradled our now 3 1/2 week old daughter; he was waiting with his arms outstretched. Looking at him this way, with that beautiful smile, at the bottom of the steps, made me remember how much I loved him.

"Let me have my baby!" he said as he moved towards me, while gently lifting her out of my arms.

He held her close, and kissed her, and rocked her, as he walked toward the couch, and sat down with her. Somehow, looking at him holding his daughter, Annette, it seemed okay for me to like him, in spite of the things he'd said and done. Somehow I felt it was okay to love Eddie Stokes, just the way he was.

"Rochelle, what are your plans?" he asked glancing up at me but quickly refocusing on Annette.

"What do you mean, what are my plans?"

"Well, what are you planning to do about school? About Annette? About us?"

"Well, I want to finish school. I want to make a good life for Annette, so I want to go to college. Okay? So that's what my plans are."

"Aren't you forgetting something?"

"Forgetting what?"

"Forgetting about us."

"Well, Eddie, I didn't think there was much of an 'us' left."

"Rochelle, you know I love you."

"Well, I guess you do. You love me and a whole lot of other people."

"That thing with Sabrina was just an infatuation. Nothing ever happened."

"Sure. Sure, it didn't."

"Rochelle, I don't know why you don't believe me. I love you. I rode 12 hours on a motorcycle to see you and to see my daughter. You don't believe that I love you?" I moved toward the loveseat, and sat down so I could look across the living room at Eddie. I didn't want him to be that close to me, not yet.

"I think you're doing what you're supposed to do. I think your parents probably called you and told you that you should come."

"My parents have no idea that I'm here. Rochelle, please. Let's give it another chance—for Annette, for our daughter."

"I don't know, Eddie. I have to think about it. How long are you going to be here?"

"Oh, just for a couple of days."

"Let me call my parents. Let me call them and see if it's okay if you can stay for dinner. You know you can't stay here at our house."

"Oh, I wasn't planning to," he quickly said. "I have money; I'll be at a hotel."

"Well, there's a cheap motel down the street. Hold on, I'll go call Mom, and get some information, and call that motel for you."

Mom seemed delighted when I called and told her Eddie had ridden all the way from Colorado on a motorcycle to see Annette. She said to have him stay until she and Daddy got home, and she'd fix dinner. My Mom, as angry as she was with Eddie and me, was so happy for him to come see us. I guess she just wanted to know that Eddie really cared about Annette and me.

That evening all was calm and quiet at my house. My brother and sister, Mom, Dad, Eddie and myself, all sat down to our usual fried chicken meal. I was really surprised at how happy my parents were to see Eddie, despite all the frustration, and how much, at one point, they seemed to despise him for the situation we had both gotten ourselves into. They showed him so much warmth.

After dinner, Mom and Dad wanted to talk to Eddie and me. My sister and I had to clean the kitchen first. Eddie sat in the breakfast area holding Annette and giving LaWanna and me a hard time about everything from school to the weather in Oklahoma. After LaWanna and I finished cleaning the kitchen, Eddie and I moved into the living room to tell Mom and Dad we were ready to talk to them. Mom quickly jumped up and said, "Let's talk in the dining room." We all followed Mom into the dining room. We had finished in the kitchen, but LaWanna had to hang around the kitchen wiping up every little thing about four times! She made sure she was there just to eavesdrop on the entire conversation that Mom and Dad were going to have with Eddie and me. God how I dreaded times like this. Eddie and I sat down on one side of the table. Dad sat at one end of the table and Mom sat at the other. We truly felt like we were on trial. Just about the time I expected a bailiff to come in, Mom and Dad looked across the table at one another, then looked at Eddie and me. Eddie was still holding Annette. They asked us what our plans were, how we planned to support our daughter, if we planned to stay together, and if we realized the challenge for us. Daddy lit a cigarette and leaned over his cup of coffee. He always sat up on his elbows when he was about to make a point that he intended for everyone to listen —not only listen, but to follow.

"I think you two need to consider getting married. I know you had talked about marriage before, but now I believe it's time for you to do it."

Marriage, I thought. Of course I love Eddie, but he's so unstable right now. But none of that mattered at this point. I was a Mom, and I was expected to do whatever was best for my daughter. If that meant marriage, I knew I would be expected to do it.

I simply said, "Dad, we are thinking about it. And we've been making plans. I thought I'd stay here and finish school first." I said this while quickly moving my head back and forth between him and Mom while trying to read their faces, tone, and body language.

"I think that's a good idea," Daddy said. "Whatever you do, I want you to go to college. You know I've always said that. But I also think you need to be married now."

Eddie looked at Dad. He never really understood what to call my father.

"Mr. McCauley, sir," he sure wasn't about to call him "Daddy." "Well, sir, I intend to take care of my daughter, and I intend to take care of your daughter. Rochelle and I love each other, and we love Annette. We plan to get married. I should finish with my training soon, and then I'll be settling in California. I'd like for Rochelle to come out there with me, as soon as she finishes high school, if that's okay with you."

Me move to California? My head was spinning and thoughts were running through my head like crazy. Eddie had not ever mentioned to me that he wanted Annette and me to move to California. My God, how can he be telling my parents this when he hadn't even asked me about it? Before my thoughts could stop racing, Daddy leaned over toward Eddie and responded.

"That's all right with me. I just want my granddaughter taken care of properly, and my daughter."

"Yes, sir," Eddie said.

After Eddie responded to Daddy, that seemed to signal the end of the conversation. Eddie started rocking Annette; she began burping, and threw up on his shirt. He quickly got up and went through the kitchen to the bathroom for a towel. After he got up, Mom and I headed toward the kitchen.

"Pamela, are you sure you all didn't plan this?"

"Mom, I *promise* I did not plan to have Annette. I love her, and I'll do my best to take care of her, but this is not what I wanted at this time. I didn't plan to have this child." There was almost a pleading in my voice as I tried so desperately to get her to believe me one more time. I said, "Mom, I was happy being a cheerleader. I want to be young and have fun. Why in the world would you think I planned to have this baby? Yes, I love her so much Mom, but I never wanted to have a child before I got married and certainly not in high school."

"I don't know. You and Eddie Stokes, you may have," her tone suggesting that she wasn't convinced. She started back toward the kitchen to do the pots and pans. She would usually put the food away and wash the pots and pans after LaWanna and I had washed the dishes. Quickly moving pots from the stove to the sink, I realized then that it was useless trying to convince her otherwise. While Mom was cleaning the stove, I was putting the food away and putting the pots in the dishwasher. I felt that same sick feeling that I felt every time she and I had one of our disagreements. I felt so terribly misunderstood. She was never going to believe that I didn't plan this. Thank God Eddie was here, so I could at least talk to him tonight. After Mom and I finished putting the food away, and I made sure every single thing was in its place, I took Annette from Eddie and sat in the living room and rocked Annette to sleep. I walked up the stairs to put her in her baby bed, and kissed my beautiful little daughter, so sweet, so sweet she was. I covered her up after I laid her on her stomach, turned the lights out, and left just a little night-light on, just in case my precious little baby awakened during the night. According to the doctor, after she'd been in the darkness of my stomach for nine months, she would prefer not to have light. Nonetheless, I wanted my baby to have a little light if she awakened. After tiptoeing out of the room, I walked across the hall to Mom and Dad's room.

"Mom," I said, "Eddie and I want to go for a ride on his motorcycle."

Mom looked up, "You're riding a motorcycle? Be careful, you know you're a Mom now. Where are you guys going?"

"Well Mom, I just thought we'd go out and get a Coke or something. We just want to sit somewhere and talk."

"Well you can sit downstairs and talk," she piped up.

"I know we can Mom, but do you and Daddy mind if we go, just go somewhere so we can talk?"

Daddy looked up from his book and said, "Sure, go ahead. Just be back at a reasonable hour." Reasonable hour meant midnight or before.

"I promise, I promise I'll be back on time." As I turned to walk out the door, I heard Mom's voice ringing in my ears, "Just make sure you don't get pregnant tonight. Your baby's not even six weeks old." As she said those words, I felt a sharp pain. How could she think I'd do this again? But then again, maybe she was right. I hadn't planned to do it the first time. I hurried down the stairs, rushed over and grabbed Eddie by the hand, and walked outside.

Climbing on Eddie's shiny new motorcycle gave me such a strange and distant feeling of freedom. Even though I truly disliked motorcycles, and was often terrified at the thought of, me or anyone else I cared about, riding one, somehow I felt comfortable on the back of his motorcycle that night. As Eddie drove down 47th Street, up Madeira Street, and down 44th Street, I laid my head on the back of his leather jacket, holding him tightly. I could feel my face warming up and the tears started to roll. I was so frustrated and confused. I wasn't even sure why I was crying. Does Mom really think I want another child? Does Eddie really expect me to move to California? Would I not be a good Mom if I didn't get married? I'm only fifteen; I don't want to get married. How did I get myself into this situation? The tears continued to roll right off of my face onto Eddie's leather jacket. Fortunately, I hadn't started to sniffle when we took off, and with the noise of the motorcycle, he couldn't even tell I was crying.

Eddie looked over his shoulder and said, "Rochelle, do you want to stop at this store and get a cold drink?"

"Sure, sure," I said, "let's go ahead and stop." I knew I'd have to dry my face quickly; otherwise, I'd have to spend the next two hours explaining to him exactly why I was crying, and he probably still wouldn't understand. We hopped off the bike and got two Pepsi's.

After we left the convenience store, we headed on over to the cheap motel where he was staying. I certainly didn't want to get involved in another predicament. In other words, I didn't want to be pregnant again, but I knew Eddie really wanted us to spend some time alone, which very likely included having sex. I would just have to be strong or so I thought. Eddie had made another purchase at the store – condoms. As much as I wanted to be strong, I was in the grip of his charm again. After a few minutes of talking at the motel, Eddie sat on the bed next to me. "Rochelle, please marry me. I'm so sorry that I hurt you with my friendship with Sabrina," he said.

"Friendship?!" I snapped.

"Yes, she was just a friend. I love you. I love Annette. Give me a chance to make a good life for us," he said leaning close to me and kissing me softly on my lips.

"Maybe he's serious," I thought. "But, does he mean it?" Being this close to Eddie quickly eroded my strength. I was so in love with Eddie Stokes. Eddie reached over and turned off the lamp. "God please forgive us for our weaknesses," I prayed.

The next evening, Eddie got on his motorcycle and headed back to Colorado. I waved at him as I stood on the porch holding Annette in my arms. Somehow the two days he'd been in Oklahoma City made having Annette seem a little easier, a little more pleasant, almost okay. We were officially back together. But now that he was gone, I knew I'd have to take on this daily responsibility by myself. My parents were there of course to help and support, but I couldn't escape the feeling of disappointing them. I came back in the house with Annette. As I was on my way up the stairs, Dad came around the corner.

"Did Eddie leave?" Daddy asked. He sounded sort of relieved at the possibility.

"Yes, he's gone." All of a sudden, all of the sadness and worry was hitting me. I was so scared, insecure, and worried.

"What's wrong, Puddin'?" Daddy asked. I always felt so special when he called me 'Puddin'.'

I wished now that he could just fix all of my problems.

"Oh, nothing." I was halfway up the stairs, but I turned around.

"Yes, there is. What's wrong?" he inquired.

I moved to the right to hold the rail on the stairs, and then I turned and sat on the steps. Annette had gone to sleep. I laid her across my lap. Daddy sat a couple of steps below me, and leaned back looking over his shoulder at me.

"What's the matter, Puddin'?"

"Daddy, I don't know. I feel badly. I just feel bad. I feel like I let you guys down, and I'm a failure. I had Annette; I'm fifteen. I'm just not the way I used to be."

"Well," Daddy started, "we love you. We love you, Pamela. You made a mistake, but you're a good girl. Even though you made a bad choice here, remember you're a good girl. The thing is to learn from this. But I love you, and I'm still proud of you, honey."

I couldn't even respond. I tried to choke back the tears, but instead I picked Annette up and covered my tears with her blanket. I think Daddy knew I was crying. He looked back and got up off the steps and walked into the living room. As I turned to walk up the steps, the tears kept coming. Lord, I love my mom and dad. I love my family. I've let them down so much. Is it possible that they could still love me and be proud of me? If it's possible, Lord, please help me. Help me to really give them a reason to be proud of me someday.

My family was high on nicknames and Annette was quickly nicknamed "Nettie." Lewis and Annie promised to visit "Nettie" and me. They mailed so many outfits and toys! It did so much for my spirits. It really mattered to me that they wanted to be a part of Nettie's life.

Now it was time to go back to school full time after the "second coming of Eddie Stokes." Annette was only a few weeks old, when I started going back to class everyday but I just had to get back to concentrating on school. I had been going to the school for just a couple of hours a day since she was a week old, just to make sure I didn't get too far behind. The first week after his departure felt like I was on a treadmill! I mean a seriously fast treadmill. Getting up in the morning, getting Annette dressed, getting myself dressed, and God knows I wanted to look "cute." Working hard to get to class on time, getting her to school, trying to stay attractive, getting all my homework done, and being able to halfway intelligently discuss matters in class, whew... it was all a bit much. And that wasn't even the most challenging part of it!

At the end of my day, I was going home to take care of a tiny baby while other people went to hang out. So, in addition to being totally tapped out with everything I had to do, I started to feel a little jealous. I was jealous of those high school students who had that footloose, fancy-free lifestyle.

Summer school was at U.S. Grant High School – a very "normal" school so I was no longer shielded from the difference in my life and other high school students, like I was when attending Emerson. Somehow I had to learn to deal with this lack of a carefree life and freedom. Somehow, I just didn't feel comfortable being in high school and being a mom at a regular high school. It occurred to me that one way to deal with this would be to finish high school early and start college where there would be more people like me.

After my realization that I needed to finish school early, I decided to call Emerson and talk to Mrs. Bennett and the counselors about what it would take for me to finish high school early. They seemed to think this was a strange request, not because I wasn't smart enough, but because everyone else was taking it easy. They outlined a plan for me that showed how I could graduate a whole year early. I would need to take another course during summer school and take a course during the fall, in the evening. By following that plan, I could be out of high school by the time I was sixteen, just a month shy of my seventeenth birthday. Sounded great to me, then I wouldn't have the continual reminder of how different my life was from most high school students. So, in the summer of 1979, I went about my plan of enrolling in another class in summer school. At the same time, I wanted some independence, so I started looking for a part-time job.

Mom said, "Are you sure you want to work part-time, with a child, while you go to school? When are you going to have time for Annette?"

"Well, Mom, I just want to have a job. I'll feel better." What I really meant was that I didn't want to depend on her, Daddy, Eddie Stokes, or welfare to take care of my daughter and me.

"Well, okay. Go on and look for a job, if you really want. I just think you should focus on your school and your daughter."

"I can still do good in school, Mom! I always did good in school. That won't change with a job."

"Pamela, before you didn't have a daughter to take care of."

"I know, Mom, but I'll do good. You'll see." All I needed was a little support from Mom to go for my job search, and I felt like I had gotten it. It was now time for me to find a job!

I went to the mall and applied for several positions at clothing stores, T-shirt shops, anywhere I thought I could get a job. Eventually one of the stores in the mall called me. I was excited—no, I was thrilled! A couple of days later, I went to work at Super Tees, making fancy T-shirts. This, of course, was 1979, the height of the T-shirt era. Everybody had T-shirts to express themselves. I was thrilled to be "making T's." Boy, did I love it! I loved the thought of having my own paycheck, more than anything. Being able to go places and buy things for Annette without having to ask anyone, I absolutely loved it! Maybe I could even pay for daycare! Well, that was when the reality of my finances hit me. Daycare was outrageously expensive. My parents had been helping with Annette and babysitting along a lady from our church. But that couldn't last more than a few weeks. How in the world was I going to pay for daycare? Mom and I must have been thinking about the same thing because a few days later she wanted to talk to me about the babysitting situation.

"Pamela, your dad and I have been helping with Annette during the day. As you know, Daddy works through the night. But it's getting really tough for him to watch her in the daytime, even though you get home pretty early. You need to get some daycare assistance." Mom was crisp and absolute in her statements. I knew the decision for Nettie to go to a daycare had already been made.

"Daycare assistance, how?"

"Well, you can go down and apply for Welfare. They'll give you daycare."

Well, I hadn't really thought much about it. I didn't really want welfare, but I didn't seem to have a choice.

"Mom, Eddie is going to send money, and now I have a part-time job," I said. "I didn't think we'd need welfare, and I didn't think they'd give it to me when Eddie has an income from the Air Force."

"They'll help with Daycare, but they won't give you any money," Mom said.

"Pamela," I guess Mom read my mind, "there's nothing wrong with getting some help. After all, your daddy and I have paid enough money in taxes for you to get a few months of daycare to help. It's not like you're trying to use it for your living...."

"I know, Mom," I interrupted. "I just thought that maybe with my job, I could...."

"Honey," she interrupted me. "You won't make enough to cover your daycare. That doesn't make sense for you to struggle to pay for daycare and not do well in school. Just go and apply."

"You're right, Mom."

"We'll go down there tomorrow, and find out what you need."

My sister, Marcella, entered the room after coming from the kitchen with my niece, MaRisha. MaRisha was my angel. She was three years old now, and the most beautiful, loving child I had ever seen. She ran to me and jumped on my lap. I reached down and picked her up, and hugged her tightly. She immediately started asking about Nettie, her new cousin.

"How ya doin' sis?" Marcella asked.

"Oh, I'm fine. Mom and I were just talking about getting some daycare for Annette."

"Are you going to go apply for some assistance with daycare?" I nodded yes, never losing my focus on MaRisha. "Yeah, that's a good idea. I know they help out with that."

"Yeah, we're planning to go tomorrow. You know about how long we should plan to be down there? Down at the welfare office?"

"No, I'm not sure. I don't really know what the procedure is, but if you want me to, I can call and find out. I know somebody that works down there," Marcella said.

"Would you please, Marcella?" I asked.

"Sure."

Mom entered the conversation; "I told Pamela there's no harm in getting a little assistance for daycare. After all, some people are on welfare for twenty years. Surely she can get some help with daycare while she's in school."

"Yeah, Mom, I think you're right. I just want to be a good mother, and want to take care of Annette," I offered. "I want to provide for her."

"You can still be a good mother," Marcella said. "There is nothing wrong with getting a little help."

"Okay, that's fine. MaRisha and I are going to watch TV."

As MaRisha and I went around the corner, Marcella and Mom began to share the family news—who was doing what with whom, details about church activities, and so on. Marcella always seemed to know exactly what was going on. Boy, she and Mom seemed to enjoy each other so much. As much as I loved her, again I felt envy and jealousy of the closeness she had with Mom. After all, she was always so beautiful, and she was always smart. She was the oldest and the wisest, and always seemed to do just the right thing when Mom wanted her to do it. She was my big sister, and I wanted to be like her so Mom would love me and let me be her "friend." I wanted to be more than like her; I wanted to be her. I wanted to be smart, and I wanted Mom to want to talk to me the way she did to Marcella. Maybe one day, I thought, but I never really expected that to happen.

MaRisha and I finished watching cartoons. I loved cartoons. My favorite was *Scooby Doo*. I especially loved it when the Harlem Globetrotters were on the show: Black people, basketball, and cartoons, all in one. It didn't get any better than that!

MaRisha grabbed my hand and asked in the sweetest voice, "Where's Nettie?"

"She's upstairs," I said.

MaRisha started pulling my hand, "Aunt Rochelle, let's go upstairs and watch TV with Nettie," she requested in her special three-year-old style.

"Okay."

As I picked up MaRisha to go upstairs, I peeked around the corner.

"Marcella, MaRisha and I are going to go upstairs and watch TV with Nettie."

"Oh, that's fine," said my big sister.

Before I left the room, I needed to ask my sister a question.

"Marcella, you know what? What do you think about me finishing high school early?"

"You want to finish high school early?" she said turning to focus her full attention on me.

"Yes, I just thought it would be good. I can start college

earlier and graduate earlier and have a job."

"Well, that sounds good! You can start college next year, right?" she asked. "I think that's a great idea." My heart leaped for joy at the knowledge of my big sister's approval. I had it! I had her approval and Mom's too! I knew Daddy would be thrilled, so basically it was a done deal.

"Well, do you think it would be okay? Do you think I could get into college?"

"Sure! You could surely go to Oscar Rose Junior College. Maybe you couldn't get into the university yet, but you could surely go to Rose. What do you plan to do?"

"Well, I'm still planning to be a doctor, Marcella."

"Oh, okay. Well, that sounds great. Maybe we could go over to Rose and get some information and talk to a counselor there," she said. "I can take you after work one day."

"Okay!" I smiled broadly. "That sounds great!"

"Okay, honey," she said, "we'll do it."

"Well, we're going upstairs." I tickled MaRisha, and she ran toward the steps with me chasing her, and we were both laughing.

As I walked up the stairs, I felt a certain satisfaction. I loved having my sister's approval, even though it seemed as though I didn't have it very often. I knew education was important to her, and this time I was certain I had her nod of approval on my choices.

The next morning I got up early. Mom and Dad were already up having coffee.

"Pamela, we need to go down to the Welfare office early today. If you're going to go down there, you need your social security card (which I had). You're going to need a copy of your birth certificate and Nettie's birth certificate. Daddy has a copy of yours in the file, and you need to get me a copy of Annette's birth certificate. We'll go on down there. They said we should try and get there early to get finished as soon as possible."

"Okay, Mom. That's fine." Just what I wanted to hear as

soon as I got out of bed! I'm about to become a welfare mother!

As I showered, I couldn't help but think: I am going to apply for Welfare. I thought back to holding Annette in the hospital, lying in the bed promising her that I would take care of her. Lord, I sure don't think this is taking very good care of her. But somehow it'll work out. It has to work out!

I made sure to get out my best outfit. I wanted to look good to go to the Welfare office. I didn't want to look like just any old body, looking for a handout. I wanted them to see that I was somebody with goals, somebody who was going to be a good Mom. I wanted them to see that my baby wasn't always going to need to depend on the State of Oklahoma for a living. I wanted them to see that we had pride.

I dressed Annette in the best outfit she had, and put her pink blanket and a big pink bow on her practically bald head. The only thing you could see from 5 feet away was a pink blanket, a bald head and a huge pink bow! We were ready. We were not going to be stereotypical Welfare recipients.

As we walked in the door at the AFDC office, Mom was in front of me, just as tall and proud as ever. God, I wish I could be like that; she's so proud and confident, I thought. I walked in mimicking Mom's stride and her "look" while holding Annette in one arm, diaper bag over my shoulder, purse in the other hand. After we sat down, I looked around. All around me I saw young women with children, who were running and playing. Some of the kids were young. Some of the kids were not so young. Nonetheless, there were children everywhere. As I looked closer, some of the women didn't look so young. Many of them looked to be in their thirties, forties, some even older. My God! Am I going to be here when I'm 30? When I'm 40? I felt a cold chill.

All of a sudden a sense of panic came over me. I felt my palms sweating. My God! Is this my future? I don't want this! I don't want this, I thought. I asked Mom to hold Annette while I went to the restroom. I went in the stall, and started crying.

"Lord, please help me, I said. I don't want a life of poverty. I don't want to be on Welfare. I don't want this life forever." I heard the restroom door open. If Mom hears me in here crying, I'll never be able to explain this; she won't understand. I peeked out of the stall to make sure the person who had just come into the restroom was not my Mom. Thank God it wasn't her. I walked slowly to the sink. I dried my face and splashed some water on it. I had to get that teary look off my face. I calmed myself, and went back to the waiting room. Mom was feeding Nettie and rocking her.

"Are you okay?" Mom asked.

"Yes, I'm fine. I had something in my eye. I think this time of year my allergies and sinuses really start to bother me." God, forgive me for lying, I said silently.

"We'll pick up something for your allergies on the way home," Mom said.

Soon after I sat down, a Case Worker came to the waiting room.

"Pamela? Pamela McCauley?" she queried.

"Yes. That's me. Come on, Mom. Let's go." As we walked back to the room and sat down, she began to ask a string of questions that I never thought would be asked of me.

"Name? Age? Child's age? Number of children? Married? Where is the child's father? Location? Do you know where he is? Does he acknowledge this child? Is there a question of paternity?" I completed the form. She looked it over to make sure all those questions had been answered.

"I have my daughter's father's name here. And his mailing address," I said, with a sense of pride. "He's very proud to have a daughter, we just don't have much money."

The social worker seemed unimpressed with my input on Eddie. "Make sure you put his full name and address on the form. We'll try to get in touch with him."

"Well, I've talked to him," I said.

"You've talked to him?" She looked across the table at

me.

"Yes, I have," I said. "You see, he's going to send child support, and he's trying to set it up. He's in the Air Force. He'll be sending money soon," I informed her.

"Well, give us that information, and we'll still make an effort to contact him," the social worker said.

"Okay. But really, all I want is daycare assistance," I said. My mom looked over at me.

"Well, I understand she's eligible for daycare assistance, but is she eligible for other services?" Mom asked.

"Right now Pamela is attending school, trying to finish school and take care of her daughter. I'm just not sure if it's a good idea for her to continue working, because she does need to get a good education." Mom continued.

Boy, could Mom take command of a situation, most often when I least wanted help! The Case Worker looked at Mom.

"Well, if she isn't working, we could give her AFDC for her daughter, but since she's under the age of eighteen, we cannot give it to her for herself. So, we would be able to offer her some assistance for her daughter and daycare assistance. However, the check will be in your name Mrs. …..? Mom broke in, "Mrs. McCauley."

"That would be fine," said Mom. "Right now, I think it's much better if she concentrates on school."

"Mom!" I said. "I like my job."

"Honey, I understand," said Mom, "but right now, it's more important for you to focus on your education and your daughter." She redirected.

"Okay," I said. I was saying 'okay' on the outside, but I felt like a tire that was deflating on the inside.

All I could think was, "Why won't she let me do what I need to do? This is my decision. If I have a job, I'll feel like I'm not becoming the thing I fear most—a dependent and a welfare mom: dependent on her, dependent on Dad, dependent on AFDC, dependent on everybody for everything!" Somehow I knew my mom had my best interest at heart, but I didn't like it. I didn't like it one bit. She should have let ME make this decision.

As we got up to leave the office, the Case Worker said she'd schedule a home visit. To me, that meant further humiliation.

"That'd be fine, just get in touch with us," said Mom. Mom stood up handing Annette to me, and we headed out of the office. We went to the car and headed home.

"Mom," I said. "Why do you want me to quit my job?"

"Pamela, right now I think you need to focus on your education and your daughter."

"Mom, can't I focus on my education and my daughter and have a job? How many times are you going to say that? Why don't you believe me?"

"No, Honey, I don't believe you, not really. In fact, your father and I have to do a lot of baby-sitting for Annette with you working. I don't think that's fair to us." She made it clear with her last statement that this had to change.

"Okay, Mom. I see." This was just what I didn't want.

I didn't want to depend on them, but I needed them so badly right then. You see, being at my job was more than a way to earn some money; it was a way for me to escape, escape from being everything, escape from being a mom, from my parents, from everything I wanted to escape from so much and to just be me. To offer help to people wanting cool T-shirts, for them to look at me as just a normal teenager, a normal high school student was such a relief. Not someone who has a child, someone who has tremendous responsibility, someone who may even be a slut, someone whom they should look down on, someone who's not what you would expect a teenager to be.

As soon as I got home, I went upstairs and grabbed the phone to call Eddie to let him know that the AFDC people would be contacting him, and to let him know that I wasn't reporting him, or saying that he wasn't going to try to send some child support. Just to let them know that he existed. After all, I did need the daycare assistance. So I dialed his number, anxious to talk to him. I was sure I had dialed the wrong number when a woman answered the phone.

"I'm sorry, I must have dialed a wrong number," and I hung up the phone, and immediately dialed again. Once again, the same female voice answered the phone.

"I'm sorry, I'm trying to reach Eddie Stokes."

"Oh, yeah. He's not here right now. Did you want to leave a message?"

"Who are you?" I asked.

"Who are you?" she asked with an immediate attitude.

"I'm his fiancée, and I need to speak with him."

"I told you, Eddie ain't here!" she said. We had a moment of silence and then she hung up; sounded like she slammed the phone down! No, she didn't hang up on me! Who does this heifer think she is? My anger quickly went from her to Eddie. That lying sack of dirt! I thought, he promised me that he was going to be faithful, and we'd start building a life together: a life for him, Annette, and me.

I couldn't even respond. As I sat there in silence, I heard a dial tone. I couldn't even move to put the phone back on the hook. What in the hell is Eddie doing to me? To me, to us, and to his daughter? This is how he shows me he loves me? This is how he shows me he wants a future with me? I thought, "This won't work. This will never work. I hung up the phone and called my cousin, Angel. I was crying and angry and hurt and mad.

Angel answered in her usual, cheerful voice. All I could say is "Angel."

"What's the matter, Pam?" she asked.

"I just called Eddie, and there was a woman that answered his phone. Can you believe that? AND, she was rude to me! I guess he has a new girlfriend; he must have a woman out there. When was this cheating dog planning to tell me? Angel, I am so tired of this! Daddy says we should get married, says it's the best thing for our future, for Annette's future, too. But I just can't do it. I cannot marry this lying, cheating dog!"

"That's okay, honey. It's going to be ok," Angel said. "You don't have to get married to him. You know you don't. You know Uncle Maurice and Aunt LaFrance would still love to have you at home." She stopped for a minute. "What we need to know is WHO is this tramp at your boyfriend's house talking noise to you?!"

"I know, Angel. I wish I could have gotten my hands on her. But I don't know why I'm angry with her! Eddie is the one who lied to me. I want to give him a piece of my mind. I'm so upset! Everything's just crazy. I need his help, Mom and Dad's help, and now I'm getting on welfare! Can I depend on him if he's a liar? It's just that I need so much help right now. I need so much help. Eddie should be the one helping me; this is his baby, not Mom and Dad's. Sometimes I still feel like they're angry with me. I know Mom's still upset. She's upset that I had Annette and that I'm so young. I'm so upset, Angel. What can I do?"

"Hon, it'll be okay," Angel said. "Do you want me to come over and get you? We're getting ready to go shopping."

It was one of her favorite pastimes. After all, she had a job, no responsibilities, nothing to do with her money, but shop and look good. She did well at both. So most of the time that's what she did—shop. "Yes Angel," I said, "come and get Nettie and me now."

As soon as I hung up the phone, LaWanna entered the room.

"What are you doing?" she asked

"Oh, I'm getting ready to go shopping," I answered.

"With who?" LaWanna asked.

"With Angel. She's gonna come get me and Nettie."

"Oh, okay," LaWanna approved.

I thought for a moment that I should ask LaWanna if she

wanted to go. But she never seemed to want to be around Angel and me. Somehow I think we got on her nerves. Also I think she and Mom blamed Angel for the lack of closeness between LaWanna and me. But it really wasn't that, it really wasn't that at all. LaWanna was sweet but she was always a tattletale, and as much mischief as I'd been in my fifteen years, I knew I didn't need anybody telling on me. Most of the dirt got back anyway. Besides, it didn't really seem to matter that much to LaWanna whether we hung out together or not.

By the time I got Annette dressed, got myself ready, and loaded up the diaper bag—boy, it was like moving to another state every time I went somewhere: loading up diapers, bottles, wet wipes, and the stroller --I thought I was probably too tired to do any shopping. I sat Annette in her seat on the couch as the phone rang.

"Pam," Mom said, "It's Annie! Annie wants to speak to you."

Oh, boy. I hope Eddie hadn't called her. After all, why would he call her? He hadn't even returned my call. What a stupid thing it was to ever believe all the lies he told me when he was here, and I was so stupid to have sex with him when he came to see Annette. God, when will I learn? I reached for the phone.

"Rochelle?" Annie said in her perky, wonderful, always happy voice. "Baby doll, this is Annie," as if I was going to mistake her voice for someone else. "We just want to know what you're doing next week. Lewis and I want to come out and see our new grandbaby! Rochelle?"

I was in shock! Were they really going to come all the way from Virginia to Oklahoma just to see Nettie?

"Well...I'm not doing anything. I'll be here, if you guys want to come see her; we'll be here."

"Okay, baby doll! We'll be out there next week. Let me speak to your mama."

"Okay, Annie." Before I could hand Mom the phone, I

thought about telling Annie what a cheater she had for a son. "Annie..." I said.

"Rochelle, how ya doin', sugar? Is everything ok? " Annie asked. Mom was within hearing distance.

"Oh, I'm fine." I didn't want to tell this story in front of Mom or start crying.

"All right. We'll see you next week," she said.

"Thanks, Annie," as I handed the phone to Mom, a certain joy started to ease my hurt. I dropped the idea of telling on Eddie. I'll just tell him off.

Wow! I thought. Yeah, they're such good people, even if their son is a liar and a cheat. They're coming all the way out here to see me? To see Nettie? This is wonderful! Somehow I had thought that if Eddie and I didn't make it, that Lewis and Annie wouldn't want to be grandparents to Nettie. I couldn't have been more wrong.

The next few days went by slowly. I waited for Eddie to call. The next day he didn't call; the second day he didn't call; finally, I got a call from him.

"Rochelle?" he said. "Did you call me the other day?"

"Yes, I did," I replied sharply. How dare he call me and try to play crazy!

"What's going on? That was my roommate's girlfriend that answered the phone."

"Well, it's mighty strange that you have an excuse before you even have an accusation," I replied.

"Now, Rochelle, don't even start." I could hear it in his voice.

Eddie had an explosive temper, and sometimes it didn't take much at all to tick him off. It was one of the things that concerned me most about him. That was one of the main reasons I didn't want to marry him or be alone with him in California. Just the same, I managed to still love him, but he was truly chiseling away my love. I think I was at the end of my rope. I was not going to play second fiddle. I felt like I played second fiddle when I was pregnant, and maybe I had little choice then, but damn it, I was not going to play second fiddle anymore, not by choice. No way!

"Eddie, listen," I said. "I am sick of you! I am sick of your attitudes and thinking that the world revolves around you! I am not going to put up...." All of a sudden, Eddie interrupted.

"Listen, Rochelle, I have been here for you. I have sacrificed for you. The allotment I am trying to get prepared to send, I had to move out of the barracks for that! That's why I'm staying here with somebody else. Yes, that was his girlfriend that answered the phone. Now, if you don't believe me, if you don't believe my story, if you just think I'm feeding you a line of bullshit, then you just go on about your business!"

"Fine, Eddie! I accept the offer to leave you 'cause you are a lying and cheating dog! Find another fool to put up with your bullshit." I said and slammed the phone down.

He was not going to intimidate me. Did he think I had to have him because I had his child? God knows I loved him. God knows I wanted him. But, I refused to live a life of frustration, deception, anger, and helplessness.

I was amazed at the strength that I had just shown; the ability that I had to just say good-bye to Eddie, even though I knew somehow that it wasn't the complete end. I don't think I had ever stood up to him like that. I don't think I had ever let him know that I could really do without him!

I was in school at U.S. Grant for the summer of 1979, but I would go over to Emerson about once a week to see LeMonia. Mrs. Bennett wasn't teaching summer school, but she told me that I could call her at home anytime. One day Angel dropped me off at Emerson to meet with LeMonia. As I sat down with LeMonia, I told her, "When I hold Annette, I love her so much. When I kiss her on her little face, and I think about this beautiful, living, breathing creature in front of me, all of a sudden I feel so badly. I feel so bad that, at one point, I could have not wanted her. How can I raise her and love her, knowing that at one point I thought about not bringing her into this world or about giving her to someone else to rear?"

I remember LeMonia leaning across the desk, saying, "Pamela, you are only fifteen years old. It is scary to become a Mother at any age. Please don't be hard on yourself. I know you want to do what's best for you and your daughter. That is all. That's all any of us can want for our children. I'm much older than you, and everything I do may not be right when I do it for my children, but I do it for them because I love them." "I believe," she said as she reached out and touched my hand, "that all the things you were trying to plan, that you were trying to do, were with the best interests of you and your daughter [in mind]."

"You're right," I said. She was right, and I knew she was right, but somehow the guilt still didn't go away. It would be quite some time before I really learned to deal with my feelings about this.

As the summer progressed, my sixteenth birthday drew near. I remember waking up on a hot July morning and thinking, "Wow! I'm sixteen today!" I heard the song "Happy Birthday, Sweet Sixteen" playing in my head, and I started to hum it out loud. As I looked out in the backyard, saw the big tree, and smelled the fresh morning air, I thought, "This is great! I'm sixteen! I can get my driver's license! This is awesome! I've been waiting for this for so long." All of a sudden, I heard my daughter cry. I reached over to get her, picked her up, hugged her and thought, "Today is your mama's birthday! Yeah, your mama's sixteen today!" As I walked downstairs with her to get her bottle, it hit me. For years I had been looking forward to my sixteenth birthday, hoping for it, wondering what I'd be doing. Never, in my wildest dreams, did I expect to be carrying my daughter down the stairs to prepare a baby bottle on my sixteenth birthday.

The day was fairly uneventful. Mom cooked a nice dinner, and the family sang "Happy Birthday" to me over a homemade German Chocolate cake. It was my favorite kind, and Mom made the best in the world. I put Annette to bed early, and went to a movie with Angel.

After I got home, I remember humming to myself the "Happy Birthday, Sweet Sixteen" song again. Well, it sure wasn't what I would've picked for my sixteenth birthday, but it finally came. I was lying in bed planning the coming year. Planning and dreaming about my future always made me feel good. The optimist in my mom had been passed on to me, and I always expected tomorrow to be better. This time next year, I thought, what will I be doing? Well, I hoped to be graduated from high school. If I do two classes in summer school and a night class in the fall, I should certainly be able to finish next fall. Then I won't be a teenager in high school with a baby. I'll be a college student with a baby. Yeah, that'll be much better and much easier to handle. I rolled over on my pillow and smiled. I could hear Annette moving in her baby bed. I rose up on my elbow to look at her. She was so beautiful, tiny, and sweet. I prayed, "God help me. Help me not to be scared. Help me to be a good Mom and make a good life for this baby. Help me to feel okay about myself and help me to be happy. I really want to be happy." A sort of joyful and peaceful feeling seemed to come over me right then. I smiled and laid my head down on my pillow. It was a good day. Completely unlike what I had planned, but somehow it was a sweet sixteen anyway.

The rest of the summer seemed to go by so quickly. Before I knew it, I was enrolling at Douglass High School in the fall of 1979. Douglas was the "flagship" high school in Oklahoma City for African-American students. My daddy had graduated from Douglas High School, along with many of the African-American people in Oklahoma City, whom I had admired and grown to respect. Good old Douglas High School Trojans, I was going to become one.

Even though I was only going to be at Douglas for a year, I had decided that I was going to try and catch the Trojan Spirit. That wasn't very hard to do. The school had been decorated with orange and black all over the place for the first week of school. Spirit ribbons, people in uniforms, and oh my God, cheerleaders! How I envied them. The cheerleaders! I flashed back in my mind of my days at Hayfield High School and my orange-and-white cheerleading suit. God, how I loved being a cheerleader! The attention from guys, the sexy uniforms, the fun and yelling that went so well with my personality! Now there was nothing, nothing that I could do to recapture that part of my life.

I decided that I would just study, study, study and graduate. School was easy. I managed to get five classes, and also took a class where I would get credit if I got a job. I told Mom since I could get school credit for having a job; this would be a good time for me to work. She reluctantly agreed, and I got a part-time job at the mall. This time I was working in a clothing store—Sales. I was good at sales; I was always a people person, and loved to talk and that was all it took. I loved this job; it was very convenient and getting school credit for it sure helped. Although it was hard to get back and forth to work, I was really glad to have a job and to be going to school.

My sister, Marcella, noticed my struggling to travel around, and she called me. She had managed to get a secretarial job near Douglas, and every now and then, she'd pick me up or drop me off at work.

"Listen, Rochelle, I've been thinking," Marcella said. "I was planning to get a new car, and if you're interested, you can have my Mustang, and just take over the payments."

Wow! I thought. This is great!

"Well, Marcella, how much are the payments? I don't know if I can afford them."

"Well, sweetheart, the payments are only $98 a month, and if you need some help right away, I'll be glad to help you out."

"Okay! Thank you, Marcella! Thank you so much!"

"Sure, sweetheart. Thank you! It'll help make it a little easier to get my new car."

"Oh, thank you, Marcella!" I hung up the phone. I was thrilled!

"Mom!" I said, "Marcella's going to let me have her Mustang! I just have to make the payments."

"Yeah, she talked to me about it. That sounds like a good deal," Mom said. I could tell she was pleased.

"Oh, Mom, this is great! Mom, you know what?"

"What, honey?" she said smiling at me.

"Mom, I'm happy!"

"You are? Well, praise God, I'm glad you're happy!" Mom said. I reached out and grabbed her arm. She turned to look at me...I said again, "I am, Mom. I'm really happy!" It felt so good to say that and mean it.

The fall was extremely busy with school, my job, and Annette. Before we knew it, Christmas had come. It was a cold Christmas. I had Annette wrapped in a thousand blankets every time we so much as went near the door. Mom and Dad laughed at how many clothes and blankets I put on her! I wasn't ever going to let anyone say I didn't take care of my baby. She always smelled so good and looked adorable in her cheap, but nice outfits. Mom seemed pleased with my parenting and often told me what a good Mom I was.

Even though Eddie and I weren't together, he still called about every other week to see how Annette was doing. Somehow every time we talked, we would get back to the conversation of us getting back together or having sex together – neither of which interested me.

Whenever he would start to talk about us, I would stop him and say, "Eddie, I just don't think it's a good idea." Inevitably, he would become upset, and we would end up angry by the time the conversation ended.

Christmas was great! Annette got a lot of toys. Thank God for her grandparents! Between my parents and Eddie's parents, she had more clothes and toys than I knew what to do with! Of course, she didn't even know she was in the world. But it sure made me happy to see all those wonderful gifts for my baby. Somehow it didn't make it seem like we were Welfare recipients. Even though I never felt I lived a life of poverty while living with Mom and Dad, just the thought of getting AFDC, when I knew that wasn't how I wanted to raise my child, humiliated me. I still remember the conversation Mom and I had when she said it was OK for me to get help. After all, I was going to need help for a little while, and then I could be a taxpaying person and help someone else. This rationale did not always help, but today it was working. It was a good Christmas by all measures. Annette was seven months old now. She had the fattest, sweetest, most kissable cheeks. Boy, was she the prettiest little "chocolate drop" in the world or what? She inherited Eddie's beautiful and flawless dark complexion, and had the biggest brown eyes and sweetest little smile I had ever seen. Yes, my life was so much harder now than I ever imagined, but I was determined to make it for my beautiful precious little doll. I started calling her Little Bitty Doll. She became my inspiration more than ever, as I rocked her to sleep on this Christmas afternoon. I had to be successful. I had no other choice.

 The cold and wind of the Oklahoma winter couldn't go by fast enough. Soon we started having warmer and longer days. I couldn't have been happier about that! In the spring I continued to work, take care of Annette, and go to school.

 Annette's first birthday came so quickly, that I couldn't believe she was about to be a year old. As her birthday came, she was not only walking, but also starting to run. She had the fastest little legs, and it was so funny to see her try to run. On her birthday, I put a pretty yellow sundress on her. She had a little hair now, and I decorated her hair with pretty yellow and white barrettes. Mom went all out, making a huge dinner and she bought a quarter sheet birthday cake that said "Happy Birthday Annette." It had a big #1 and yellow flowers on the cake. We had lots of family and friends, and, of course, Mom took lots of pictures.

School was very easy, it was not challenging me in any way, except for my algebra class. Algebra II had a way of keeping my attention, and keeping me motivated and challenged. Daddy made me take Algebra in the 7th grade, so I was used to math classes but this was hard. As I planned for graduation, I started to talk to Daddy about what I wanted to do in the future. I was so glad that my plan to graduate early had worked out.

"Well," he said one day as we sat at the kitchen table, "you're smart, you are good in math, and you like science. You'll make a good doctor. Isn't that what you were planning to study?"

"Yes it is Daddy, but I just wanted to talk to you about it." I had thought seriously about medicine before I got pregnant, and then Mrs. Bennett brought that dream back to my mind. I was so glad that Daddy still thought I could do it.

My matter of fact response must have made Daddy think that I wasn't really interested or serious about medicine. He looked over at me as if to offer me an alternative and said, "Well, whatever you do, get your education. I have these young kids who come in [to my job] and, because they have the degree, they end up making more money than I do. Get your education." He always pointed two fingers at me when he was emphasizing a point, and today was one of those days.

"Okay, Daddy." I said, "I'm going to study medicine." One thing I was sure of was that I would get my education. Despite negative people, people doubting me, people saying I would never do it, people wondering if I'd ever graduate high school, somehow I knew that I was going to graduate from high school and get my higher education. I wasn't sure how I would do it, but I knew that I would.

"Daddy?" I said. "I've been thinking about how to pay for school. Um...I called Rose State, and they sent me some information. I think that's where I should go to school to begin, because it's cheaper, it's close to home, and I could stay here with you and Mom, so you guys can help me with Annette."

Mom interrupted. "Pam, I've heard about grants and financial aid. Have you thought about applying for those? Dr. Ryder, my boss, said his kids get financial aid, and he makes good money at the Health Science Center. He's a doctor. So, I know if his kids can get financial aid, we can."

Dr. Ryder was Mom's boss. He was a physician and a teacher at the Health Science Center. He had confided in her that even though he had a good salary, his children managed to get financial aid each year that they were in college, mostly loans, but he said it helped a lot.

"Surely if Dr. Ryder's children can get financial aid, Pamela, you can." Mom liked to say the same thing over and over when making her point.

"Okay, Mom. I'll apply for financial aid. I'll call tomorrow and get all the paperwork. Maybe I can get a scholarship." I wasn't in the top 10% of the class, but I did have what was identified as "scholastic distinction." "I'll ask them about scholarships too," I said. I was excited that the family was discussing my future. "They believe in me," I thought. Maybe they are even a little bit proud of me. I know I've messed up, so I have to do something to make them be proud of me.

I was so excited when graduation came around. There I was, finally going to graduate from high school. As I put on my robe and my cap and looked at myself in the mirror, I thought, "This is it!" I loved my gold cap and gown. My hair even looked good on that day. I looked over at my daughter. I bent down to pick her up, and started dancing with her and singing. She was just over a year old.

"Look at your mama, honey. She is going to *graduate* today! She is going to be a college graduate! Whoops! I slipped, didn't I, baby? I didn't mean college; I meant high school. This is a big day 'Nettie Girl.' One day you're going to look at your mama, and she is going to have another one of these on. Then she will be a college graduate. You believe it! You don't pay any attention to what those people say about your mama, the ones that say she's not going to do it, because she's going to do it baby!"

Annette was laughing and putting her head back – that was her cue for me to spin her around. Whenever anybody came over, they'd always ask, "Where's Nettie? Bring her here, and let me kiss on those jaws!" In fact, my dad always said, "Let me bite on those jaws!" He would kiss her and rock her and play with her. Boy, did they love their granddaughter!

Later that night, as I walked across the stage to receive my diploma, I felt a sense of accomplishment. But as I watched many of the other students embracing each other and crying, talking about how far they had come, I didn't really have the same feeling. Even though I was very proud to be finishing high school, I knew that this was just the beginning of a very long journey—a journey to an education, to independence, to accomplishing the things that so many people believed that I couldn't. I maintained my job throughout the summer. I was so excited about starting college that I enrolled in Rose, and decided to take one course in the short summer session.

As I walked on the college campus, it was an exhilarating feeling. I felt so important, so grown up, so normal. There were other people on the campus that had kids. There were other people on the campus who were moms, who had jobs, who had responsibilities. But the thing I liked most was that I didn't have to see any cheerleading uniforms!

I went by the financial aid office to pick up my application. I had already enrolled and informed them that I would be applying for financial aid. Unfortunately, I didn't know how to complete the forms correctly, and two weeks after I completed them, they came back to me indicating that there was an error on my application.

Once again I went back to the financial aid office. Hopefully this time, I thought, I can get it filled out correctly, and get the money to pay my tuition. In the meantime, I was still at the mall, working as a shoe salesperson at Thom McCann. Thom McCann was a great place to work. It was in Crossroads Mall, close to home, and I could dress nicely for my job. The best part of it was that I saw some of the finest men in Oklahoma City walking through the mall! That certainly made the job worthwhile.

One day as I was preparing to close the store, a man walked into the store casually checking out the boot display. Not a bad-looking man, not what I would choose as someone I wanted to date, but I could feel him looking at me. Wanting to make a big sale, I thought, hey, he's looking at an expensive pair of boots. Maybe I can have a good sale here to end the night. So I walked over to him.

"Can I help you, sir? Would you like to try that boot?"

"No," he said. "I'm just looking." But now he wasn't looking at the boot anymore, he was looking at me. All I could think of was, no he didn't come in here at ten minutes to nine talking about he's "looking," and then try to "check me out." He better buy some boots if he wants my attention. But I quickly fell back into my courteous mindset.

"Okay. Well, you let me know if I can help you in any way," I said. I smiled and turned to walk away, and felt his eyes on me.

I stopped to straighten up a row of shoes. As I stood there I could see, out of the corner of my eye, that he was still looking at me. He started to walk towards me. I looked over.

"Did you find something you're interested in, sir?"

"Yes, but it's not a pair of shoes."

"Well, if he's not going to buy boots, I guess he should at least flatter me," I thought. I smiled and blushed a little.

"What's your name?" he asked.

"Rochelle," I said, still sort of embarrassed by his continuously looking at me.

He extended his hand and gave me a warm, firm, handshake. Then he smiled and had the warmest, most beautiful smile I'd ever seen. "My name is Joshua....Joshua Smith." He spoke in a warm, deep, and even soft voice. He was only a little taller than me, but between that beautiful smile, sexy voice, and golden complexion, I did not need anything else to know I was interested.

"Well do you think maybe we could get together some time and have lunch?" he asked.

"Well, I'm very busy most of the time. You see, I'm in school, and I have a daughter," I promptly replied, while turning to straighten another row of shoes.

"You're in school?" he asked. He seemed surprised.

"Yes, I'm in college." It always made me so proud to tell people that I was in college.

"Well, you know, maybe some time we can get together. I'd like to take you and your daughter to lunch," he said.

I looked at him quickly, and then looked back to the shoes. I was certainly interested, but I was hesitant. Seemed like most of the time the men, the boys, whatever you want to call them, that I had talked to since Annette was born, immediately thought that I was an easy sex target. Just because I was young and had a baby signaled an easy target to them. He seemed different somehow. He looked older, older than most of the "men" I had talked to. Maybe he'd understand; maybe he'd be fun to talk to; maybe he would enjoy talking, and wouldn't want to just get with me so we could have sex. After all, he did offer to take *me and Nettie* to lunch.

"Well, maybe," I said, still not looking at him. I was starting to feel nervous, the kind of nervous I get when I like a man and I hoped he liked me, really liked me and not just wanted to sleep with me.

"Could I have your phone number?" he asked. I was so relieved that he asked. I thought for a minute that my hesitation turned him off.

"Yeah, let me go write it down. Give me just a few minutes. I've got some things to get done, then I'll give it to you." I walked to the back room.

"Sure," he said. "Take your time." I appreciated his patience.

As I went over and wrote the number down, I thought, who knows? Maybe he'll be different. Maybe he'll be the one.

CHAPTER 3

MAKE ME WANNA HOLLA!!

Going to school at Rose State College in the fall of 1980 was tough, a lot tougher than I expected. I had pretty much breezed through my final year at Douglas High School, and expected to do the same thing at Rose State. It seemed that the courses took a lot of time, a lot more time than I had, or maybe a lot more time than I was willing to expend. Yes, I'm sure I could have spent more time studying, but after all, by now I was seventeen. I wanted to go out, I wanted have some fun, and of course, I had to be a mom. Although Nettie was barely a year old, I liked reading to her, showing her bright colors, and singing to her.

Her favorite word that summer was "Be-ba Be-ba," and she said it all the time! Toddling around and saying "Be-ba, Be-ba, Be-ba," we had no idea whatsoever what she was talking about, but we sure loved to hear her saying "Be-ba."

After our initial meeting, I had gone out to lunch with Joshua a couple of weeks later. He picked me up in a strange little burgundy sports car. We went to a really nice restaurant, and talked for hours. He was in the Air Force and going to school at night to finish college. He was smart and worldly. He had been all over the world – wow, and he wanted to spend time with me! I felt so lucky. We talked for hours. Even though I should have spent some of this time studying, I allowed myself the time to have these wonderful conversations with Joshua. There was only so much I should be expected to sacrifice, I thought. As a result, my grades weren't nearly as good as they should have been, not nearly as good as they could have been. On top of that, I was starting to have problems at home. It seemed like Mom looked for every opportunity to fuss at me. I was an adult. Why was Mom treating me like I was still a kid? I'm in college. I have a kid of my own. Why does she want me to be in the house by 1:00 a.m.? Why does she want to know every move I make? This doesn't make sense. "I'm getting tired of this!" I reasoned. "I've got to get my own place!" is all I could conclude on the matter.

As I continued to mull over the frustration in my mind, I decided to call Joshua and to talk to him about it. I was sure he would help me feel better. He sure seemed to understand all my worries. He was a mature man – not a boy. After all, he was a few years older--actually, 10 years older--than me, twenty-seven. God that seemed old to me then, but he had a certain sense of stability that attracted me, perhaps because he was in the Air Force. Being in the military seemed to offer such a sense of security to me; I'm sure that was because Daddy had been in the military for twenty years, and whenever we were with Daddy, everything seemed so secure. I equated this sense of security with Joshua, and I often went to him, talking to him about my problems. Talking to him about how no one understood me, how Mom didn't understand me, and how Dad always took her side. I would confide in him how she would always tell my brother and sisters, when I messed up and why. Why didn't any of them seem to understand me? Why didn't they even try? Joshua was all too eager to listen, so eager to help, and he quickly became my refuge. He offered encouragement in his soft, caring voice, and always told me that I would be ok. He always said that God would take care of me. He was a Christian man, too. I was so thankful to have him in my life. Soon, we were talking every day.

Looking back on it, I certainly understand my mother and father's position. But back then, all I could see was their lack of trust, their lack of faith in me, and them thinking I was going to go out and have another baby. I agonized, "Why don't they chill? I'm going to school; I'm doing all the things I said I was going to do, despite getting pregnant. Why do they think I'm going to get pregnant again?"

One day it seemed as though I had more than I could stand. We were sitting in the dining room eating dinner. I got up to leave as Mom started in, again, on how I needed to stop seeing

Joshua. How he was too old for me, how he didn't mean any good, how the only thing he was concerned about was having sex with a young woman.

"And also," she continued, "Why would he want someone who's ten years younger than he is? Don't you understand? He only wants to use you."

Even though Mom may have been right, it hurt so much for her to say those things in front of my brother, my sister, and my dad. I felt so humiliated. I stood up at the table, and got ready to leave.

"Sit down, Pamela! Sit down!"

"Mom, I am grown. I am tired of this," I said turning to leave the room.

All of a sudden, I felt a hand connect with my face, and the next thing I remember, I was on the floor looking up, as my mother reached down to grab me. Thankfully, my father came to my rescue, grabbing my mother, and pulling me up by my shoulder.

"Pamela, don't you ever talk to your mother again like that! Do you understand me?" Daddy said as he stood between Mom and me. He looked directly at me while holding Mom off of me. Mom was shouting over him as he spoke sternly.

"Who do you think you are? You're grown? You're grown? Get out of my house if you think you're that grown! That's the problem! You're over there with that nigger. He's tellin' you all this mess...get outta my house if you're grown!"

"Fine," I said, tears in my eyes. "Fine, I'll leave." I pulled away from Daddy and ran toward the stairs. Nettie was crying because of all the commotion. My face was still stinging from Mom's slap, and my tears were coming faster than they could roll down my face.

As I went upstairs crying, I could barely see my way. I grabbed my purse and my keys.

"Come get your baby! Take your daughter with you!"

"Oh Lord," I thought, "how could I be leaving without my

child?" I needed to calm down. I don't want to upset my baby. "Calm down," I said to myself. "Calm down."

As I grabbed my daughter, I turned, not making eye contact with my parents or anyone in the room. I rushed to my car. I put Nettie on my lap, and dried my tears with the sleeve of my shirt. I looked over at her, while still sniffling, after I settled her in the seat next to me. I smiled or tried to smile and said, "Baby, we're going to be okay." I turned on the ignition, and the only place I could think to go to was Joshua's. I drove the fifteen minutes to his house, silently crying all the way.

Joshua heard me pull into his driveway. He opened the door with a big smile. He was always very happy to see me. As I took Annette out of the car, he could see that I was crying. He walked over to me, and hugged me.

"What's wrong, sweetheart?" he asked.

"It's my family. It's my mom; it's my dad; it's everything. I don't want to go back there. I'm so tired of this. Why don't they trust me? Why don't they like you? I just don't understand this! I don't think I can take this anymore."

He took Nettie from me and rocked her, as he opened the door, and we went into his house.

"Well, Rochelle, if it's that bad, you know you're welcome here. You know you can come live with me." Josh said with genuine concern for me. I loved being with him; I started calling him Josh soon after we met. I don't think anyone else did so it was my special name for him.

I thought about it, but how could I think about "shacking up" with a man. I never thought I could live with a man without being married to him. Maybe it was time for me to change my rules and expectations, I considered. I needed to get out of that house. I went in the house and laid Annette down; she had gone to sleep on the way over. I kissed her cheek and covered her up. I had forgotten her diaper bag. I didn't care about that tonight. I thought, "I'll go buy some more diapers and baby food."

Josh and I settled in the living room on the couch to

continue our conversation. "Well, Josh," I said, "I really don't want to just live with you. I mean, I love you, and I think we can have a future together, but I never really wanted to live with anybody unless, of course, I was married to them." I looked up to see his response to my mention of marriage.

"Well, Rochelle," he said, "I understand your feelings, but I'm just not ready to get married. I mean, anyway, marriage is just a piece of paper. If we love each other, and you respect me and I respect you, what difference does it make if we have a piece of paper between us? God sees our hearts," he said moving closer to me on the couch.

"Well, Josh," I countered, "I'm a Mom. I'm not sure I want to shack up in front of Nettie even though she's a baby. Also, what about church? And Reverend Parker? And my family? My mom will die if I move in here with you." I put my face in my hands just at the thought of how upset my family would be if I moved in with Josh.

Josh got up to go to the kitchen. "It's up to you. You know you're welcome. But I'm telling you, marriage is just a piece of paper." He opened the refrigerator. "Rochelle, let me fix you something to eat. You just relax."

As I was lying on the couch relaxing, I thought, maybe it wouldn't be so bad if I moved in with Josh. He was a good guy, and I would take good care of him and this new house. He could see what a great wife I could be, and then he'll want to marry me.

I really wanted to marry Josh. Marrying him would give me the stability and support that I needed with no more arguing, no more fighting with my mom and dad. Then, not only would I be grown, I'd be grown and in my own house, and have a husband. I'm sure I can convince Josh that we should get married, I continued. I'll just move in, and he'll be so happy to have Nettie and me with him, he'll be asking me to marry him in a month.

"Rochelle," he said, "I fixed you a sandwich. Eat this. I

know you didn't finish your dinner at home."

"Thanks, Josh," I sat up and ate a few bites of my sandwich, but I was so sleepy. I put the plate down and lay back on the couch where Josh was still relaxing. I drifted off to sleep on the couch after I felt Josh snuggle up behind me.

"Yea," I thought, "It will be great to be with Josh."

When I woke up, it was almost daybreak. Oh my God, I thought, another night, all night out. Mom is going to be furious with me. I have no choice but to move now. I went back home. Mom and Dad were up having coffee as always in the morning.

"Mom," I said, "Nettie and I are going to move in with Josh."

"You what?!?!" she exclaimed.

"I just think it will be better right now, Mom. And you said if I think I'm grown that I should have my own house. I just think this is the thing to do." I couldn't make eye contact with her. I put Nettie in her high chair and started fixing her breakfast.

"My Lord, Pamela! What are you thinking about? I guess I sure have raised a fool." She looked at me with so much frustration. "Well, I'll tell you one thing, I'm sure glad I have my other daughters. I'd be in trouble if you were the only daughter I had." I knew she would say something like that, but oh my God, it hurt so much to hear it!

I went upstairs, and gathered my things. It didn't take more than two trips to get everything I owned and everything of Annette's. I put those things in a few garbage bags, and placed them into the trunk and the back seat of my car. As I drove off, I still felt confused about my decision, but I also had a strange sense of relief. I thought, "Hey, now I am riding to freedom! Now I'll be able to do whatever I want! Now I'll be in my own house. Now I'll be able to call the shots." I would soon find out how very untrue that thought was. Boy! Was I wrong. Was I so wrong!

When I got to Josh's house, and started to unload things, he was thrilled. He was very happy to see me. He had bought a bedspread and some sheets for a twin bed, and said we could use those for Annette's room. He had a nice house, small but very nice with three bedrooms, a nice living area, and a patio. I thought this could really be a nice home for all three of us. So, over the next few days, I started settling in as a "wannabe Mrs. Smith."

Annette really seemed to like Josh. He'd read to her and always picked her up to give her a hug and kiss before he left the house. She'd run around the living room playing with her toys, making all the noise she could. I really enjoyed spending afternoons with her when I didn't have to go to class or I didn't have to go to work, which unfortunately was not very often.

I started establishing a schedule to get myself ready, get Annette dressed, have breakfast, and fix lunch for me and Josh to take to work, all by 7:45 a.m. This gave me enough time to drop Nettie off at the daycare center and get to class or work by 8:30. Rose State College was working out as a good place to begin my education. Also, with my financial aid, I got a work-study job on campus. This made it so much easier for me to study, earn a little money, and take care of Nettie and Josh. I always tried to get home before Josh – just to make sure the house looked good, and so I could be there for him. Whenever Josh came home, I tried to have something ready for dinner. I also tried to have Annette rested and quiet so we could spend a little time together because sometimes when he came home he wasn't in a very good mood. I never understood why. Sometimes he would come in and he wouldn't want to talk; he wouldn't say anything. He was mostly upset that he was not an officer in the Air Force. He said he wanted to be a pilot and an officer, but he never got the support from his family or first wife to make it happen. I knew this bothered him almost daily.

He always wanted to know what I did each day, who I saw, who I talked to, and if there were any men who tried to talk to me when I was at school or work. I didn't really understand at first. At first, I just thought it was petty jealousy, and then it escalated.

He'd come by the campus at Rose State to see what I was doing. I thought it was that he missed me and wanted to visit with me. Then I found out that he would come and sit in the parking lot sometimes and just watch me walk to lunch with my friends. He would call throughout the day, sometimes on the hour, to see if I was at the office when I was supposed to be working. He would always call the moment he expected me to be home from school. If I were still at work more than 10 or 15 minutes late, he'd want a full explanation of why I didn't leave on time. He was insistent that I leave work, get Annette, and come straight home. It started to scare me a little bit, because when I wasn't where I was supposed to be, he would get angry. He would interrogate me by asking whom I saw and what I did. Josh wasn't a bad person, but he seemed to be very, very confused sometimes. I'm sure a big part of the confusion was his upbringing and a very bad marriage he'd had when he was only nineteen years old.

I met his mother. She was a very nice woman, but unfortunately, she had Josh when she was seventeen or eighteen, and she allowed his grandmother to rear him. After giving him to his grandmother, she had other children, married and reared them. For that reason, Josh felt very unimportant and very insignificant to her. In some ways I could relate to his feelings. All that his mother tried to do to change his feelings still hadn't worked. He loved his Grandma, who had since passed away, but had a love-hate relationship with his mother. He also never really knew his father. This added to his frustration and insecurity.

I tried to reassure him that I understood his feelings because I was the middle child. I, too, felt a little unimportant in my family. My sister, Marcella, was always the most important. She was the oldest; she was the smartest; and she was Mom's friend. She was always number one. My brother, Maurice, was the only son. After all, he was Maurice, Jr. My sister, LaWanna, was the baby of the family. Everybody loved LaWanna. She was sweet, always said the right things, and never got into trouble. Then there was me, stuck there in the middle, just kind of hanging out, growing up. Even though I'm sure it was never intentional, and I knew my parents loved me just as much as they loved my other brother and sisters, for some reason, most of the time, I felt fairly unimportant in my family. As such, I could relate to Josh's feelings. I knew what could lead to frustration and insecurity, so I really tried to be understanding of him, and show him love, understanding, and encouragement.

However, his upbringing wasn't the biggest problem, it was his early marriage. He married his high school sweetheart after they had a baby. Well, after he went away to join the Air Force—reminding me very much of what Eddie had done to take care of Annette—she didn't stay faithful to him, or so he said. Apparently she started using drugs and cheated on him with his close friends. Then, she sold his clothes, sold his furniture, and even had men coming into the house where they lived. To add insult to this, his mother knew about it; his sister knew about it; and so did a lot of folks in the neighborhood. So, he was further humiliated in front of his family and friends. Therefore, Josh returned home to Miami, Florida to a bad situation. However, he tried to forgive her, and gave her another chance; they tried reconciling. Even after that, according to what he told me, she was still unfaithful, deceitful, and continued to destroy what bit of a marriage they had left. He told me she became pregnant by someone else while they were still married, and tried to convince him that the child was his. I felt so badly for him while he shared these painful memories with me. Eventually Josh divorced her, and decided to move on with his life. After a series of relationships, traveling across the country and the world with the Air Force, he settled in Oklahoma City. That's when I met him.

All of his actions, feelings, and expectations were not just because of me, but also because of previous hurtful experiences that he had not addressed. At seventeen I didn't understand that at all. I simply thought that if I called him as soon as I got home, if I got home on time, if I called him from the office, if I showed him lots of love, then eventually his efforts to control me and his anger would go away. I was sure it would. After all, I really was going to love him. I was going to love him better than his mother did, better than his ex-wife did, better than anyone else had, and he was going to have to love me back. Unfortunately, I didn't realize the depth of the scars that Josh was carrying.

One day after school, I decided to go to lunch with my cousin, Barbara. After lunch we went to the mall and had a great time. A couple of hours later, Barbara and I were headed home. We had picked up Annette from the daycare center. Barbara took me back to the school to get my car and Nettie, and I drove home. Nettie was so sweet, even when she was tired like today. I put my sleepy baby down to bed as soon as we got home. Just a few minutes after I walked in the door, Josh came in.

"Hi, honey! You're home early!" I said.

"Where have you been?" he said in a calm but questioning voice.

"Well, I went to lunch with Barbara," I said walking over to give him a kiss.

"Don't lie to me!" he shouted walking quickly to me and grabbing me by my shoulders.

"What are you talking about, Josh? I went to lunch with Barbara, and then went to the mall." I was shaking and totally confused. I had seen Josh upset before but never like this, not with me.

"What's wrong Josh?" I asked trying to pull away from his grasp.

"Don't you lie to me," he shouted. "I'll slap the shit out of you if you lie to me."

"Josh! What are you talking about?" My hands were

trembling. I couldn't even think. "What are you talking about? I mean, Barbara and I just went to the mall," I said. He pushed me away from him.

"I went by the school and saw your car but you weren't at work", he said staring at me. I told him quickly that I rode with Barbara.

I was trying to tell him again that we were just at the mall. I started to stutter, and this angered him all the more. I guess he thought if I was stuttering, I had to be lying. As he came near me, his eyes were big, sweat was on his forehead, and his voice was like I'd never heard it before.

"Don't you deceive me!" he yelled. "Don't you do this to me!"

All of a sudden I felt a slap on my face. It was a hard sting and it knocked me to the floor. As I hit the floor, I started crying.

"Joshua! Why are you doing this? I just went to lunch! I went shopping with Barbara. Why don't you believe me?"

"Then where is she?" he quizzed. "If you went shopping with your cousin, where is she?"

"She went home. Barbara went home. I promise I just went shopping with her." I was still crying and yelling now, trying to get him to believe me. "Call her; she will tell you we went shopping."

"I'm not going to have you lying to me nor deceiving me. This is my home! I'm the man of the house. You are going to do what you're supposed to do. You're going to do what I tell you to do. Do you understand me?" he demanded, walking up to me and standing over me as I sat on the floor.

"Yes, Josh, I understand," I complied. "I'm sorry. I'm sorry."

He walked away, went to the table, and sat down. A couple of minutes later, he walked over to me. I was still sitting on the floor, trembling. He seemed as if he had calmed down.

"Rochelle," he said, "I'm sorry. I just love you so much.

When you do stuff like this, when I don't know where you are, it worries me. It scares me. I love you. I don't ever want anything to happen to you. I just have to know you're okay." He seemed like a totally different person from a few minutes before. But this made me even more afraid.

His words sounded so smooth, so soft, and full of concern, but I couldn't stop trembling. He reached for me; I quickly pulled away.

"Rochelle, I'm sorry. You know I never want to hurt you. It's just that you make me like this when you don't do what you're supposed to do, when you aren't where you're supposed to be. I love you. I love you so much, Rochelle. You're the best thing that's ever happened to me, and I can't bear not being with you. I can't bear something happening to you. If you do what you're supposed to do, this won't happen again."

This time as he moved towards me, I didn't pull away. He sat on the floor next to me, and pulled me close. He held me really close and told me he was sorry and that he'd never do it again.

"I promise, Rochelle, I'll never raise my hand to you again," he whispered in my ear.

"Okay," I said. "Okay, Josh."

After that, I realized it wasn't a good idea for me to go to lunch with my friends or to do anything after school and work but come home. Even if I told him I wanted to go to lunch, he would still have an attitude. By the time I told him who I was going to lunch with, where we were going, how long we'd be there, I was not even in the mood to go out with my friends. So, I just stopped even trying to hang out at lunch. Josh really liked being at home, and he really didn't want me going anywhere either. So I would make fancy meals on what money he budgeted for groceries, watch movies, and watch professional wrestling on Saturday. Nettie loved being at home and playing with her toys. On most weekends, I would take her to my Mom's or Marcella's, so she could play with my niece MaRisha.

Other than that, we didn't do much else. Professional wrestling was the highlight of the weekend. I remember the "Junkyard Dog." He was our favorite wrestler. Every Saturday morning we'd get up, make Ramen noodles, put some ground beef in it, then lie around watching professional wrestling -- me, him and Annette, whenever she was home. We really enjoyed it, but somehow, I knew there was more to my life than what was being offered to me in this situation.

I started to feel discontent, and I also started to feel like I was being isolated—isolated from my friends, from my family, and from my church. Josh didn't even like me to go to church anymore. He said he knew some of the men in church were looking at me, and that if he couldn't go, he didn't want me going. This was really hard at first to accept. After all, this was my home church. How could he feel this way about my church? But I wanted so much to make Josh happy. I thought I'd take a break from my home church. Just until Josh saw that he could trust me, and there was nothing for him to be concerned about with my church and men looking at me. I offered to go to a church that was close by or even a "white church." No one's going to "look" at me there, I told him. "No," he said. "God is here. He's with us; we don't have to go there."

"Josh," I said, "that's ridiculous. I need to go to church. Nettie needs to go to church." That comment made him even angrier, and he was really determined not to let me go back to my church or any church.

"No, let's just pray together. Let's read our Bible together. If you want understanding," he said, "you need to read the book of Proverbs." "You don't need some man interpreting the Bible for you. Read it yourself," he said.

Well, one thing I can say about Josh, and one thing I will always thank him for is directing me to the book of Proverbs to gain wisdom and understanding. I remember one night I was so frustrated. He had come home in a bad mood and gone through one of his shouting spells. He didn't hit me, but I was terrified.

As he got angry, worked himself into a frenzy, calmed down, and then stormed out of the house, I sat on the couch with tears in my eyes trembling. I reached for the Bible, and dusted it off. Since I hadn't been going to church, I hadn't read my Bible. I remember opening it to the book of Proverbs. The first chapter I read was about understanding. God, did I need understanding!

"Lord," I said, "I don't even understand what I'm doing. I don't even understand how I got here. If anybody ever needed understanding, Lord, it's me."

And then I prayed and prayed and prayed.

CHAPTER 4

NEVER CAN SAY GOOD BYE

Over the next few days, I read a lot in the book of Proverbs. I felt a certain comfort, a certain sense of security as I read. Lord, I thought, "I'm not sure what the right things are to do in everything. I don't know if anybody knows. But it says here to listen to my mother and father, to listen to wisdom, to gain wisdom, to seek understanding. I'm not even sure how to seek it, but I'll continue to ask for it."

One scripture that really stuck with me was Proverbs 3:5-6, and it read, "Lean not into your own understanding, but in everything you do, ask God for guidance, and He will direct your path." I wasn't exactly sure what this scripture meant, but I liked it. For one thing, it told me not to count on my own understanding of situations – well that was not hard for me because I didn't seem to understand much of anything. But then it read if I asked God for help, He would direct my path. Lord knows I wanted somebody to help me figure out which way to go. "Lord," I prayed, "I sure hope this scripture will work for a teen mom who's living in sin." I could only hope and pray at that point. I later learned that it would work for me and anyone else who believed.

About two weeks later my mom called. "Well, Marcella's going to the hospital. She's going to have the baby." My older sister, Marcella, was pregnant. They knew it was going to be a little boy; she was so excited. Although she and her husband Charles, whose nickname was Spike, had had some problems, they managed to work out their differences and stay together. They bought a cute little 3-bedroom house, and then decided to have another child. Those nine months went by fast, and now it was time for the baby to come.

I went to the hospital to see Marcella deliver Charles Alexander Washington, her second child, and her first son. We quickly nicknamed him Alex. The first son in her family! We were all elated. The first grandson, that was. "We all have a little boy," we said. My brother reminded us all that he was "the son" of the McCauley family.

I remember taking a dozen roses to Marcella when she was in the hospital. It felt so good to be able to give her the roses, to go and see her. See, Marcella and I never had much of an opportunity to be much like sisters since I always felt like she was a second mother to me. Doing something like this made me feel rather sisterly. So I took the roses up to her. She was so glad to see us. She was beautiful. She was smiling and holding her son, Alex. He was so precious! Mom and LaWanna arrived soon after I got to the hospital. We all instantly fell in love with Alex. We all took turns holding him. Marcella got out of the hospital the next day and went home. I remember going over the following week to see how she was doing, and we went out to lunch. She asked me how school was going, and I told her things were fine. She really wanted me to do well in school. That was so important to her. She asked me how things were with Josh, and I lied and said they were fine. I told her I really didn't want to be there, not under those conditions, and I hoped we'd get married soon. But I couldn't dare tell her that he slapped me. She'd tell Mom, and it would be a major family problem. I just didn't want to deal with being wrong again.

"Well," she said, "I don't know if he's going to marry you. He doesn't have any incentive to, with you living there." She looked at me as if she thought I would disagree. I didn't have the strength to disagree – all my energy was being drained trying to deal with Josh. I always had to think about what to say, how to say it, and when to say it, all of this had really taken its toll on my energy.

"Yeah, Marcella, I know." I changed the subject. I wasn't in the mood for a lecture; I was enjoying this pseudo-sisterly time. I went home and went about my usual chores of taking care of Josh and Nettie and being a student.

A couple days later, I remember Mom calling me around 11:00 a.m. on a Saturday morning. She said, "Marcella passed out. She fainted. She went to Captain D's to get some lunch. We can't find Spike, but the people called us from the restaurant. So LaWanna and I are on our way over there now."

"Mom, Marcella is so sickly and weak! Why did she go to the restaurant by herself and why did she faint?" I asked. "She's so sickly and she just had Alex. What was she thinking about?"

"Honey, you're right, if she wasn't feeling good, she shouldn't have left the house, but that's not the issue. I'm going to go over and pick up some chicken for her and her husband, and I'll stay at her house with until she feels better. LaWanna and I are going now. They just called us."

"Okay Mom," I said. Marcella had fainting spells when she was too hot so we all knew that she was a bit on the fragile side.

I hurried to clean the house, so I could go see Marcella. "It's crazy for her to be leaving the house when the baby's so young, and she's still so fresh out of the hospital." I thought, "Well, hey, this will teach her a lesson. She's not a wonder woman, and she needs to take better care of herself." A few minutes later, the phone rang again. It was my sister, LaWanna. She was crying hysterically.

"Rochelle, it's bad. It's bad," LaWanna said through her tears. "It's really bad."

"LaWanna? What's wrong?" I asked.

"It's Marcella, it's Marcella! She didn't just faint or fall; they don't know what's wrong. She doesn't know who we are! She's here on the floor at the restaurant, she doesn't know anything!" LaWanna was screaming and crying now. "The ambulance is here."

"Oh, my God, where are they going to take Marcella?"

"I don't know, I don't know. Momma's upset. Momma's crying and nobody can tell us anything," LaWanna said.

"Are you going to Midwest City Hospital? Are you going to Oklahoma Memorial Hospital? Where are you going? LaWanna please try to calm down, and tell me where they're taking her!"

"I don't know, I don't know. I'll call you when we get there." She hung up the phone.

Oh my God, what is going on? I don't know anything. I can't do anything. I felt so helpless; there was nothing I could do. I paced the floor. I called my dad, I called my brother -- nobody was home. I waited for what seemed an eternity. About 45 minutes later, the phone rang. I didn't even let it ring one full time. It was LaWanna.

"Rochelle, we're at Oklahoma Memorial Hospital. They said Marcella had an aneurysm. A stroke. She had a blood clot that traveled to her brain. They're doing surgery. They're taking her to surgery right now." She started to cry again.

"LaWanna I'll be right there!" I said. I jumped in my car and drove that Mustang faster than it had ever been driven. All I could think of was getting to the hospital. I didn't even know what an aneurysm was, but I asked God to please take care of my sister. By the time I got to the hospital, Marcella was already in surgery. Mom was numb. She just sat there. LaWanna was sitting next to her. I ran to get right in front of her. By now Daddy and my brother were at the hospital too. I knelt down in front of Mom. "Mom," I asked, "what did the doctor say? What happened to Marcella?"

A nurse walked into the waiting room. Mom looked past me, and stared up at the nurse.

"How can this be happening? Marcella's twenty-three years old! My daughter is twenty-three- years old, nurse. What is this? I don't understand."

"Ma'am, I'm not sure. The doctor will be in to talk to you as soon as he's out of surgery."

All of my aunts—all six of them an my Mom's three brothers—started arriving, one by one. They sat there holding Mom, praying with her, praying with us, quoting scriptures, and sounding strong. Nettie and MaRisha were at Mom's with my cousin Angel. Angel had come to the house to take care of the kids while we went to the hospital.

After the surgery, the doctor came out of the room, and told us the aneurysm had burst, and this had caused something similar to a stroke. However, he thought that they had taken care of it. He said she would be in the intensive care unit for a while. She was not out of danger completely, but she could make it. He said that we could go into ICU, one at a time, and see her. But right now probably wasn't a very good time because she wouldn't know who we were. That didn't matter to us; we just wanted to see her.

Mom and Dad were the first to go in. When Mom came out, she was crying.

"Mom," I said, "she's going to be okay. You know she will, Mom. The Lord is taking care of you all the time. He's taking care of all of us. You know she's going to be okay." I didn't even know what I was saying, but I had to try to comfort Mom. I had never seen her hurt like this. Marcella's husband, Spike, went in next. He was only in with her for what seemed like two minutes. We saw him walk out of ICU and quickly walk by us. He didn't make eye contact or stop to talk to any of us. He went right by the waiting room and headed to the elevator. I walked into the ICU by myself – I was sure I could handle it. As I opened the curtain to see her, the shock and pain of seeing Marcella, knocked the breath out of me. I couldn't breathe, and I felt light-headed. I prayed out loud, "God help me."

Seeing my beautiful sister like that devastated me. They had to shave her head to perform surgery; there was a large incision, and half of her beautiful, long, thick, black hair was gone. I touched her hand; it was still warm. I lifted her hand and put her hand on my face, and I told her that I loved her. I knew she probably wondered sometimes if I did. Right now I wished I could take back every negative thought and mean word I had ever had for my sister. I loved her so much. I wanted to help her so much, and right then she couldn't feel any of my love or desire to help her.

"You're going to be okay, Marcella. You're going to be okay," I said while rubbing her right hand. "I love you, and you're going to be okay."

The family maintained a 24-hour vigil beside Marcella's bed. At least one, and sometimes two, of us were always there at all times. I took my books when it was my turn. I read my homework from school and textbooks while sitting. I would go in holding Marcella's hand, and tell her how much I loved her, and tell her how school was going. She made no response whatsoever. During one of my sittings, I wrote a letter for Marcella. In this letter I poured my heart out to her. I told her how much I loved her, how beautiful I thought she was. I thanked her for being a second Mom to me. Then I apologized to her for being jealous of her and for not listening to the good advice she often gave me. Then I promised her that I would never be jealous again, and that I would always tell her and show her that I loved her. The last part of my letter begged her to get well. As I was reading this letter out loud to her, my tears started to fall on the paper. "Marcella," I said looking directly in her face, "please get well...give me a chance to be a good sister to you, to make you proud of me, and to tell you that I love you. Please, please, please get well." I touched her hand again and turned to leave the room. My brother was there to relieve me.

About a week later, the doctor said Marcella's condition seemed to be improving.

Mom called and said, "Marcella's going to be moving out of ICU later this week. In fact, the doctor said he might even do it tomorrow. So I'm going to get some of her things, so we can make her hospital room look homey. Praise God!" This was the first time I'd heard hope in her voice since Marcella's incident.

"Oh, Mom, I told you everything's going to be okay. Everything's going to be fine!" This was the best news I'd heard in some time. I was so happy.

The next day I woke up early to go to the hospital. I called

Mom. She said that she was on her way to the hospital. I told her I'd be there soon after. I started to get myself ready and immediately the phone rang again.

"Rochelle." It was my sister, LaWanna. "Rochelle, Mom's going to the hospital. The nurse just called and said Marcella's not doing very well. They said she started hemorrhaging in her brain. Mom's on her way to the hospital." LaWanna was crying. "Daddy is with her."

I jumped in the car; Josh ran after me. "Rochelle, move over. I'll drive." He drove me to the hospital. I barely let Josh park. I ran into the hospital and to the stairs to get to the second floor like I'd done so many times over the last two weeks. Josh stopped the car and ran behind me. When we got there, my mom and dad were coming down the stairs. They both looked right past me – they didn't even recognize me. She and Daddy walked right by me. My aunt Camille and her husband walked right behind them.

"Pam," Aunt Camille said, reaching for me.

"Aunt Camille. What is it, Aunt Camille?" I asked.

"Marcella didn't make it, honey." She responded, while trembling and with tears in her eyes.

"What?! What are you talking about? She's doing better! That's what the doctor said. She's doing better." I was crying. I pulled away from Aunt Camille– this didn't make sense to me.

Aunt Camille reached out, and put her arms around me again. "Your sister didn't make it, honey. They said they did all they could. She didn't make it." Aunt Camille turned and walked away to go to Mom and Dad.

I turned to Josh. He reached for me and held me. I pulled away and dropped to my knees. I couldn't say anything; I couldn't think anything. I just cried and cried. I screamed in the stairwell and cried again and again.

The next couple of days were just a blur. As we tried to prepare for the funeral, my mom realized that my sister's husband had not maintained her insurance after she quit work.

No life insurance? What kind of man had no life insurance on his wife and no money either? Unfortunately, this financial burden quickly fell on my parents. In addition to the unbelievable hardship of losing a child, now they had the financial burden, which they had expected her husband to carry. They handled it like champs, arranging and paying for the funeral. The church and our family were really there for us. Every day somebody brought food to the house and prayed with us. During all of the planning, all I felt was hurt, deep pain, and confusion. I felt such hurt and anger at losing my sister, hurt in seeing my Mother and Father suffer. I had never seen so much pain in either of their faces. One of my aunts went to buy Marcella's burial clothes and a wig for her. Since they shaved her head, we knew that to have an open casket funeral, she would need a wig. My aunt brought a beautiful lavender dress and an afro wig. Years earlier, Marcella had a big, beautiful afro, and my aunt thought that this would be a beautiful way to recapture my sister's beauty. Spike was totally out of it. No one in our family seemed to be able to catch up with him, even though we had heard that he was at his mom's house. He'd dropped MaRisha and Alex off at my parents' house the day after Marcella died, and we hadn't heard much from him since. I think we all knew that he just couldn't handle losing Marcella, and he certainly was not up to making any of the required arrangements.

  The day of the funeral, we all gathered in the family car, and went to St. James Baptist Church, our family's church. As Reverend Parker delivered the eulogy, I cried, and then I cried some more. All of a sudden it seemed I had no more tears. I looked at my mom and my dad. They were both so motionless. Mom cried, and I saw tears on Daddy's face. But they just sat and stared. Both seemed like their minds had left them. As they opened the casket, and we got up to walk around, Josh held my hand. He had been there for me, listening to me, holding me, letting me cry, and being strong for me. As we proceeded to view Marcella for the last time, it seemed as though everyone walked in front of me, and I couldn't see her. I let go of Josh's hand and tried to get closer to the casket.

I was standing on my toes, saying, "I can't see her, I can't see her!" All of a sudden, I was on the floor, and I remember people looking down at me, reaching for me, trying to help me up. Two of the male ushers helped me up and guided me to the pastor's study. Immediately, Josh walked in.

"Are you okay?" Josh asked.

"Yes...yes, I'm okay. I just wanted to see her. I couldn't see her. I couldn't see my sister." I said

"Are you okay?" he asked again.

"Yes, yes, I'm okay," I confirmed.

"Are you going to stay here with her?" the usher asked Josh.

"Yes, I'll be here with her," he stated. As everyone left the room, Josh held me while I cried.

"I just wanted to see her one more time, Josh. I just wanted to see her one more time!"

As we left the funeral and ended the day, I got home and opened my Bible. Somehow the words of Proverbs didn't give me the comfort that I wanted. I turned to another book. I found no comfort there. I closed the Bible, and I sat.

"Lord," I said, "I don't know if this hurting will ever stop. Help me, Lord! I'm not even sad. I'm so far beyond sadness and hurt. I'm devastated." I prayed more. "God I know you don't want to hear from me since I'm living in sin, but God I need you." I pleaded. "I can keep hurting like this – please help me through this Lord, please send some type of comfort to me."

CHAPTER 5

THE 48 HOUR DAY

The weeks and months went by slowly after Marcella's death. Mom and Dad were raising Marcella's children, MaRisha and Alex. My entire family was very disappointed in the way that Spike responded to losing Marcella and taking care of his children. Sure he was hurting, but so were we. As far as we could see, Spike did nothing to make losing Marcella easier on his children. He wasn't even there for them. In a time like this, there was so much hurt, we couldn't even begin to understand. Maybe this was the only way he knew how to cope. We were just hurt, disappointed and trying so hard to handle this devastating situation.

Mom and Dad were raising MaRisha and Alex and dealing with the sudden and unexpected loss of Marcella. I admired their strength; I admired them so much. But any time I wanted to tell them I admired them, the hurt of losing Marcella, of dredging up the memories once again would get in the way. So unfortunately, I don't know if I've ever let them know how much I admired them for what they did -- for being wonderful, not just grandparents, but parents to MaRisha and Alex, despite the hurt, the anguish, and the pain that they were enduring.

Seeing how my sister's husband lacked the responsibility and the maturity to be a good father in a crisis made me think about my situation. It forced me to think about my life, my relationship with Josh. How would he handle a difficult situation like this? I was still reading Proverbs regularly, and sometimes calling my Pastor to talk to him. Reverend Parker started sensing that something was troubling me. After all, he'd known my family for years. Marcella adored him, and he adored her. I remember her telling us one time that she dreamed that God came to earth to reveal who his chosen men were. In that dream, she said God told her Reverend Parker was chosen. I really loved Pastor Parker. I hadn't spent a lot of time with him, but he baptized me when I was about five years old. So he had a special place in my heart. I knew I could trust him and that he would be praying for my family and me all the time.

I remember telling him how unhappy I was one day. I explained that I was unhappy with my relationship with Josh and my accomplishments. I told him I really wanted to do what God wanted me to do.

"Well," he said, "you know what the Bible says, and you know what the Lord would have you to do." As I hung up the phone, I knew he was right.

Actually, I knew the Lord didn't want me there with Josh. Not only did the Lord not want me there, I didn't want to be there. But I'm gonna look so stupid, I thought. After I've lived with him for six months, I'm gonna move out, just like everybody said, he was never going to marry me. But I knew I had to do something.

Before I could talk myself out of leaving, I heard Josh come in the front door. I walked up to him, and gave him a hug. "I need to talk to you, Josh." He backed away.

"What's wrong? Is everything okay with your family?" he asked.

"Yes," I said, "my family is okay. Josh, I need to leave." Even though I thought it was going to look stupid to my family and my church because they were going to be proven right about him not marrying me, it was worth it. I had to go!

"Why are you leaving, Rochelle?" he asked.

"Because we're not married. I can't stay under these conditions. It's wrong, and it makes me feel bad. I just can't do it." I could feel the tears and lump in my throat – I didn't want to start crying. I needed to make my point.

"Rochelle, God knows what's in your heart. He knows what kind of person you are. Whether or not we're married has nothing to do with it." He reached for my hand.

"Josh, I know. I know that, but I just have to go. I have to do this." I walked into the room, and started packing my things. I called Mom and asked her if she could come and help me. I just wanted to make one trip as I had accumulated a few more things than I could carry in my Mustang. Before I could finish asking, she was grabbing her purse and was on the way. I felt so much love for her right then.

God, I love my mother! Despite all the hurt I'd caused her, despite all the arguments we'd had, despite all the things she'd said to me which hurt me, there was never a time in my life when I didn't feel her love. There was never a time when I didn't know that she would be there whenever I called her. She helped me put the things in her car. I put Nettie in the car with Mom, and buckled her in. Mom got in her car. I went back in the house to get my keys and to tell Josh goodbye. I followed Mom as we drove slowly back to 47th Street.

When we got home, we sat down at the breakfast table. I knew I needed to explain what was going to my Mom. "Mom," I said, "I want to do good. I don't want to live with Josh if we're not gonna be married."

"Well," she said, "I told you that before you moved in with him. You need to stay at home and finish your college degree and just focus on your daughter." This started up one of her lectures, but somehow it didn't bother me too much that day.

"All right, Mom," I agreed. All I wanted right then was to do the right thing, to feel happy; to feel like I was doing what God wanted me to do.

Moving back home was tough. Once again, I was subject to Mom and Dad's curfews and their rules. Somehow it was a little easier this time. Josh called several times throughout each day.

About two weeks later he called, and sounded really down. "What's wrong Josh?" I asked. "Nothing," he said.

"Tell me," I said.

"Rochelle, I miss you, and I love you. I need you with me." He said this in every conversation, but he sounded different that day – more sincere.

"I love you, too, Josh. But I can't come back. Not unless

we're married." A few days later, he very reluctantly agreed that we could get married. I don't know if I should have been happy or sad, but I was elated.

In the conversation that led to his agreeing to get married, we started out as usual – with the I love you; I need you dialogue, but I could sense that he was getting irritated with my usual response of marriage. He interrupted me. "Okay, we'll get married," he said. "We'll get married. You want to get married? We'll get married."

I was so happy. "Yes, Josh – I love you, and I want to be your wife," I responded. "You'll be so happy – we'll be so happy! I love you!" I ran downstairs, skipping the bottom two steps, and yelled to Mom as I ran in the kitchen. "Josh asked me to marry him. Mom, we're getting married!!" I yelled as I embraced her, and started jumping up and down. The truth was that Josh didn't exactly "ask" me to marry him, but he agreed to my conditions for moving back – minor details. I thought, "I'm getting married!"

"Congratulations, Baby," Mom said. "Congratulations! See what happens when you do things God's way? Congratulations, Sweetie, I'm so happy for you."

It was October of 1982; I was 19 years old when Mom and I set about planning a small wedding in the backyard. We'd invite my aunts, uncles, and a few family friends. Daddy went to the Commissary at Tinker Air Force Base and bought several hundred dollars worth of groceries. He and Mom were always such great hosts. Dad barbecued, and Mom fixed desserts and several hors d'oeuvres. We ordered a cake, a small wedding cake from Beachler's IGA grocery store. We had a small, sweet ceremony, but it almost didn't take place.

I had bought a full-length yellow formal dress at Wall's Bargain Outlet Center. I remember paying all of $15 for it, and I loved it! It was perfect! Then Mom took me to a fabric store, and we got some yellow net, and we made me a veil. Certainly wasn't what I expected my wedding to be like, but somehow, it was coming together, and I was happy. As I prepared for the wedding, a few of the guests started to arrive. Unfortunately, there was no groom. The wedding was set to start at three o'clock.

Three o'clock came and went, and there was no still no groom. Three-fifteen came and went; still no groom. By 3:30, I was a nervous wreck.

"Mom, do you think he's going to come?" I asked nervously.

"Honey, I'm sure he'll be here. He'll be here." She answered with total confidence but a bit of annoyance that he would do this to her baby and in front of the family.

A few moments later, I saw Josh's car pull up. I headed to the front door to meet him.

Ms. Bennett and her little daughter, Tara, were sitting in the house with Mom and me. Tara was about nine years old, and she rushed over to me before I opened the door. "Pam, you're not supposed to see the man before the wedding, are you?"

"No, Tara, I'm not. But I really need to talk to him," I said. "It's okay to see him for up to ten minutes." I bent down and hugged her then proceeded out of the door.

I went out onto the porch, and closed the door behind me. Mom looked out of the curtain. I waved my hand for her to go.

As Josh walked to the porch, I noticed he had his sunglasses on, very dark glasses, which I removed. His eyes were red, and I smelled liquor, no, whiskey, on his breath.

"Josh, you're late," I dryly stated.

"Yeah, I know. But I'm here." he said with an attitude.

"Are you sure you want to marry me?" I asked. Now I was irritated. He arrived late, drunk, AND with an attitude? I don't think so! How does he think this is supposed to be okay with me? I was so mad – but how could I not go through with this? I've told everyone I'm getting married, we've got people here; Mom and Dad have gone through so much trouble; I can't stand to go through the embarrassment of telling people we decided not to get married because Josh showed up drunk!! All of these thoughts went through my head in a few seconds. Oh God, I don't know what to do. I prayed silently. God help me.

I said again, "Josh are you sure you want to marry me?"

"Yeah, I'm here, Rochelle. Let's go on," he said.

"Okay, Josh."

"Yeah, let's go on. Let's get this over with." he said. I thought, what a way for my groom to arrive—late, drunk, and in a bad mood. I should have asked myself if I wanted to marry him. But oh well, I'm sure we'll find a way to make the best of it. I don't know how, but we will.

We went through the ceremony with my Uncle Lee McCauley serving as our minister. Uncle Lee married us; we had a few hors d'oeuvres; and Mom took pictures like she always did. We managed to make this little wedding quite an occasion. At least it was for me. Some of my aunts bought small appliances and pictures, and wished me well in my marriage. Each had quick words of wisdom that they were very happy to share.

As we left the house, I was relieved and happy; I felt complete. Even with the rough start for this marriage, I started to feel confident that Josh and I would be okay. I was really going to do what God had said He wanted me to do. I was going to school; I was going to be a good mom. I was even going to be a good daughter because now I wasn't doing something that Mom really didn't want me to do. I wasn't going to be living in sin. And I was going to be a good wife. God, I hope you're happy with me. I really think you are – I prayed silently.

After the ceremony, Josh and I got in the car, and began driving. He turned to go south on I-35. I was still wearing my yellow wedding dress, and he looked so nice in his suit. The liquor smell had diminished somewhat, and he seemed to be relaxing now that it was just the two of us.

"Where are you going?" I asked him.

"Oh, I just want to go look at this car. I want you to see

this car I'm looking at." Well, how romantic, I thought sarcastically. Our wedding day, and he wants me to go look at a car? I sat silently but tried to seem interested as he started telling me about a BMW that he'd seen at a car lot in Norman.

We drove to Big Red's Auto Imports. Josh pulled into the parking lot and looked over and pointed.

"See that white BMW?" he asked. "That's the car I want to get." Well, I thought, now that I'm Mrs. Josh Smith, I'll have some say in this.

"Josh," I said, "that's just not a good idea. We just got married. I'm in school. You're in school. If we're both going to be going to O.U....."

WHAM! All of a sudden, I felt a stinging on my face. Josh had slapped me! Slapped me hard and backhanded me!

"I don't want to hear that mess from you! You're my wife. You'll support my decisions," he said staring at me.

Although we'd been through this once before, I couldn't believe he hit me. He promised! I was in shock. I was too shocked to even cry. Here I still sat in my wedding dress with my bouquet on my lap, and my groom had just slapped me. Oh, my Lord, what have I gotten myself into? I was too shocked, mad, and ashamed to even cry. I looked out of the front window of the car. "Whatever you want is fine, Josh," was my only perceptible response.

He drove closer to the white BMW studying it closely. Then he turned the car toward the exit. We drove back to Oklahoma City in complete silence.

I sarcastically said to myself, "Welcome to your new life, Mrs. Smith."

Josh and I both continued to go to school and work. But his jealousy got worse. Not only did he not want me going to lunch or shopping with my friends, but also, now, when he called and I was on the other line, he'd be furious. He'd want to know to whom I was talking. Or if it took me a long time to answer the phone, he wanted to know what I was doing. "Why didn't you get to the phone sooner?" he inquired. His angry spells became more frequent. He even slapped me more often.

Each time, he'd apologize, he'd tell me it was just because he loved me, and that somehow I was making him do that. I was provoking him, and when I stopped provoking him, and started being the kind of submissive wife the Bible told me to be, his anger would stop. He told me that I was the one in control of whether or not he got mad, and it was all in my hands. Somehow I believed it. I didn't want to think that Josh was a bad person or that I had married an abusive man. But something in me knew that this wasn't right. I hadn't grown up around this kind of behavior. I knew that a real man didn't hit his wife. I knew that a real man wasn't provoked into slapping a woman around. But I couldn't quit yet. I wanted to try to make it work. After all, we'd only been married for a couple of months. It was Christmas time. I wanted so much to try to make things work. Unfortunately, things just weren't working out at all.

Christmas was lean in the Smith home. We didn't have much money for gifts or decorations. I wasn't used to Christmas like this. No matter what was going on, my family always had lots of decorations, food, and gifts at Christmas time. I didn't have much money at all, but I'd managed to save a few dollars. I had about $40 to spend, and I had about 10 gifts for Annette, two for MaRisha, and one for Alex. Lewis and Annie sent Annette toys too. Mom and Dad, as always, showered her with gifts, toys, books and clothes. I bought Josh a present, and he bought me one. This was not my idea of what I wanted my first Christmas to be like with my husband, but Annette was happy, and that was really the most important thing.

The spring semester started at Rose State. It was almost time for me to graduate, and I was so excited at the possibility of graduating and moving on to the University of Oklahoma. Here I was about to get my Associate's degree, and some people thought I wouldn't even graduate from high school. I was excited about the spring semester too. I was truly moving toward my goal of completing my college education.

After I bought my books, and began preparing for the spring semester, Josh told me that I needed to start thinking about what I wanted to do after the semester was over.

"What do you mean?" I asked. "I'm going to O.U. I want to get my Bachelor's degree and then go to medical school."

"Well, I think you need to get a job. Remember that car I showed you? I want to go buy that BMW." All I could remember was being slapped, so I didn't dare tell him not to buy it, but I had to say something.

"Well, Josh," I said, carefully, "I'm sure that with my part-time job, your VA benefits, and you working part-time, we can afford it."

"Well, the only way we'll be able to afford it is for you to sell your Mustang, and maybe you'll need to get a full-time job too," he said.

Well, I thought, if I sell the Mustang, and we only have one car, at least it will be a nice car.

"Okay, I'll sell my Mustang." I mean, that's okay, I thought, as long as he doesn't want me to quit school.

"All right, that should do it," he said. "So let's go down there tomorrow, and I'll take care of the deal. We'll trade your car and mine. I'll also put $1,000 down on the car."

Just as he promised, bright and early, we were at Big Red's. We went down and closed the deal on the white BMW. We drove home in the new car. As I waved bye to my yellow Mustang, I also waved good-bye to any thread of independence that remained, as I was now Mrs. Joshua Smith, without my own car. When I got home, I called Mom, and told her we got a new car.

"What did you do with yours?" she asked.

"We sold it." I said.

"So now you don't have a car, Pamela?"

"No, Mom."

"My God! Are you really that stupid?" she asked.

"Mom, I need to go." I knew she was about to start.

"Listen...I'll let you hang up in a few minutes, but you listen to this. Are you that ignorant? Why would you let that man trade your car, and you end up without a vehicle? You know he's not going to let you drive that one! Did he ever let you drive his other one?"

"No, Mom, he didn't." I figured agreeing with her was the best way to get off the phone.

"Then what in the world makes you think he's going to let you drive this one?" She was yelling by now. "Did I raise someone who's that big of a fool? To let the man totally disregard your needs? I'll talk to you later!" Mom hung up without even saying good-bye, but I didn't mind – I just wanted to be off of the phone with her. I really was feeling like a fool. A dependent, confused, fool--with no one to talk to, and I didn't need her to confirm my thinking that I was stupid.

As it turned out, Mom was right about me *never* driving that BMW. I knew she was right. I was hoping somewhere inside that she wasn't. But unfortunately, Josh never so much as let me sit behind the wheel of "our" new BMW!

This is exactly where he wanted me. He would drop me off at school; my part-time job was on campus, still doing work-study. He'd pick me up from school. He knew every move I made, everything I did.

By the spring, when I got ready for graduation, I had made friends with a couple of people at school. After all, that was the only place that I had any opportunity for any outside, adult interaction. One student that I particularly enjoyed talking to was Patrice.

My new friend, Patrice, and I decided that we would get together sometime and let our daughters play. Her daughter, Courtney, was about the same age as Annette, maybe a little bit younger. Unfortunately, Courtney was a terror. She was the worst child I had ever seen in my life! She'd push Annette and I'd tell Patrice that this was not the way she should act. But

Patrice insisted that she didn't want to tell Courtney not to be aggressive because she wanted her to grow up to be a strong, assertive woman. I didn't understand her approach. But, Annette and I needed company sometimes. So, we'd get together with Patrice and her daughter, every now and then, despite Courtney's unruly behavior. I began to confide in Patrice that I wasn't happy with Josh and that he didn't seem to trust me. Patrice was about five years older than I was, so I felt like she might understand since she was mature.

Patrice was a refreshing change in my life. She'd come back to school to finish her education after her daughter was born. She was single, too; so we had a few things in common. I always looked forward to our conversations. She talked fast and smart. She also cursed a little, but I really didn't mind much. But the most amusing thing about her was how she talked about the pistol in her purse. "Well, anytime you want me to bring my pistol over, you let me know!" she'd joke when I'd tell her some of the things I was going through with Josh. I never told her he hit me. Just that he was jealous, and he got mad very easily. Sometimes I wondered if she was really joking when she'd talk about her pistol. I never did have the courage to look in her purse to see if she really did have the pistol she talked about.

May 1983 rolled around quickly, and soon it was time for graduation. Mom and Dad were so happy about me getting my Associate's Degree. I remember Mom calling each of her sisters when I went by the house with my graduation announcement. She was so glad to tell them that I was graduating from Rose State College. Her baby was getting an Associate's Degree. Patrice and I ordered our caps and gowns, and talked about how excited we were about going to the University of Oklahoma.

I started talking to Josh about going to school because now we were both going to be attending O.U. He had finished his B.S. on a distance-learning program, and now he was hoping to start law school at O.U. Each time I started talking to him about us carpooling, he changed the subject. I started worrying that maybe he was going to start up about me not going to school.

I tried not to worry too much. Maybe Josh didn't want to discuss me going to school at OU because he just expected us to do it. He had started to talk about me having a baby.

He can't be serious I thought. I'm only twenty years old. I don't even have enough education to get a good job, and we're barely paying our bills each month. He didn't bring up the subject too much, but when he did, I gently disagreed. I told him how much I'd love to have our baby, and that we should pick a date in the future, a time when he wasn't so stressed with bills and plans for law school. Somehow my strategy worked because he talked less and less about having a baby. LaWanna had just had a baby about six months prior and had gotten married, so the demands of pregnancy and a newborn were fresh in my mind, and I didn't want anything to do with it!

Graduation day finally arrived. It was a beautiful May morning in Oklahoma City. I heard the birds chirping outside my bedroom window. Before I could get out of bed, Mom called to tell me how proud she and daddy were of me. I loved their 6:30 a.m. wake up calls – especially that day. I knew it would be a great day. I fixed breakfast, and got Nettie dressed. The graduation was outside and started at 1:00 p.m. I had plenty of time to get ready.

Josh was still in bed when I came back after dressing Nettie. He didn't say a word. He didn't even look at me. "Good morning, Mr. Smith!" I said. "How does it feel to have a wife that's a college graduate?" I playfully asked, while grabbing my cap and tassel off of the dresser. "Guess what" I said excitedly, "I got my letter of acceptance from the University. O.U. wants me," I said with even more enthusiasm.

He still didn't say a word. All of a sudden, I became really concerned. Oh my God, I thought. What if he gets mad and hits me or acts crazy in front of my family? What if he doesn't take me to graduation? My fears calmed a little when I realized that I had asked my parents to pick me up to take me to graduation early because Josh had to study. Since he still had another week of school, I didn't want him to have to be there early with nothing to do. Mom and Dad were so proud of me; they didn't mind getting there early at all.

The morning had its usual routine of breakfast and cartoons for Annette. I started getting dressed early. I knew my Dad would be 30 minutes early to pick me up. He was never late and usually early! I'm sure it had something to do with military background. Today I was thankful for his punctuality and his military career – I definitely did not want to be late.

I got dressed, and had my makeup on perfectly. I was combing my hair when Josh walked in the bathroom.

"Rochelle, it seems to me like all you care about is school," he said. "The only thing you talk about is how you're going to school, and how you're going to be a doctor." He stood about three to four feet from me and was looking me up and down, checking out my outfit. I prayed he wouldn't say anything about it. I made sure it was "acceptable" to him. I had on a long skirt, had absolutely no cleavage, or even skin on my chest showing, and my blouse was loose. He didn't focus on my outfit too long, so I assumed it passed his inspection.

I heard a car pull up outside. Of course, today my Dad was not his usual thirty minutes early. He was actually forty-five minutes early on my graduation day – thank God, I thought.

"Josh," I said, "you know that my wanting to be a doctor is for me, Annette, AND you. This will help our entire little family. I'll be a good wife, a good mom, and a doctor. You know the most important thing to me is you and Nettie." I continued, "It's not at all that I only care about school – I love you Josh." Daddy was knocking on the door. I kissed Josh on the cheek, and I eased by him to get to the front door.

"Hi Daddy," I said.

"Hey Puddin'," he said. "Congratulations, College Graduate." As Josh walked into the room, Daddy extended his hand.

"Hello Mr. McCauley." Josh said.

"Good morning." Daddy said warmly. "We got the grill going for the barbeque celebration today after graduation. Rochelle, your Momma is trying to cook up the whole house for this thing." Nettie had run to jump into her Grandpa's arms, and he was holding her.

She was wearing a pretty little red and white dress that I'd gotten for $8.99 at a clearance sale at Montgomery Wards. She had on white tights and black patent leather shoes. Her hair was perfectly done in red and white barrettes. My baby looked so precious. I wanted her to look her best for her Momma's graduation. "I was a teen mom, but I was a good Mom and a college graduate," I thought. This all felt so good today.

"Let's get going. You don't want to be late for your own graduation," Daddy said looking at his watch.

"Daddy, I'm ready," although there was no chance I'd be late for graduation seeing how Daddy had made sure I would be there at least an hour before the scheduled time for graduates to arrive. But today, I didn't mind – in fact, I was thrilled!

I gave Josh a quick kiss. "We'll see you at the graduation, Honey," I said. "Remember it starts at 1:00 PM." I hugged him lightly and followed Daddy and Nettie outside.

Daddy dropped me off at Rose State College, and he and Nettie went home to pick up Mom and the rest of the family. I was sure that they'd be there in a timely fashion with Daddy in charge.

Soon the professors and all the eager students were in the auditorium ready to begin the graduation ceremonies. As we walked out in the processional, I was eagerly searching for familiar faces in the bleachers. I heard someone yelling, "Pamela, Pamela!" I looked over and saw my Mom, Dad, my sister, and my brother waving. Then, they picked up Nettie and MaRisha – they both waved. My cousin Angel was a couple of rows down, and she waved at me too. I waved back, but at the same time, I was desperately searching the stands for Josh.

"I'm sure he's here," I thought. I never saw him during the traditional graduate march into the ceremony.

I was looking for him during the entire program, and I probably would not have been paying attention when they called our row had the entire row not had to stand up. As they called my name, "Pamela McCauley Smith," I heard screams from the bleachers! I looked over again, seeing my family, but no Josh. I managed a smile and waved at them as the prestigiously clad professor handed me my college degree.

"Well, I sure hope Josh was here to see this; I'm so proud of myself. How can he miss this?" I questioned.

As soon as graduation was over, Mom and Dad walked up to me and handed me a bouquet of flowers. Nettie ran over as fast as her four-year-old legs would carry her. "Congratulashuuuunnnns Mommy!" she said grabbing me around my legs. "Thank you Honey," I said bending down to kiss her but still scanning the area for my husband.

Mom seemed to notice that I was looking for Josh. She could see the concern and sadness in my face, but rather than let this become a moment of anything but joy, she took charge as she was so good at doing. "Roche" she said, using one of her most playful nicknames for me, "We got a lot of good eating to do for this celebration. Let's get to the house." She leaned over to me and kissed me on my cheek again. "Honey, this is the Day that the Lord has made, let us rejoice and be glad in it. And today we have so much to rejoice about." She looked at me seriously and said, "Pamela, you have a college degree. This is a blessing, a blessing for you and our entire family. Daddy and I are so proud of you." I reached over and hugged her so tightly. When I let go of her, she said loudly, "Now, let's go to YOUR party!"

Josh finally showed up at Mom and Dad's. No one asked him about the graduation, if he was there or not. Thank God! I really didn't want a fight on that night, especially not with my family and Josh! Josh was quiet at the party, and didn't have much to say. He knew how my parents felt about him. They tried to accept him for my sake, but really did not like the way he treated me nor did they care for his lack of interest in our family events, church, and expectations. But I appreciated him coming to the party to celebrate my graduation because I knew he did not want to be there.

When we got home from the party, he insisted that I plan to get a full-time job, and not go to school at O.U. in the summer or fall.

The next day, Josh started to discuss school again. "Well," he said, "I've been accepted in this program at O.U., and if I'm successful, they'll admit me into law school. So I can't be worrying about the bills. I need to do well in the summer program and do well in law school. That means you're going to have to get a job and work."

Well, I thought to myself, I didn't even want this damn BMW, and he wants me to quit school? He wants me to quit school and pay for his car that I don't even get to drive, and a house that he reminds me regularly that belongs to HIM? I don't think so! Brother has gone too far this time. I was angry that he wanted me to give up so much and he didn't even have the decency to come to my graduation! I wanted to yell at him but I knew that approach would not be effective. So instead of responding in that manner, I simply pulled a piece of paper that I'd been working on. I had done a budget and list of other anticipated expenses for the next year.

"Josh, I've worked it out. This is how much money we need to make it. Between our part-time jobs, we can do it. We can both go to school."

He turned quickly towards me.

"Don't backtalk me, Rochelle! I said you're going to get a job. You've got your Associate's degree. Now you need to get a job." He was already raising his voice.

"Josh," I said, "that's not fair! How come you get to go to law school? And you don't want me to even finish my

Bachelor's degree?"

Before I could even finish the sentence completely, his hand had connected with me, and he slapped me. This time I wasn't crying; I was angry! The slap threw me off balance. I grabbed my face and said again, "This is not fair, Josh!" I was yelling.

"Rochelle, don't you disrespect me in my house!" he commanded coming towards me again. I started to get scared.

"Okay, Josh, okay. That's fine." I didn't want him to get more upset. All I could think of was getting away.

I had seen what a bad marriage could do to people in my family. I had seen what happened when you died, and you didn't have a good husband. There wasn't anything good left in this relationship. How could he want to destroy my dream? To take away my future? Did he realize that this was destroying me? Did he know that he was killing my love for him – no, it was worse that that, he was *making* me hate him because he was trying to destroy my dreams! I hated him. I hated Joshua Smith at that moment, and I was determined to get away from him. "I'll play along with this arrogant bag-of-dirt until I can get the hell away from him. And I planned to get away from him right then! Thank God Nettie's not here," was all I could think. We got in the bed, and I felt him reaching over for me. How in the world could he think that I want to have sex with him? He was destroying my dreams for a stupid BMW, humiliating me in front of my family by not coming to my graduation, and physically abusing me. But of course having sex was not for me. It was all about him. Our lovemaking used to be so beautiful and special! But there was nothing special about this now – it was just sex. I consented to avert his rage and prayed that it would end soon and morning would come quickly. The next morning I called Patrice.

"Patrice do you have your gun?"

"Oh, shit!" she said. "What's going on?"

"Patrice, I need to get out of here. I need to get out of this place. Josh just went to work; he'll be there all day. Can you come and get me? I don't have time to explain."

"I'm on my way!" She hung up without even saying bye. I hurried around the house gathering the necessities. Thank God for Patrice! I couldn't call Mom – she'd told me how stupid I was to let Josh sell my car, and this would have been total validation that she was right.

By the time Patrice arrived, I had loaded some of my things in a few garbage bags. I had Nettie's toys in another bag. We threw the stuff in the trunk and then, within a matter of minutes, we were walking out of the house. I turned to lock the door.

"I got my gun on the seat," she said. "In case this nigger drives up, I'm not takin' no shit!"

"Okay, Patrice, let's just get out of here. Let's get outta here."

She drove me to Mom and Dad's. While we rode, I told her the whole story about him hitting me and telling me I was quitting school. She cussed at every statement I made. By the time I got to 47th Street, I was calming down. I still had a key to Mom and Dad's house. Thank goodness no one was there. I went in the house, and unloaded my things. After I did that, I called Mom at work. Nettie had spent the weekend with them after the graduation party, and Daddy had dropped her off at the daycare center on his way to work.

"Mom," I said, "I'm at your house."

"You're what?"

"I'm...I'm home. Nettie and I need to move back home with you and Daddy."

"What do you mean, you're home?"

"Mom, I'm not happy with Josh."

"Well, Pamela, he *is* your husband."

"I know, Mom, but I'm just not happy."

"Well, you'll always have a home. But you know, if it's your husband, you should really try to work it out."

"No, Mom. If you knew what was going on, you would not want me to try to work that out. Mom, he hit me."

"He what?!?!" she cried.

"Yes, and he wants me to quit school, and he gets mad and yells at me. I just don't want Nettie to be in that environment all her life, Mom. If he hits me, and he doesn't want me to go to school, I'm not going to be happy. And if I'm not happy, Nettie won't be happy. I just can't see living like this."

"Well, Pamela, you'll always have a home. I'll try to leave early today."

"Okay, Mom. Thanks." The front door opened and LaWanna came in with her baby, LaTisha. She and her husband had an apartment about two miles away.

"Hi Rochelle," she said. "I just stopped by to get Tisha's bottles that I left here yesterday. What are you doing here?"

I briefly shared a few of the details, and that I was planning to move back in the house that day. LaWanna listened closely while making bottles for LaTisha. She gave me a hug and said, "I'm sure Mom and Dad will help you figure out what to do."

"Thanks LaWanna," I said. I went to the living room to take a nap on the couch.

Apparently Josh knew how upset I'd been that morning when I left because he came home for lunch. When he came home to find nothing there, he called my parents' house immediately. When I answered the phone, he had his usual soft, charismatic voice, the voice that I fell in love with.

"Hey, Rochelle, how you doing, sweetheart?" he asked.

"I'm fine," I said. How dare he ask me that after the mess he pulled last night?

"Honey, I'm sorry. Why don't you come on back home? Guess what? We got our income tax check today. Let's go to Denver. Let's go to Colorado."

As I sat on the other end of the phone, I thought, why in the hell would I want to go to Colorado with you? You've beaten upside my head while I was ten miles away from my family. Now why in the world would I go hundreds of miles away with you for you to beat me up and throw me in a snow ditch? But, my response didn't require all that. I simply said, "No, Josh," it simply isn't working out. I'm not going to be treated like this. I'm not quitting school, and I'm not going to be unhappy all of my life."

"Rochelle, God wants you with me. You're my wife."

"No, Josh! God wants me happy! Remember, the fruits of the Spirit? You remember; you're the one who encouraged me to read my Bible. The Bible says the fruits of the Spirit are love, joy, peace, and happiness." I stopped without reciting the entire verse. He got my point. I started again. "And one thing we can be sure I don't have with you is happiness. I am tired. I am tired and frustrated with you, and I am not coming back."

"Rochelle, listen. It's all going to work out. You're my wife, and we need to be together."

"It's not working. I'm tired of you slapping me around and then blaming me. I'm tired of explaining my every move. I'm sick and tired of you not trusting me. And I can't believe you want to take away my dreams. I want to go to college and get my B.S. degree, and you're trying to force me not to go. I'd said all I needed to. "Josh, I need to go." And I hung up the phone. My sister, LaWanna, was in the kitchen.

"Rochelle, what's wrong?"

"I can't be with him, LaWanna. I can't."

"Okay," she said. "I understand." She had been listening to my conversation. She walked over to me and gave me a hug.

"Rochelle, you'll be okay. I know Mom and Dad won't mind you being here. Alan and I are just down the road, so if you call me, I can come and get you. You can visit with us too," she said sweetly.

She didn't know how much I appreciated her right then. I gave her another hug and looked at my watch. I went to the daycare center in her car to pick Nettie up. We came home to

Mom and Dad's, and both took a nap. When I woke up, LaWanna was still at the house.

"LaWanna, I'm going over to Patrice's house. She's going to come pick Nettie and me up. She and I are taking the girls to an outdoor concert. If Josh calls, please don't tell him where I am; please don't tell him where I am, okay? Cause I'm afraid of him, and I don't trust him."

"Okay. What time are you going to be home?"

"We'll probably be home around 8:30 or 9:00 tonight."

"All right." She gave me a hug.

I went upstairs to wake Annette up. She was so happy to be at Grandmother's house and to see me there too.

Annette and I got dressed a few minutes before Patrice and Courtney arrived. We went over to Patrice's house, and she poured me a glass of wine while she and Courtney finished getting dressed. I called home to see if Mom had gotten home from work.

"LaWanna? I just called to let you guys know we'll probably be home a little later than we had planned to. The concert starts later. Is Mom home yet?"

"Not yet," she said. Oh, Rochelle," LaWanna continued, "Josh called."

"You didn't tell him where I am?"

"Well, Rochelle, he said he was sorry, a bunch of times, and he even came by the house and...."

"You didn't tell him where I am, LaWanna!"

"Rochelle, he wants to talk to you! You are his wife. He said he loves you."

"LaWanna! Why did you tell him where I am?"

"Rochelle, don't worry about it." Oh, my God! I thought, he's going to be so mad that I stood up to him.

"Patrice!" I yelled. "LaWanna told Josh where I am." Almost at that very instant, the doorbell rang. Oh my God, I forgot that he knew exactly where Patrice lived because I had to return a textbook to her one night. Josh had taken me to her house, and he was already familiar with the area since one of my aunts lived nearby.

"Oh, Pam, this fool is out here! Let me call the police, Pam. Let me call the police. Oh shit, where's my pistol?" Patrice buzzed.

"There's no need to call the police. I'm not afraid of Josh any more. All of a sudden, my fear turned to anger. How dare Josh slap me around, try to destroy my goals, deceive my sister into believing he's sorry, then track me down at my friend's house? I was feeling heat coming out of my nostrils as I walked past Patrice and motioned her to wait inside. And please don't get your gun. I can handle this, Patrice."

I heard her tell the girls to go play in her room and stay! She closed the door to the room. Thank God Nettie didn't know he was there, then he'd have really played up seeing her to try to get me confused and to convince me that he would change one more time.

"I'm just going to tell him it's over, and I don't want to be bothered with him ever again in my life." I went to the door and closed it behind me. I didn't want Patrice to hear me and think I was being too nice, even though nice was not what I was planning.

"Pam, at least let me come out there with my gun," I heard her yell from behind the door.

"Patrice, just sit down. Everything will be okay." Patrice reluctantly waited in the house with the girls. The last thing I wanted to do was cause problems for her by getting her involved in my marital "bliss." I was really afraid that Patrice might shoot him.

I walked onto the porch. "Hey sweetheart," he said. "How are you?" He said, trying to turn on that charm that made me fall for him. But it wasn't even coming close to working today and I didn't think it would ever work again.

I didn't want any small talk. "Josh," I said, "it's over. I'm not happy with you. I don't want to be with you."

"Rochelle, you're my wife. I love you, and I want you to come home."

"No, Josh, I'm not coming home. Please leave. I am not interested in talking to you about this. I need some time away from you. Please leave." And I turned to walk into the house.

As I turned, he grabbed me, picked me up off of my feet, and was running with me. He threw me in the back seat of the car. I was screaming! I thought, "This couldn't be happening. This was a scene out of a *Penelope Pittstop* cartoon!"

"Patrice! Patrice! Help me!" I was yelling, and hitting him on his back. I struggled, but he was holding me so tight; there was no getting away. Tears of anger started rolling down my face as I kept hitting him and struggling to get free.

He raised up the front seat; then threw me in the back seat of the car, and sped away as I tried to fight my way out of the car. He locked the doors, and started yelling. He hit the gas so fast, that I fell back hard on the seat.

"You're my wife! You are not leaving me! You are not leaving me!" He was furious, and he was yelling louder and louder. "You're never leaving me!"

"Josh, stop this car and let me out!!! Let me out!" I yelled. Oh, my God, I thought. Oh, my God. As I sat up in the back seat, I dried my face, and tried to calm down. "Where are you taking me?" I asked, still talking loud but not quite yelling. I started to pray, "Help me, Lord, please help me. I'm not sure what to do." I don't really remember what came over me, but I managed to calm myself down even more. As I sat in the back seat, Josh drove and drove and drove. It seemed like he drove for hours. We passed a church that we had visited before, which was very far out in the country. As he went past there, I had no idea where we were going. Maybe he was taking me to Miami where his family lived; maybe he was just trying to take me out of Oklahoma.

Soon we started coming to a few old houses with very big trees. Then he pulled into a parking lot of what looked like a high school. It was a large building with a huge parking lot in front of it. He drove over to the side of the building.

As he turned the car off, we sat in silence for at least ten minutes. By this time I was afraid, truly afraid. I'd seen Josh with a gun once before, so I didn't know if he had a gun or knife or what was going through his head. He finally turned around, looked at me and said, "We need to talk."

"Whatever you say, Josh. Whatever you say. I'm just not happy right now, and I just know that I can't go on like this, but maybe, maybe we can work it out."

"You are my wife."

"I know, Josh."

"No, Rochelle, you are my wife. You are not supposed to leave me," he said.

"Josh, I just can't take this. I'm not happy. But, Josh, if you promise to get better and get some help and not hit me again, I know we can work it out. I know I can stay."

Deep inside I knew there was no way that could be true, but I was simply trying to say whatever I could to calm him, to get him to let me leave. But he seemed to see right through me.

"You're lying, Rochelle! You know you want to leave me! I'm tired of you. I'm tired of you hurting me. Why are you always shuckin' and jivin' and playing games with me? Why are you doing this?" His tone was angry and he turned to stare at me.

I could see that he was getting upset. I reached for his hand and started to hold his hand.

"Josh, you know I would not do that. You know I love you. I love you very much." And I suppose somewhere in me I did love Josh, but there was no way I liked him. In fact, I hated the way he treated me since we'd gotten married, and what he was trying to do to my dreams?

So, while I loved the way he listened and encouraged me when we first started dating, I did not love him enough to be with him, and probably never loved him enough to marry him. I also felt bad for him. He wasn't a bad person. He was just very confused, and needed so much help that I had come to realize I could not give it to him. Seeing him in this state convinced me more than ever that Josh desperately needed help. My focus quickly went back to my present situation. "Lord I know You hear me. I need You to help me now!" I prayed, "Show me what to do so I can get out of here, so I can get back to my daughter and my parents. Help me Lord!" I started to massage Josh's shoulders. This always seemed to relax him.

He started to relax a little bit, and then all of a sudden seemed to realize what I was trying to do. He turned and looked at me with a glare! "Rochelle, you need to be obedient to me. Stop playing games with me," he said in a calm but almost scary voice. He got out of the car and walked over and sat along the school building. I spotted the keys in the ignition. Although I was still sitting in the back seat, I figured with one jump I could reach and lock the doors in a split-second. I could lock him out, and start the car, and drive away before he could do anything.

Although he was sitting a few yards away, he never took his eyes off of me. When he reached down to tie his shoe, I decided to make my move. I jumped over the seat, and reached for the door. Before I could even get to one door, he was in the car.

"You thought I'd let you leave me? You thought I'd let you get away? Is that what you thought? Do you think I'm stupid?" he demanded. "No, Rochelle. I'm not stupid. I know what you're doing. Get out of the car. *Get out of the car!*" he yelled loudly. He grabbed me by my arm, and pulled me out of the car.

He grabbed the keys. "Oh God," I thought, "what is he going to do to me now? How in the world am I going to get out of this?" I started praying, "God You've got to help me. This man is totally irrational. Please help me Lord." It was starting to get dark. Dusk was upon us. The road that the school was on was extremely deserted; it seemed as though a car only went by every five or ten minutes at the most. So I sat on the ground, and again tried to talk to him, but more than talking, I was pleading with God to get me out of this situation – alive!

"Josh, I only wanted to leave because you are scaring me. I never know what to do when you're like this. Here we are out in the middle of nowhere; you're yelling at me; and I don't know how to make you understand what I'm saying."

"Yeah, right! You're not trying to help me 'understand' anything. You want to leave me. You want to leave me just like everybody else did! You're no different from anybody else!" We were sitting on the ground, but as he started to speak, he stood up and started pacing back and forth.

"Josh, that's not true! You know I love you. Stop and think about it…how I've tried to be there… how I've tried to do things. I know I'm not perfect, but I love you."

"No, Rochelle. You're just like everybody else." He stopped and leaned against the building. He was a few yards away from me, but I could see the sweat on his forehead, the anger in his eyes.

All of a sudden I heard a noise, like a car approaching. It was a very loud noise, which sounded more like a big truck approaching. I thought if I ran toward the street and waved the truck down, it would pull over and get me. Surely, a big truck would notice a woman along the street and offer to help. Also, if he didn't stop, maybe he'd use his CB, and call for help. "Lord, please help, I prayed" – this has got to work!

Josh had taken my shoes. Guess he was concerned that I might try to walk away. He had kept my shoes inside the car. As I heard the truck approaching, I looked to see how far Josh was away from me. I was closest to the street and if I ran fast, recalling my days of running track, I was sure I could make it before he caught me. Finally I saw the truck coming, I ran for the street, yelling and waving my arms.

"Help me! Help me!" I yelled. Josh was right behind me. "Help me!" I was running harder than I'd ever run in any track meet, but I could feel Josh gaining on me. I felt him grab my shirt. I tried to pull away, but he had me in his grip.

The truck slowed down, and the driver looked over at us. I was still yelling, but by now Josh had me fully in his grasp. He had picked me up, and threw me over his shoulder. I was kicking and fighting and trying to get away. I was still yelling. He looked at the driver and waved his arms.

"Oh, we're just joking!" he said. "Just joking! Go on!" I was screaming at the top of my lungs. Josh was smiling and waving at the truck driver.

"Help me! Help me!" How could this man think we were joking with the terror in my screams?

Josh just kept smiling and laughing as though we were joking, carrying me back to the car over his shoulder. As I struggled, the truck sped up and disappeared down the road. Josh threw me in the car.

"Now we have to leave here! You think you're slick, don't you?" He got in.

This time I couldn't even muster up a tear. I was so angry, I was so mad. I was so disgusted with everything about him, everything about this situation. I was sick and tired of this fool! I was through being nice.

We drove a few miles until we came to an area with a lake. I guess he could see the disgust on my face. I tried so hard to hide my anger because of the way he looked back at me. When he saw my face, it made me think he was really going to kill me.

After he stopped the car, he got out. "Get out of the car!" he said. I got out quickly without even making eye contact with him, except for rolling my eyes at him.

As we walked toward the lake a little bit, he was in front of me. I still didn't have my shoes. He'd left them in the trunk. My feet felt terrible walking on the damp ground, stepping over sticks and rocks, as we walked down to the lake. Josh bent down, picked up a stick, and turned around. The stick was about three feet long and about the diameter of a nickel. As I looked at him, all I could think of was how mad I was. He must have seen the disgust and frustration again on my face. Without even taking his eyes off me, he swung the stick at me.

"Don't look at me like that!" he said as the stick made contact with my thigh. "Don't look at me like that!" he yelled again, "I've told you not to disrespect me!"

I turned and looked away from him. I knew. I could see it in his face. He was going to kill me, and throw me in the lake. He had gone down by the lake and started to draw with the stick. Oh, my God, I thought. This certainly isn't the way I expected my life to end! At the hands of a man that I married, one that I thought I loved. A man who had encouraged me to read the Bible, and who had at one time, made me feel so special. Lord, help me – this doesn't make sense. He's going to throw me into the lake I thought, Lord- help me! My thoughts continued, "My parents have already lost one daughter; I cannot, I will not die, not today and not like this!" I started to pray and pray harder than I ever prayed before. The look of disgust and fear must have disappeared from my face. Lord, my life is not going to end like this – I need your help NOW! After this prayer, I turned to Josh.

I said, "Josh, I'm hungry. Honey, I'm so hungry and so tired. I promise I won't leave you. Let's go somewhere and eat. Can we please go get something to eat, Honey? I'm getting dizzy, and I'm hungry, and I just want to go lay down. I want to lay down with you, and I want you to hold me." I reached for him, and I embraced him. He hugged me back.

The hardness in him seemed to soften. As much as I didn't want to, I started to kiss him, and told him everything would be okay.

"Let's just get something to eat and go home. Let's go home to our house, yes, our house, and start over."

"No!" he said. "Your parents are going to be at my house. They're going to be waiting for us."

"Josh, I will tell them not to bother us. I will tell them that

I'm okay, that everything is okay. Please, let's just go home; go home to our house; get in our bed; and rest." I reached for him again. "Let's go home and forget about this whole thing." For some reason, it got through to him. It had to be a miracle from God. He stood up and hugged me, and as I embraced him back, he said, "Okay Rochelle, I'm tired too. Let's go home," he said.

We walked toward the car, and I kept holding his hand. When we got there, he seemed to have calmed down a little bit. I remember driving back, being awake for a few minutes. But I was totally exhausted. After starting to see familiar sights close to Oklahoma City, somehow I fell asleep. I'm sure it was from sheer exhaustion. We went to Kentucky Fried Chicken. I woke up as he went through the drive-through and ordered something.

We got home. It must have been about 10:00 p.m. I remember eating a few bites of chicken and then collapsing into the bed. When I had been asleep for what seemed an eternity, all of a sudden, the light came on, and I heard screaming.

"Rochelle!" he yelled. "Why are you doing this to me? Why are you lying and deceiving me?"

"What are you talking about, Josh?" I asked. He grabbed me by the arm and pulled me out of the bed. He started pulling me out of our bedroom and into the dining room.

"Why are you doing this to me? Why are you lying and deceiving me?" We were standing in the doorway of our bedroom.

"Josh, I'm not lying to you. I'm not deceiving you."

He pushed me away and walked into the kitchen as he continued yelling, "Yes you are! You know you're lying and deceiving me!" I could hear him yelling as he walked away.

I walked closer to him and said, "What are you talking about Josh? How am I deceiving you? I'm not lying to you. Josh, I don't know what you're talking about." All of a sudden, I felt a sudden fear. "Oh my God – he's getting a knife," I realized.

He grabbed the longest knife out of the butcher's block,

and held it about eight inches from my face.

"You know you're lying to me! You know you're deceiving me!"

As he moved the knife closer to my face, I leaned back on the counter. By now his left hand was pressing down on my chest as my whole upper body was down on the kitchen counter. He held the big knife in his right hand as if he were going to stab me in the throat. He was still yelling, still holding the knife. All of a sudden, he brought the knife toward my face. I closed my eyes, "Lord save me," is all I could say, and I yelled it. I heard the knife make contact. Apparently he had stabbed it into the counter, right beside my head, and I heard the blade break. He threw the knife down, and walked away. I collapsed on the kitchen floor, crying and screaming.

"Josh! Don't do this to me! Please don't do this to me!" I was crying and screaming, and seemed to have lost complete control. Josh walked into the kitchen, bent down, and picked me up off of the floor. My whole body was trembling and shaking. He carried me into the room and put me in the bed.

"Just lie down. Just lie down and go to sleep," he said. I remember crying and sobbing into my pillow, not even able to think. I lay in the bed and Josh got in the bed next to me. He had sex with me. I didn't have the presence of mind to consent or resist. All I wanted to do was survive.

I lay awake all night completely motionless, listening to him breathe, and praying that I could get away from him. I must have dozed off for a minute and when I opened my eyes, I looked at the clock. It was about 4:00 a.m. Josh had to be at work at 5:00 a.m. I expected him to be getting up at any minute. Instead, I looked over, and he was already out of the bed. I looked, and saw the bathroom light. As he walked out of the bathroom, I pretended to still be asleep. He stood and looked at me, and I knew he was trying to decide whether or not to make me go with him. He probably expected me to be out cold, after the way I had been so upset the night before. He stood and looked at me for five or six minutes; I could tell he was trying to make up his mind. Then he turned and walked out the bedroom door. I heard the deadbolt lock on the house. I still lay silent, wanting to make sure he had left. I heard the ignition on the car start, and I thought I heard the car drive away. Without turning any lights on, I reached over and grabbed the phone. I called my cousin, Barbara.

"Barbara," I was already crying so, I could hardly even speak. "Barbara, come get me! Come get me!"

"Where are you?"

"Come get me. I'm at home. Come get me! Now! Come now!"

Barbara must have arrived within fifteen minutes. I barely let her car stop before I ran out the door, got in the car, and we sped off. I was just crying, trying to explain to her the horrible, terrible nightmare I had just experienced. If I never knew before, I certainly knew at this point that my life as Mrs. Joshua Smith was over.

CHAPTER 6

I GOT WORK TO DO

Joshua called several times a day, every day, for the next two weeks after I moved in with Mom and Dad. I refused to speak to him and when I finally did speak to him, it was to tell him that I was filing for divorce. He didn't seem to believe me, but it didn't matter. I hung up the phone, not even caring about being courteous to him anymore. All I could do was thank God for saving me from that situation. I promised the Lord that if I had anything to do with it, He'd never have to save me from a situation like that again. Lord, I promise!

According to the plan and budget I'd made, I needed to work full-time for six months and go to school part-time. This would give me enough money to make my car payments and move to Norman, Oklahoma to be closer to the campus within two semesters. That way, I could start full-time by the spring term of 1984. I was really trying to plan for a life – a good life for me and my baby. I knew I wanted to study medicine, and one of the counselors at Rose State had a great suggestion when I told her I was a Mom. She encouraged me to pursue an undergraduate major that would give me an opportunity to do summer internships – paid summer internships. She also said that if I wanted to take some time off between finishing my Bachelor of Science Degree, I would be able to get a job if I picked an undergraduate major with earning potential. So I started looking at majors that would allow me to do just that – make money while in school. When I compared course requirements, internship opportunities, and salaries for a few majors, I quickly settled my mind on being an engineer. It sounded really tough, but I liked math, and salaries were great with just a B.S. degree in almost any field of engineering. So, I decided in 1983 while preparing to attend O.U. that I had to change my undergraduate major to engineering.

I was still working part-time, and I'd applied for a full-time job at the university. I thought I should work full-time for a few months to cover all of my expenses. I got called for an interview at O.U. for a full-time position. I went; it was a receptionist's position, in the College of Engineering, Dean's Office. Wow! I thought. This could be a great opportunity. I could get to know some of the faculty; I could get to know the right professors to take; and this could make my life a lot easier once I enroll at O.U. I decided to enroll in the fall and take maybe one or two classes, just to get my feet wet. I was excited about my plan.

Jacquine Littell, the lady who interviewed me, seemed very nice. She also seemed fairly impressed with my experience. In fact, I'd met her a few months ago when I applied for another position at the university in the College of Engineering. Unfortunately, I didn't get that position; they had to have someone more qualified. However, this time I was sure I was going to be the right person for the job. I put on my most cheerful smile, and I felt really good about my suit, one that Aunt Camille had given me. It was my very best suit! I was sure I could convince her that I was the only person for the job. My interview went well. Jacquine remembered me from my first interview with her earlier in the spring. She seemed impressed that I was interested in a career in Engineering. She also seemed impressed that I was willing to work full-time and go to school part-time, in spite of the fact that I had a daughter.

Oh, this could be great, I thought. She was even excited about me being an engineering student! She'd be a wonderful boss. I explained to her that I could be available immediately, and, although it would be a 30-minute commute each day, it would be absolutely no problem. I could stay late if she needed. She seemed eager for the help that I so enthusiastically offered; I left the interview feeling very optimistic.

A few days later, Jacquine called. She wanted to know when I could start work. I was absolutely elated. Finally, finally, I'm getting my foot in the door at the university. Not only that, she told me that once I'd been working for six months,

I could get six hours per semester of free tuition. This was exactly what I wanted! It was truly a happy day.

I told my mom that I had gotten the job, and that I would probably be staying with them only for a few more weeks. After that, I would probably move into some low-rent housing in Oklahoma City. I still needed to be in Oklahoma City, I thought, so I could have Mom and Dad to help with Annette at least while I got settled into O.U. and into being divorced.

I made an appointment with the Oklahoma City Housing Authority, and got on the waiting list. They told me that there were low-income apartments immediately but not in the area where I wanted to live. Will Rogers Court was the name of the apartment complex where a 2 bedroom was immediately available. These apartments, even though they were low-income, were fairly decent. Many of the residents were older people. After I went and took a look around the area, I noticed that there were just a few children, and there was a nice little playground for them to play in. Besides, I thought, Annette probably won't be here that much; she'll be over playing with her cousins most weekends. This will do just fine.

After I decided to move in and made my initial deposit, I felt a sense of freedom. For the first time I was going to have my very own place! Not a place provided to me by someone else, not a place that someone had given me. Low-income though it was, it was going to be my very own. I was so happy I didn't know what to do. Then it dawned on me. I didn't have any furniture! I didn't have a stick of furniture. I also didn't have any dishes, cooking utensils, or towels. I didn't have anything! I didn't have much money either, but I looked at my checkbook calendar to see when I would have some money. I set my moving date to be the same weekend that I got my first paycheck from O.U. I decided that I would go to Wal-Mart and buy a few utensils. Mom was eager to help and gave me several things since she could see how excited I was about having my own apartment. She went through her cabinets, and loaded up a box with one of everything extra that she had for me to take to my new apartment. She also went through the linen closet and gave me a couple sets of sheets and towels. This was great! I beamed.

The next day my cousin, Angel, and I went to a garage sale. I found a dinette set for $20! Rickety though it was, it sure was going to serve the purpose; Formica-top with steel chairs, and all. My daughter and I now had a place to eat! Also, the best find was a sofa. I found a sofa for $20! My house was going to be complete! Mom gave me a twin bed out of one of the bedrooms she wasn't using.

"Take this," she said. "I want Nettie to have a nice bed to sleep in. Daddy and I just replaced this mattress and box springs." I was so happy. "Thanks Mom," I said with a hug.

Everything was perfect except for my room. But I didn't mind sleeping on the floor if I needed to, for a while.

A few days later, I started to gather everything—my dishes, my dinette set, my sofa—I put it all in Mom and Dad's garage to prepare for the move. Angel looked through the stuff and said, "Hey, Pam! I forgot! I have an old bed you can have. It's at Daddy's house. I'm sure you can use it," she said. "Angel, can we go look at it now?" I asked eagerly. "Sure," she said, so we got in the car and drove over to her Dad's house.

Uncle Dave was my Mom's big brother, and I do mean BIG – he was a huge man. Angel's dad, six feet, ten inches tall, wore the warmest smile you've ever seen. He had a garden and whenever I saw him, he had fresh vegetables.

"Come on in, girls!" he said with his usual beautiful smile, deep dimples, and a big hug.

"Daddy," Angel said, "where is that old bed of mine? You know; the one I used to use?"

"Oh, it's back here, hon." He walked slowly through the small living room, into the hall, to the back bedroom. Uncle Dave was so tall he always had to duck down when going through doorways.

"Is it okay if Pam has it?" Angel asked.

"Sure, that's fine, hon." Before we knew it, Uncle Dave had the bed loaded up on his truck. He drove it over to Mom's house where we stored everything in the garage until the next day when we started to move in.

Moving day finally came. I was so excited I woke up before daybreak. My dad and my brother loaded everything into an old truck that we'd borrowed from one of my cousins. We drove all the things over. I moved each piece in as if it were a showplace. Annette seemed so happy that we were going to have our own place.

Even though this was low-income housing, having my own place and being able to afford it, would be a challenge because although I was working full-time, my earnings were only about $750 a month. My rent would be subsidized a bit, but I still had to pay electricity, buy goods, and buy gas for my car. One of my cousins told me I might be able to get a few food stamps. I made myself a budget, and promised to keep to it, although it only left me about $10/week after my bills were paid. I went and applied for food stamps, sure to tell the caseworker that I had goals and only needed food stamps for a short time.

In the meantime, school was starting for the fall semester. I was going to my two evening classes and working full-time in the College of Engineering. I enrolled in Physics I and Calculus I. I went to class early, anxious to be an O.U. student. Immediately I saw a difference in the pace of the classes at O.U. versus Rose State. The classes were tough, very tough. I never expected to feel, in the first couple of weeks of school, so lost. I also never seemed to have enough time. Enough time to study, enough time to get caught up, enough time to spend with Annette, enough time to do anything that needed to be done at home or for myself.

One thing I did make time for was to file for divorce. I called one of my friends from Rose State and asked her which attorney she'd used in Oklahoma City for her divorce. When I got the information, I quickly called and made an appointment to go see him. I filled out the necessary paperwork, and he even let me post-date a check to pay for his services. I told him I wanted the divorce to be done as soon as possible. I had so many things to do; I didn't want this divorce to be hanging over my head for months and months to come.

Meanwhile back at school, things were really getting difficult. My job was taking a lot more time than I expected. I thought I'd have a few minutes during the day to study, but that never seemed to happen. The only time I had to study was at 10:00 or 11:00 p.m., after I had cooked dinner, cleaned the house, and put Annette to bed. It just seemed like I was too exhausted to read more than a few pages, much less do physics problems and calculus homework.

One night before a test, I sat looking at the material. It looked like a foreign language to me. I felt so frustrated. I started to think, maybe they're right. So many negative thoughts started going through my mind. Maybe everyone who says that I can't do all of this is right—this is so hard. Maybe I can't go to school; I can't have a good job; I can't be independent—maybe they're right. Frustration overwhelmed me. But, instead of starting to cry like I felt like doing – something inside of me asked, "How can I do this? How can I make my dreams come true? I've worked so hard to get to this point. I don't intend to fail." I started to think of my options.

Okay, so what? If they say I can't do it, what if I try? I got a piece of paper, and wrote on one side "Success" and on the other side, "Failure." In order to be successful, what did I need to do? At the top of my list was finish school. To fail, hey, that didn't take much. There was nothing on that side. Do nothing.

Another thing I put on my list was that, in order to be successful, I needed to be a good mom. Failing to be a good mom, well, that didn't take anything either. There was still nothing on that side of the paper.

Another thing I put on the "Success" side was "try." Try,

try, and try. Without even realizing what I had done, I had motivated myself. I knew that it took absolutely nothing to fail. Just do nothing; believe the negativity that other people speak about you and your goals; mix that with a negative attitude; and you have sure failure. But success, on the other hand, would someday be mine if I just tried. If I just continued to try and if I tried to think positively, even though it didn't seem like I was getting very far, then success, at some point, at some level, might be mine! Would it happen? I wasn't sure, but I hoped with everything in me that it would.

Even though I was in school and sometimes it wasn't going that well, it still made me feel good to be doing something worthwhile. It made me feel good to know that I was putting forth an effort to make a better future for myself and for my daughter. When I met people and they asked me what I was doing, I was glad and happy to report that I had a job in the College of Engineering as a receptionist. But it always made me even more proud to tell them that I was in school and I was working on an Engineering degree. Most of the time they were very surprised, especially when I told them I also had a daughter. Well, the next question that always came was, "How do you do that? How do you go to school and take care of a five year old?"

"Oh, well, I just manage." That was not completely true. I was hanging on by a thread! Even though I managed to maintain a "D" average at that point, somehow that information didn't seem to be pertinent. I just told them I managed.

One weekend Angel and I decided we'd try out a new jazz club that had opened in Oklahoma City. We usually tried to find a place where we could listen to her brother, David, play since he was in a band, and he played the saxophone so well. David Carr, Jr., was awesome on the saxophone and it was a nice way to end the week. It had been an especially long week for me, and Angel had worked really hard that week, too. While she was working full-time, she was also taking classes four nights a week in order to become a certified electronic technician. So on

Friday evening, we were ready to relax and have a few drinks, listen to some good music. This particular Friday, we ended up in a new jazz club near the mall in northwest Oklahoma City. Although we were both only 20 years old, David could always get us in the clubs. The legal drinking age was 21 and we rationalized that it was ok for us to drink since we were almost 21. It didn't occur to us how very wrong we were and that we were actually breaking the law. All we wanted to do was chill. As we sat there sipping on our White Russians, laughing and talking, I spotted someone from across the room. He was a very elegant, but sort of rugged looking man that sat at a table visiting with his friends, I could hear him laugh – he had the richest, fullest laugh. Before long, he noticed I had been looking at him, and he had the waitress bring a drink over to me.

"Angel," I said excitedly, "The guy with the beard is offering to by me a drink."

She turned around to get a glimpse of him. He was looking in our direction now. Angel turned back to look at me. "Say thank you, he's looking over here." We'd been out to a few clubs before, so we knew if someone was interested he might offer to buy a drink, but this didn't usually happen.

I nodded with a look of approval, and he came over and introduced himself. I was interested in hearing his laugh up close and seeing him up close too. It seemed like all I was doing was working, going to school, and being a Mom. So I thought it would be nice to talk to a gentleman, even if only for a few minutes, to keep my mind off of all the demands on me every day.

"Dave—Dave Scott," he said as he extended his hand.

I extended my hand, shook his, and introduced myself. I motioned for him to sit down. As he pulled out a chair, I noticed he was wearing cowboy boots, jeans, and a sport coat. He had a beard and a mustache. He looked about six feet tall and had broad shoulders, your typical Marlboro man. God, he sure is nice-looking, I thought. But I sure hoped he didn't smoke,

seeing how he fit this Marlboro image.
"How are you this evening?" he asked. I loved his voice. Calm down I told myself – I was always a fool for a sexy voice!
"Oh, just great," I said. I introduced Angel to him, and she soon noticed his friend walking over to talk to her. Dave and I continued our discussion.

We talked about what we did and what our goals and aspirations were. He was a positively charming Texas gentleman. It was absolutely wonderful talking to him. It was delightful talking to a man, a black man, who was interested in hearing about my dreams and my goals. He was someone other than my father or my brother, a male someone, who could appreciate the fact that I did have dreams and goals. He seemed to be very impressed when I told him that I was working toward an engineering degree.

I didn't want to tell him how old I was because he looked quite a bit older than twenty and I didn't want him to know that I wasn't old enough to be in the jazz club! Also, now that I had built up what I perceived to be a decent image in his eyes, I didn't want it to appear that I was a stereotype. If he thought that maybe I was 23 or 24, he wouldn't think that I had Annette so young. He certainly wouldn't expect that I lived in federally subsidized housing or used food stamps. In fact, I'm sure I still had some food stamps in my purse, right there in that jazz club. I thought, if he thinks I'm a little older, maybe he would think that I'm the kind of woman that he would want to take out. Someone he'd want to take places with his colleagues. He was a real professional man. A professional man, yeah! That's what I was interested in, a charming, professional, gentleman like Dave Scott.

Over the next few days, Dave and I talked several times. We managed to go out to lunch the following Saturday. It was a wonderful lunch. We sat and talked for at least two hours, continuing to talk about our dreams and our goals. He had a great sense of humor, and I loved to see and hear him laugh.

When he laughed, his smile would be really broad and his beautiful white teeth all showed as his roaring laugh escaped from his smile. He was a delight to be around. After lunch, he kissed me softly on my cheek, and told me he'd look forward to seeing me again in the future.

I was having a great time laughing and talking with Dave during our few conversations throughout the week. That made my social life better, but school did not seem to be getting any better. I had gotten a tutor, even started trying to do more homework. Unfortunately, it just didn't seem to get any better. Nothing was helping, and I was running out of time.

The end of the semester was drawing near. I went to see one of my professors. I told him that I had been going through a divorce, was having difficulty in the course, and that I was also having a lot of financial problems. He was very cordial, but did not seem to care at all that I had personal problems, which didn't involve calculus.

"Well," he said, "you can take it again next semester. Don't worry about it; my daughter's making her first F or D this semester too." He seemed sincere, but it was clear that there was no hope for a better grade.

Well, there was my answer. I guess there wasn't much that I should have expected at this point. I should have talked to him earlier in the semester, and maybe he could have given me study tips or helped me understand. At least he would have known that I was trying.

Though I appreciated his cheerfulness that was not exactly what I wanted to hear. I loaded up my book bag, and slowly walked out of his office. "D's" and "F's", my God, this was no way to get an engineering degree! How in the world was I ever going to graduate at this rate? I thought, "Lord, help me to find a way to do all of this. You gave me this dream or so I thought." I continued praying as I walked to my car and drove home.

I studied hard for my final exams. Even though I put in several hours, it didn't seem to help. I considered that semester a complete academic failure. I knew I would get a D or an F in each class. This is hard, but there has to be a way that I can do this, I thought. The following week after school was out, I wrote down a plan to accomplish my goals. I began questioning myself, how many times am I going to do this? I kept writing and writing. Am I getting any closer to accomplishing my goals? Last semester was nothing but frustration and my writing goals did nothing for me. I could feel the frustration and despair creeping up on me. I knew the best way for me to fight this frustration, despair, and depression was to take action. But, before I could take any action, I had to figure out what my problems were.

I started writing a list of all my problems. I didn't have time to study. It also seemed like when I did have time to study, I had other things to do, so I couldn't concentrate. The commute down to school was taking a lot of my time, 30 to 40 minutes each way. Feeling guilty about not having time with Annette, was really weighing on me. And also, I wanted so much to have money, to do things for Annette, and I really wanted to keep my job. The list was long and I read it again:

a) No time to study
b) School is hard –so hard for me
c) Commuting is taking too much time
d) I don't have enough time with Annette
e) I don't have enough money
f) I feel like everyone in my classes is smarter than I am

I concluded that working was taking too much time-- that was the bottom line. It was affecting my goals and my time with Annette. I couldn't maintain my full-time job. However, Jacquine had been so nice to me, and I didn't want to let her down. Also I wanted so much to be responsible in Annette's eyes, and to myself. I liked having a job. It meant I was taking care of my daughter and me. But, I thought, if I'm going to make a better future for her, it's going to take some sacrificing today.

As nice as Jacquine had been, I reasoned that maybe she'd understand that as a single mom, I needed more time to study and couldn't work full-time. I decided to talk to her. The next day before I left, I asked if I could visit with her. As I sat in her office, I told her that my grades had been really bad, and that it was going to be necessary for me to work part-time or quit work completely in order to get my engineering degree. Surprisingly, she seemed to understand completely. She told me they would start looking for a replacement, and asked if I would stay on until they'd found one. I gladly agreed. At the same time, I started looking for another part-time job.

I contacted some of the other offices in the College of Engineering. Luckily, one of the other directors in the department was looking for some part-time help. He offered me a position, and I told him that I could accept it as soon as the Dean's office found someone to replace me. In the meantime, I was trying to figure out how I was going to make ends meet, now that I was only going to be working part-time.

I made another budget and figured I would need another $300-$400 a month if I was going to make it. At that time, Eddie's child support checks were irregular, unpredictable, and fell tremendously short of what I needed. AFDC, I thought. But my next thought was, God, I don't want to apply for Welfare. I really don't want to apply for Welfare again. I received AFDC and food stamps for a short time before Joshua and I got married, and I hated it. However, I knew that if I was going to change my life and make it better for Annette and me, I needed some help. I wrote AFDC down as a possibility for getting myself through school.

The next day I went to the Financial Aid office at school, and made an appointment to visit with a counselor. As I sat there, I took my piece of paper out. On one side I had my goals and on the other side I had a short budget of my monthly financial expenses. I explained to my financial situation to the counselor.

"Well," she said, "as long as you completed the financial aid form, we'll see what it says about whether or not you can get assistance." That's right, I thought, I needed to complete that God-awful, long, financial aid form. I had done it when I was at Rose State.

I took a few hours over the next couple of days to complete the financial aid form. I called the Financial Aid Office at least five times with questions about what my answers should be on certain parts of the paper work. I completed the form, and mailed it in. On my next visit, I met the same financial aid counselor. By now she had my results.

"Well, you can get a student loan," she told me. "You can also get a Pell Grant."

That was good news to me. I had planned to enroll for about 14 hours. Three to four classes, that is. And I knew that working full-time was completely out of the question if I was going to have any success academically.

Not only did I need my Pell Grant and my student loan, if I was going to do well in school, I needed to move. I needed to move to Norman immediately. The drive was absolute suicide on my academic situation. She explained to me that she couldn't help me move right away because the student loan wouldn't be there for several days.

"Listen," I said. "I know something is available. I have got to move. You don't seem to understand. If I don't move, I'm not going to do good this semester. It's out of the question for me to stay in Oklahoma City any longer and commute back and forth as a single parent."

She paused for a minute and seemed to be thinking.

"Hold on," and she got up and walked out of the office. She came back and said, "Here's an application. You can apply for an emergency student loan." She looked pleased. "These funds can be available in as little as three days," she said.

"When your other aid comes, you'll need to pay this back."

"Thank you so much," I said. "You have no idea how much I appreciate this." I was so thankful that I wanted to hug her, but I resisted the urge. I completed the paperwork, and left it there at the office.

Within three days I had a $300 check as an emergency student loan. I called my dad and my brother, my regular movers, and asked them to help me move to Norman. I'd looked into the university apartments, the married student housing. Married student housing was basically apartments for students with spouses or children. I chose to live in these apartments because they were on campus, safe and affordable. There were two or three complexes to choose from. I didn't have much choice; I chose the least expensive one. It was considerably smaller than the subsidized housing apartment where I was living in Oklahoma City, but it would certainly meet the needs that Annette and I had. The wonderful thing about it was that there was an elementary school directly across the street. Annette could go to kindergarten there during the coming year. Also, I wouldn't even have to drive my car to go to campus since the apartments were right on campus, and a bus came close by. I also found a local daycare center that was glad to accept Annette, even with the payment of her daycare bill by the Department of Human Services. Everything seemed to be working out so well.

Now, this was my second semester at O.U., spring semester 1984, and it started out extremely demanding. I kept studying hard for my classes. Four classes seemed like an awful lot, with a part-time job, while taking care of Annette. I worked so hard, and it seemed like my grades got better, but they certainly didn't seem to improve in proportion to the rate that I increased my studying. I was going to tutoring. I was staying up late doing homework. And it seemed that I was just barely getting by. It became so discouraging. Some days I sincerely thought that maybe I was on the wrong track. Maybe the goals that I wanted were too lofty. Just maybe I didn't need to be trying to become an Engineer. But I felt so much in my heart that I wanted it. I knew that I just could not give up on my dream.

I remember one day deciding to go on campus to pick up my Calculus II exam. I took Annette with me. We'd go to the campus, and pick up my exam, and I'd go back home and fix us some soup. Later, I'd study while she played and colored. I felt especially good about this exam. I knew I had gotten at least a "B" on this one. Every question, I knew! I knew I had gotten the right answers. I saw the cardboard box out in front of the professor's office. I sifted through the papers to look for my grade.

As I found my paper, I couldn't believe the grade I saw on the front of it. Forty-eight. Forty-eight! I thought. Maybe the number was transposed; maybe it was supposed to be an 84. I stared at the paper. Still looking back at me was the forty-eight. An "F", I thought. How could I have made an "F" on this? I tried so hard. I studied so hard. Lord, I don't understand this.

"Hurry up, Mommy. Hurry up! I'm getting hungry!" Annette said.

"Just a minute!" I snapped. My God! I threw the paper in my bag, and hurried out of the building. I grabbed Annette's hand. "Hurry up! Let's go home."

"Okay, Mommy. Come on." As she skipped along, I practically dragged her out of the building.

We went outside, and as we waited for the bus to come to take us back to the apartment, Annette said, "Mommy, I'm cold. It's cold."

I was so wrapped in the poor grade I had received that I couldn't even hear her.

"Mommy!" she said. "I'm cold!" All of a sudden, I turned and snapped at her.

"Just deal with it, Annette! Don't you think I get cold sometimes? Don't you think I have to put up with things I don't want to deal with? I'm cold, too. Everybody out here is cold."

Her big eyes filled with tears. She turned away from me,

and pulled her sweater tighter around her. I felt so awful. I felt two inches tall. I knelt down beside her, and hugged her. The tears started to flow.

"Don't cry, Mommy. I'm not that cold," she said.

"No, honey," I said, "I'm sorry. I'm so sorry I yelled at you. I know you're cold, baby. The bus will be here in a minute. We'll go home, and I'll make us some hot soup, and we'll watch cartoons." I was holding her little body close to me.

"That's okay, Mommy," she said. "But I'm not that cold, really, I'm not."

I felt so badly. Not only was I flunking school, I wasn't even a good mother. I was snapping at my daughter over something I had no business getting upset with her over. Could this day be any worse?

As we got on the bus, we walked by several students, several carefree-looking students, as they talked about their plans for the weekend. God, how I envied them! I grabbed my baby, and sat her on my lap. She was the only child on the bus, and everyone seemed to notice her, waving at her as they walked by.

As much as I loved Annette, I thought, it would be so nice to just be like them, to not have such demanding responsibilities like all of the other students, to be talking about the weekend, to be wearing a sorority sweater or sweatshirt. I wished I were thinking about all the silly things I had planned, but instead I was thinking about how I was going to prepare a future for my daughter. How I was not only going to prepare a future, but also how I was going to take care of her immediate needs? I was trying to decide how big to buy her clothes, so that she could possibly wear them again the next year. I was hoping that the child support would come so that I might go out and buy a few extra things that she might need. I wanted so much to shield her from poverty, for her never to know that we were on Welfare or used food stamps, for her never to know about the times when we didn't have things. I wanted her just be a kid, to be carefree. After all, I had made this bed; I needed to lie in it, not her. It became clear to me that I could no longer have a carefree life, but it was completely within my power to make a good life for my daughter.

I had gone to apply for AFDC, daycare assistance, and food stamps in Norman since I was now in a different county. The caseworker was nice, and she approved me for daycare assistance. The caseworker told me she needed to schedule a home visit to approve me for AFDC. She seemed very surprised when I told her that I was pursuing an Engineering degree.

"Oh, that's good, that'll be just fine. Well, I'll be out to visit you soon."

As I left the office I thought, well, that wasn't so bad.

A few weeks later I was approved for AFDC and food stamps. Having the food stamps and the AFDC made it a lot easier to manage my budget. I paid my rent, thank goodness I didn't have any utilities, and bought all of the groceries I could stand to eat. I got all of Annette's favorite cereals, all of her favorite snacks. Everything that she wanted, I got. I always made sure I had plenty of fresh fruit in the house. I'd read so many things about young mothers not fixing good meals, about them not giving their children good diets. In fact, the insert that they sent out with the food stamps had details on nutrition and how important a healthy diet was for children. I knew that several vegetables per day and enough dairy products were key to her development. Annette loved fruit and vegetables when I seasoned them with butter. But my baby hated milk, so I bought ice cream and yogurt to make sure she was getting enough calcium. I encouraged her continuously to eat these things. She seemed to love the yogurt most of all, the cherry and the pineapple flavors. She'd ask me to mix them for her. I was glad to do it. I was glad to do anything for her to get her calcium. I always loved for her to ask for yogurt because she couldn't pronounce it quite right. She'd ask for "yoga", and I'd snicker as I corrected her for the hundredth time on the pronunciation. As good a child as Annette was, she definitely required some extra discipline without my parents around. I had managed to make friends with a couple of black women who were engineering students. Karla Green was not only an engineering student, she was a little older and in graduate school working on her Master's Degree. I was so impressed with her. Not only was she smart and successful, she was so nice. She offered to help with Annette and baby sit for me whenever I needed help.

One night I really needed to meet with my study group for Physics I class, so I took Karla up on her offer. I explained to Annette that she would be with Karla for a little while so Mommy could study. She seemed very comfortable with the idea, so we proceeded. I took her to Karla's apartment and reassured her that I'd be back soon. The study session went well, and I hurried back to Karla's apartment in less than 2 hours. Well, my sweet Nettie must have smelled Karla's inexperience like dogs smell/sense fear! Karla was calm and gentle in describing how Annette ran wildly around her apartment, talked loudly to Karla – even when she was on the phone-- and insisted on watching only what she wanted on television. I apologized several times to Karla. She assured me that it was fine, and she'd even be glad to keep Annette in the future. Annette sat silently as Karla gave me this report. She was embarrassed. She knew she had done something wrong, and she knew I was going to address this with her. When we got home, I made sure I explained what she did that was wrong. I also told her that she had to be disciplined. I'm not sure how much of this she understood but the next time Karla babysat for me, we didn't have any problems.

Annette was such a precious child although she had her moments of being unruly. Had she not been such a well-disciplined and independent child, it would have been a lot harder to get through school. She'd play in her room by herself for hours. Playing with her dolls, playing with her chalkboard, and setting up all her stuffed animals as if they were her students in a class were all a part of her playtime regimen. I guess she'd seen the inside of enough classrooms with me when I didn't have enough money for a baby-sitter. So she knew just how the professors would act. She'd line up her dolls on one row, her teddy bears in another row, and they would all be students in Miss Annette's class. I'd hear her scribbling on her chalkboard, and then she'd tell them it was naptime, then lunchtime. It was such a joy to peek in her room and watch her without her noticing it. What a delight she is, I thought. How precious my little baby is! On days like that, that somehow seemed to make all the struggling worthwhile. It seemed to make it okay there wasn't much money; that sometimes I didn't do very well in school. It seemed to make everything okay just watching my daughter be happy, be content, and enjoy life, just as I wanted my child to do. Whether I had her at fifteen or at thirty, all I wanted was for her to be happy and to enjoy life, and to grow up healthy, confident, and strong.

Sometimes to escape the monotony of school and work, Annette and I would go to a dollar movie. At other times, even a dollar was tight! We'd go to the library. I loved going to the library; there was always so much to do, so many books to read. Annette would go in the children's section and read picture books or books with very simple words. I'd also go in the children's section with her sometimes and sit on the floor and read her a story. Most of the time we'd check the books out and take them home with us. Then we'd plan our excursion to the Duck Pond. The Duck Pond was a park area on the edge of the university campus. It was a beautiful area, particularly in the fall and spring. During that time of the year, the trees were responsive to nature by displaying breathtakingly beautiful shades of red, yellow, and eventually brown, exquisite leaves. A beautiful green field and dozens of large trees surrounded this little pond. After the leaves fell, we always made a point to get back to the duck pond before winter set in to see the first snow that was generally very pretty without the bitter cold.

I remember one spring afternoon we made sandwiches,

packed chips, cold sodas, fruit, and yogurt in a cheap picnic basket. We each grabbed a book, and I grabbed a blanket. We drove over to the duck pond and laid our blanket out and had lunch. Annette didn't want her entire sandwich, so she took part of the bread and walked over to the ducks in the lake. She threw the bread at them. At first she was afraid of them, but then she seemed tickled as the ducks ran toward her, fighting for the bread on the ground. It was wonderful to see her interacting with nature. We'd also see several couples in the park, couples lying on blankets, laughing, talking, and being romantic. There were also several families out. Each time we went, we'd see different people, some familiar faces. That was one of Annette's favorite activities, and I loved it because it was fun, free, close to home, and I could study.

The end of the spring semester came. Although my grades improved, they were a far cry from what you would call good. I decided that summer that I would work part-time as a waitress and put a few dollars back. . That way, maybe I wouldn't have to work a full twenty hours per week during the school semester. I would also put back a few dollars to buy some things for Christmas. Maybe I'd do better in school if I had a few less financial worries.

Annette's birthday was coming up, and I wanted to do something special for her. I could always count on my mom for a birthday party. Never once did she think her children or a grandchild should go without a birthday party. So we did the usual ritual. I called Mom; I bought a cake. She fixed a spectacular dinner, and we went up to her house and sang "Happy Birthday": me, Dad, my brother, my sister, and my nieces and nephews. Annette was as happy as she could be. Mom and Dad had bought her several toys. I had bought her several outfits and a couple of toys. Her other grandparents, Lewis and Annie, could always be counted on to send a nice present, and her Aunt Felicia always managed to throw something in the box that her parents were sending.

Unfortunately, Eddie's gift didn't always arrive, and when they did arrive, they usually weren't on time. Annette didn't seem to mind. His parents would always put, "from your grandmother and grandfather and your daddy, so she always felt a presence from him, even though I knew the real deal.

After the party was over, I told Mom and Dad that I was going to work a lot that summer. I asked them if they could help me more with Annette. They didn't seem to mind at all.

"Any time she needs to come up is fine," Mom said.

Daddy added, "You just call me. I'll come get my girl. You know I love having Nettie up here."

Even though I knew I could count on them to keep her, I always felt a little better explaining to them what I was doing. I never wanted them to feel like I expected them to take care of my responsibility. So I always made it as clear as possible that I was asking for their help, not expecting it. But the help was so appreciated and needed! Some days – no, most days, I was so stretched with all of my demands.

When Annette and I drove home that night, she went to sleep in the car. When I got to our apartment in Norman, I picked her up, and carried her into her room. As I put her into her bed, she woke up.

"Mommy," she said, "will you read me a story?"

This was one of her favorite pastimes. She loved for me to read to her when she went to bed. I snuggled in the bed next to her, and started to read. Before I could even get to the fourth page, she had gone to sleep. I kissed her on her forehead and pulled her covers up. As I left her room, I thought, I want so much for you, Annette. I want so very much for you, darling. And I promise you; I'm going to work hard to see that you get it.

After returning home from a few hours of ice cream and cake with my family, I had renewed strength. I was prepared to go and talk to the school counselor about my summer school plans and my plans for the future.

As I got my file and went into the office, the counselor had a grave look on his face. I told him I was planning to enroll in two classes for summer school.

"Well," he said, "you haven't been doing very well."

"Yes, I know," I told him. "But that should be improving soon. I'm not going to have to work as much in the future. And my parents are going to help me more with my daughter. They've agreed to keep her every weekend for me if I need them to. You see, we live down here in Kraetli Apartments right here on campus...."

"Well, well, that's fine. It's just that your grades are looking really bad, and maybe you shouldn't be in an Engineering program." I didn't know what to say as he spoke those words. I simply leaned back in my chair as he went on.

"Let's just say that you do squeak by and get an Engineering degree. Even if you do get this degree, nobody's going to hire you. Your grades are low, and you're a single mom. I'm telling you, in my experience, when they hire these engineers, they want you to be mobile; they want you to go places and do things. They certainly want you to have outstanding grades. Perhaps you should think of a change of major. Don't let me discourage you or anything. I just don't think it's going to work out too well for you in the college of engineering."

I was crushed. I was absolutely crushed. I managed to part my lips to defend my desire to stay in the engineering program.

"Well, I kind of think I want to stay in engineering. But I'll think about what you said. Thank you."

"Okay," he said.

"I'll come back later to plan my schedule," I said as I prepared to leave his office.

As I loaded my book bag up and left the office, I felt my face getting warm. I felt the tears stream down my face. I hopped on the campus bus, and headed straight back to my apartment. In my apartment, I looked at my records.

"Yeah, he's right. My grades are awful; they're absolutely terrible. Maybe I don't need to be trying to get an Engineering degree." I laid on the couch and thought, "I'm probably not even the engineering type. But it's what I want to do; it's part of my goal, part of my dreams." All of these thoughts raced through my head.

Once again, I pulled out a sheet of paper, and wrote down my goals and my dreams. I wrote down what I wanted to accomplish, what I wanted to be. And this time I didn't just write them, I wrote them, and wrote them, and wrote them. I wrote so many of them, I pasted them on the refrigerator; I put one on my bathroom mirror; I put one on my bedroom mirror. Everywhere in my apartment I could think to put one, I put one. Everywhere I turned, I would see my goal; I would see my dream. I wouldn't let him or anyone else decide what the future was going to hold for me.

I decided that I wasn't unrealistic. I knew I'd had some setbacks. I knew my grades were a lot worse than most of the students. But one thing I knew, I had determination. I knew I was willing do what needed to be done for me to get my engineering degree. I had a daughter that I wanted to make a better future for, and I was determined that I was going to accomplish my dreams. I just had to figure out a way that I could do this and be successful. I knew I needed help. I needed inspiration and guidance.

As I started walking around my apartment to make sure my goals were shown in every room, I noticed an old book. I dusted off this old book that my dad had given me several years ago. I remembered reading bits and pieces of it, but I couldn't remember ever having read it completely. I liked the title. It had "power" in it. So I sat down to take a closer look at this book. I started reading it, absorbing every word. It was *The Power of Positive Thinking,* by Dr. Norman Vincent Peale. I thought, "I couldn't control what people said to me; I couldn't control what people thought; but, according to this book, I could control what

I thought, and that would determine my success!" There's power in this positive thinking, the book told me. I thought, "This applies to me too if it worked for all of the folks in this book!" I understood that there was positive power in what I said. I had nothing to lose by trying what the book said in my life. So I began to transform my thoughts and behavior.

I started to speak confidently to myself about my goals. I'd tell myself that I could accomplish my dreams. Every now and then, when I got frustrated, I'd say I was stupid. Every now and then I'd say that I was the dumb one in my class. But, as my transformation took place, I decided, no more would I say those things to myself. Whenever I started to think something negative, I would change my thinking. Then I adopted a new rule. When I thought something negative about myself or anyone else for that matter, I'd make myself think three positive things. At first it felt strange and sort of pompous. But everything that I said about me was true, so it wasn't a lie. This was a new feeling. Three positive things about myself! Sometimes these were small things such as, I cook great spaghetti or I cleaned out my linen closet, but no matter how small the item or activity, it counted because it was a positive thing about me! So every one negative equaled three positives. I thought, that should change my thinking and eventually help me reach my goal. So, I practiced the power of positive thinking, and practiced it, and practiced it.

That summer of 1984 I continued to practice my positive thinking, along with taking two classes and a part-time job as a waitress at a local steakhouse. I enjoyed the waitress work. Waitressing was fun and gave me interaction with people; I enjoyed that. I was also very good at it, and managed to make excellent tips. This was great 'cause it always meant that I had a few dollars in my pocket. I would pick up little gifts for Annette. I would pick up little toys and put them in her room to surprise her when she came home from school or after her weekend with Mom and Dad. She loved finding the surprises in her room. I'd always tell her, "You're such a good girl. I just want to do something special for you." This helped me not feel so guilty about working so much, and it also helped Annette see some immediate benefit from me working all the time. It was also necessary to do a bit of reconditioning after each weekend with Grandmother and Grandpa! She rarely, if ever heard "no" from them, so she had to be reminded that she was back at home with Mom after each weekend. This was usually accomplished with a stern look if she responded negatively to my instructions to get ready for bed or turn the TV off. I rarely had to raise my voice to her, and she hardly ever got spankings. If I gave her a hard look, she would straighten up quick. If I followed it with a loud, stern command, she was directly "in-line", and her great big brown eyes would usually fill with tears as she did what she should have initially done.

Even with the regular reconditioning I had to give Annette, it was well worth the support I got from my parents. Lewis and Annie were still very involved in Annette's life. They called at least once a month to see how she was doing, sent Christmas presents, and birthday presents. And since she was age four – they would fly down to pick her up to spend two weeks with them in the summer. I appreciated this so much because I wanted Annette to be close to her Dad's family and him, even if we weren't together. Eddie was in D.C. now, so he would also see Annette when she spent time in D.C. over the summer with her grandparents.

Sometimes working at the steakhouse part-time didn't have many daytime hours, so I signed on with a temporary agency. I was always very good at clerical duties: had good phone manners, typed well, knew how to file, and managed simple office matters. Soon the temporary agency was sending me out two or three days a week. Sometimes going from one job to the next, I got confused about my work schedules, so I started leaving an extra waitressing uniform in my car. I also kept an extra pair of hosiery in case I ran them going from my office job to my waitress job.

In addition to working at the steakhouse, I also got a job working on the weekends in an upscale restaurant in Oklahoma City. I thought if I could work a couple of days a week there and bring in a few extra dollars, that would make it that much easier. They didn't require me to work early on Sunday, so I could still go to church with Annette and my family. That summer I worked so hard that sometimes I felt like my feet were splitting in half. I would go home and soak my feet, take long baths, pour myself a glass of wine, and just rest. Then most nights I'd have to try to study for at least one hour. But most of my studying was done in my car while I waited to start the next shift at work.

Even though I was working long and tiresome hours, I felt a sense of satisfaction. It felt good to know I was working toward my goals. Some Friday nights the girls from the restaurant and I would go out. We'd go out and dance all night long, then get up early Saturday morning and start the routine over again! Nonetheless, I really didn't mind. Annette was spending the weekends with Mom and Dad and having a great time. And even though I worked hard, hanging out with the girls my age gave me an opportunity to feel like a carefree twenty-one year old.

On my twenty-first birthday, three of my girlfriends took me out dancing. We drank a lot more than we should have, and thank God I didn't have the keys to my car when we left there. The next day I remember celebrating with Mom and Dad and having what had to be the worst headache of my entire life. Even though my parents had an occasional drink, I was embarrassed to have a hangover. I felt so bad; I had to see if Mom knew of anything that would help me. I told Mom that I'd had tequila the night before.

"Mom, it was awful!" I said. "How do people drink that nasty stuff regularly?"

"Well, sugar, you probably got some bad tequila." She fixed me a cup of warm tea, brought me a couple of aspirin, and she even seemed to feel sorry for me.

This sure wasn't the response I expected. I expected her to yell and to tell me how I shouldn't have drunk so much. But I guessed that would come later. It was clear that right then, she just felt sorry for me. She refreshed my cup of tea, and asked if I wanted anything to eat. I was too hung over, sick, and tired to enjoy my birthday dinner. The family gathered around the table and sang our usual "Happy Birthday." Right after dinner, I went upstairs and lay down on Mom and Dad's bed and dozed off. I must have slept for three hours because they woke me up when they were ready to go to bed.

The next few weeks seemed to zoom by before school started. That summer I did okay in school, but I still needed to do much better. I'd managed to put back a few dollars from my three jobs. I quit my job at the temporary agency and the job at the restaurant in Oklahoma City. I also told my manager that I would need to cut back to fewer hours at the steakhouse in Norman. She was glad to work with me, because I seemed to have such a good rapport with the customers.

Prior to the start of the semester, I knew I would have to go talk to a counselor. God, I thought, who am I going to talk to? Nobody thinks I'm worth it; nobody there thinks I can succeed. Lord, send me in the direction of a nice counselor that's going to help me. As I sat and thought, I remembered the nice man I'd met while I worked in the Dean's office. "Ced "Dr. Ligouris," I thought. He was always so considerate, so friendly, and so thoughtful. I could explain to Dr. Ligouris how hard I'd been working, and that things hadn't gone as well as I'd hoped. He could help me. He could help me figure out a plan to get through my engineering degree. I made an appointment the next day to visit with Dr. Ligouris.

As I went in his office, I had my head down. I was a little embarrassed that someone I knew, someone that knew me, was now going to know the terrible grades that I had. I handed Dr. Ligouris my folder.

"Well," he said in his wonderful French accent, "you've done better this summer semester. But your previous two semesters could have been a lot better. Also, Pam, you haven't done very good planning. When you didn't do well in some of these courses, instead of trying to continue, you should have repeated them."

"But I thought that if I worked hard, I could just go ahead and get through the other ones," I responded. I raised my eyes to look at him. He didn't sound like he thought I was stupid. He sounded like he wanted to help me.

"Well, I understand your thinking, Pam. But what you did was set yourself up for more frustration. If you didn't do well in the previous course, you're not likely to do well in the next one because you don't have a strong foundation." What Dr. Ligouris was saying made perfect sense to me, but somehow I thought that I could just manage my way through it. But obviously, my plan wasn't working.

"Yes, Dr. Ligouris, "I agree. I think what you're saying makes good sense."

"Okay, Pam. So, let's get a plan for you." This was wonderful, I thought.

Dr. Ligouris understands the challenges I've had, and he understands that my grades aren't as good as they could be. But he still wants to help me; he still believes that I can make it. Thank you God, Thank you God!

"Pam," he said, "you're trying to take too many classes at a time."

"Well, I want to hurry up and finish, Dr. Ligouris. I'm a mo"Pam, if you try to take too many classes, then it's going to make it very hard for you to finish." Once again, I knew he was right. "Let's cut back to just three to four classes. That will be enough for you this time." He began writing courses on the forms.

I agreed quickly with Dr. Ligouris, thankful to have someone to help me, someone who was concerned about me, and wanted to offer some insight and direction. We made up a schedule for me, and he shook my hand.

Handing me my file, he smiled broadly and said, "You'll be fine, Pam. You just have to work very hard. Make sure you stay in touch with the tutors, and if you have any problems or need any help, please come by and see me and let me know."

I responded with a firm, polite thank you, but I could have reached out and kissed him! I was so happy! I bounced out of the office, determined that I was going to do better this semester, determined that I was going to succeed.

This was now the fall semester of 1984. I worked very hard. I worked harder than I thought I had ever worked. My grades gradually improved, but I still thought they could be better. At this point I was earning B's and C's on my exams, and maintaining passing grade point averages in each class. Nonetheless, I wasn't deterred. I kept working.

I was also spending as much time as possible with Annette. About every other weekend, she went to visit Mom and Dad in Oklahoma City. But I also thought it was very important for her to have some time with me. I didn't want her to feel like I wasn't being a parent to her. I didn't want to lose my position as her primary parental figure. My parents were great with Annette, but sometimes I felt like they let her get away with too much. After all, they were grandparents. It was so hard, going back and forth, trying not to contradict them, them trying not to contradict me. Some days were really tough. When Annette wanted to do certain things in Mom and Dad's house, I would tell her no. Then Mom and Dad would say they'd been letting her do it! This was really frustrating, so I made every effort to try to keep her at home at least two weekends a month. I tried to let her go to Oklahoma City on the weekends when I had an exam or a major project coming up. This made it even harder to schedule things, to try to work part-time, and also try to study.

The next couple of semesters went by slowly. It seemed as though the work was getting harder, and I was spending more time and energy preparing, and I was just barely getting by. At the same time, Reverend Parker had asked me to teach a Bible study for our church at O.U. There were about seven or eight students from our church there. I think he picked me because I was the oldest student. Also, he knew my family very well. So, in addition to trying to juggle everything else, I was also teaching Bible study one night a week. Even though I wasn't sure why I agreed to do it, it turned out to be one of the best things I've ever done. Once a week we'd all get together at each other's apartment, read the Bible, talk about the lesson. We would also eat, snack, and talk about how terrible and how hard school was. We'd discuss if any of us were going to make it. But soon, I started to apply my positive thinking and encouraging Bible verses to our Bible Study. Everyone seemed to appreciate the shift and before long we were all trying very hard to be encouraging to each other. We decided that we would apply a particular scripture to our tough situations and speak victoriously about our goals. That Scripture simply said to "speak those things that be not as though they were." So we figured we'd try this one.

  I remember that spring semester one of my classes got particularly hard. Also it seemed like the frustration was building in all areas of my life. I still needed more money, I never seemed to have enough time, and things hadn't worked out in any of my recent relationships. I was really cautious about dating guys at O.U. because I thought they wouldn't be serious about a single mom. Also, Dave and I saw each other every now and then, but that hadn't worked out the way I wanted it to work out either. He was a Marlboro man with a charming personality, but he was not interested in charming me alone. He said he did not want a committed relationship. So in this semester the disappointment was running as high as it had ever run.

  I went to visit Mom and Dad. I talked to them about me possibly staying out of school for a semester. I remember going up to their room and lying on their bed telling them how tired I was. That I was so depressed that I didn't think I could keep going.

I remember Daddy saying, "It's going to be tough, but it's worth it. You don't need to take a semester out of school."

"Okay, Daddy," I said, not really thinking much about it.

Mom said, "Well, you've been going for a long time. I know your final exams are coming up, but it seems like you've been studying all semester, you would know it. It doesn't seem like it should be that hard, honey."

I knew Mom meant well, but unfortunately, just because I'd been in class all semester, sure didn't mean I automatically knew everything. Sure, it made sense what she was saying, but the frustration of trying and trying so hard, and just barely getting by was becoming unbearable. It also seemed like so many of the other students put in one-tenth of what I put in, and they just breezed by. God, it didn't seem fair. Oh well, like I'd heard before, who said it was going to be fair? "Lord help me figure out a way to do this, despite the pain and despair! I can't go on like this," I prayed.

I decided to stay for dinner with Mom and Dad; we talked a little bit more about school. Later Mom told me she didn't want me to get too worried. She didn't want me to get depressed about it. There had been a number of suicides at O.U. over the last year, and she was getting worried that I was just making all of this school stuff too important.

"You know, Pamela," she said as we had dinner, "we're very proud of you, and we'd like for you to graduate. But if it's too much, if the stress is too much on you, we'd rather you just didn't go to school. I mean, we know you have goals. We sure will be proud, 'cause you know me and your daddy didn't go to college, but we managed to do very well. And Marcella was in college when she died, and I'm sure she would have finished by now, but you know, honey, you'll be the first one to graduate from college. But that's not the most important thing to us. You are what matters most to us. If you feel like the stress is too much, don't do it, honey."

    I really appreciated Mom telling me that. For so long it seemed to me that I was working hard to make them proud, especially Mom, because of the many challenging times that she and I had over the years. But I wanted to disprove what other people had said, even though I never really felt like my parents thought I would never do anything with my life or I'd be nothing. It was so important to me, so very, very important to make them proud, to prove to them that I was something, that I was going to do things with my life, despite my many bad choices, and me being a teen mom. So even though Mom encouraged me to just take it easy and relax, when she said that, it made me feel so good. I think it encouraged me to work even harder.

    So I went back at it, starting to think about my goals again. Once again rewriting them, writing everything that I wanted in life. Writing my short-term goals, my long-term goals, writing things that I wanted to do for my daughter, writing the things that I wanted to do for my family. Somehow rewriting all these things just renewed my energy. It helped me to focus, to visualize the things I wanted so much for my future. Unfortunately, the one difficult class, Rigid Body Mechanics, didn't get any better. I think I started to give up on it. I also didn't like the way I was feeling. I was feeling like a victim, feeling helpless, starting to feel sorry for myself. Even when I started writing my goals again, it seemed like the power of my dreams and encouragement started to diminish. I needed a little reinforcement from somewhere!

    I had met some really great people at O.U. I talked to a good friend of mine, Karen. Karen was a little older than I was; she had been married before, but she didn't have any children. She was an older student, so I felt a little more comfortable talking to her because so many of the other students, it seemed like, just couldn't identify with my situation. Karen also babysat for Annette sometimes and she continued to be one of my most trusted confidants. I talked to her about how frustrated I was; told her how tough school seemed some days. At that time, Karen was dating a psychologist. Once or twice a month we'd get together at one of our apartments, share a can of chicken noodle soup, and talk for hours.

As I confided in Karen, sharing my concerns about how I was feeling, she got her frequent look of wisdom. That look that told me she was about to share some very useful information! "Well, Pam, maybe you ought to talk to somebody. Maybe you ought to get some therapy."

"Well, Karen, I've thought about that. In fact, I remember when I was in high school, how much it helped to talk to the school counselor, Ms. Parker. But right now, I can't afford counseling."

"Oh, no, honey! There's a counselor right here on campus! You can walk right over there and get free counseling."

"Are you serious, Karen?"

"Yes, I'm serious. Let me talk to John and see if he knows anyone over there [that] would be good for you to talk to," she said. John was Karen's boyfriend and a dedicated child psychologist.

"I sure appreciate it, Karen." I trusted her insight and her wisdom. She'd been through a number of difficulties in her life, and no matter what, it seemed like we could solve any problem over a shared can of chicken noodle soup. As tight as money was for both of us, and most of the time both of our student loans were late, this was a great monthly activity to look forward to with Karen.

Having a circle of friends to relate to represent some of the best times I had at O.U. It was always so nice to talk to someone who, I felt, understood my struggle and who was also going through similar things. Although Karen was white, she'd had her share of frustrations as well. She wanted so much to complete her degree. She wanted to complete it quickly, and she wanted to do well. Being one of so few women in the College of

Engineering, Karen and I both experienced a lot of the stereotypes and poor expectations that we often felt professors had for female students. When we'd share all these frustrations, it somehow made it better over our chicken noodle soup or a cup of herbal tea to share.

I also had another friend who I managed to become very close to while I was at the university, Marcie Turner. Marcie was Miss Black O.U. her freshman year. Miss Black O.U. was the African-American version of Miss University of Oklahoma. Due to the small number of black students at O.U., we thought it unlikely that we'd ever have one of our own represent us as Miss O.U., so we had our own queen. It was kind of unusual how we came to be friends. During her reign as Miss Black O.U., Marcie became pregnant. At that time there were so few black women in the College of Engineering, probably less than 20 of us out of over 1,000 students. Marcie just happened to be a brilliant engineering student and her parents encouraged her to stay in college. After having her son, Brandon, she came back to complete her Electrical Engineering degree. Well, Marcie knew I was a mom, and somehow we started talking about taking care of kids and going to school. Though it would be years before I realized it, Marcie said my being there had truly encouraged her not to give up on pursuing her engineering degree when she knew she was going to have her baby.

Marcie and I got to be very good friends. Sometimes we'd babysit each other's kids while one of us had a test or just get together and talk about the juggling that was required to go school and take care of a kid. We'd also talk about how we couldn't wait to graduate. How nice it was going to be to be an engineer. These times really helped me get through the frustrations, but I still felt like I really needed someone, a professional counselor, to help me sort through my feelings and frustrations.

Joe Marshall – God bless Joe Marshall – was just the person to help me to do that. Karen talked to John and almost immediately got back to me. Joe, she said, was a friend of John's and would be a good counselor. A few days later, I called the O.U. Counseling Center, and made an appointment to see Joe Marshall.

When I first met Joe, I trusted him almost immediately. He had graying hair, a mustache, and a warm, inviting, trustworthy smile. As we sat for our first meeting, I started to tell him about myself. I told him I didn't think I had many problems, but sometimes I just got a little bit confused. I told him I had made quite a few bad choices in my life. I started to tell him about my family, my divorce, about Annette, about my dreams and goals. The thing that I remember most about Joe was that he seemed to believe in me immediately. Almost immediately he seemed to see that I was going to accomplish my dreams and goals. Whether he believed in me or not, I felt like he did. I don't think he had any idea how much that meant to me. But I detailed all the activities that I had planned for my future, then all of the things that I had currently going on. "My life is complicated, huh?" I asked Joe. He just smiled and said, "Not much more than many other students' on this campus." Hearing him say that was like being healed from leprosy! Here I was feeling like everyone was looking at me strangely and pointing a finger at me when that was really very far from reality. Later, I learned that most of us would part O.U. with the same dreams and goals of graduation, and each and every one of us had our problems to deal with on a daily basis. Some problems more obvious than others, but nonetheless we all had our challenges.

I would meet with Joe Marshall once a week for the next several months, talking with him about the things that were bothering me. One by one, we sorted through them. Also I talked to him about the things that really mattered to me. Over that period of time, I learned several very important things, things about myself. I learned that forgiveness was very important, most of all forgiveness of ourselves. I don't think I had ever forgiven myself for getting pregnant when I was fifteen.

I felt like I had disgraced my family, and becoming pregnant was a very stupid thing to do in the first place. While it may have been a very stupid thing to do, just as we're taught to forgive each other, it's very important to forgive ourselves. I also felt like my mother was upset with me, that she'd been upset for years. What I learned was whether she was upset or not, she'd always been there to help me and to support me. I'm not exactly sure why I held on to this feeling. Perhaps it was partly because I was not forgiving myself. But I soon learned that in spite of the mistakes that I had made, in spite of feeling like I had let other people down, that I was okay. We all make mistakes. Also I learned that it was okay for me to acknowledge the difficulty of parenting, studying, working, and trying to have a social life. The load that I was bearing was difficult, and it was okay for me to feel hurt, frustrated, and tired. Joe also helped me resolve the jealousy and guilt issues that I had with my sisters. I knew I was jealous of all that Mom and Marcella had in a relationship and to make it more difficult, I was feeling guilty for all the years since her death. I was envious of LaWanna too because she always seemed to do the right thing. It took some time, but my sessions with Joe helped untangle much of my confusion and hurt. I was so relieved to know that I was not the only person who had experienced these feelings, but more importantly, I learned that I could get over these feelings. Now that I was beginning to understand this, I was preparing myself to work on the problems, and get to solutions.

  Those lessons were so helpful to me. In the process, one of the most important things that I learned to do was to forgive Joshua. I was very angry with him for not being the kind of husband that I expected him to be and for taking advantage of me when I was so young and vulnerable. But I learned, too, that Joshua also had some problems. And later on, I learned that he had also chosen to get some professional counseling and to improve his life. Those lessons helped me to ease the burden of frustration that I was carrying, and then I prayed to completely forgive him. Joe and I also got around to discussing my first love, Eddie Stokes. I had a lot of anger at Eddie. While we were both responsible for bringing Annette into the world, I felt like his life was minimally impacted and mine had been turned upside-down. He got off so easy – all he had to do was send money and sometimes he didn't even do that. But in those many afternoon sessions with Joe Marshall, I learned to resolve my anger and even to forgive Eddie.

I remember one day talking to Joe about the things I wanted to do. I'd had a particularly good week before this counseling session, and I shared with him some of the things I'd managed to get accomplished. Joe got a big smile on his face, and said, "You know, Pam, one day you're going to be a big star. You're going to do it, kid!" I knew he didn't mean like a movie star but instead, that my dreams would come true. If it had been professionally acceptable, I'd have reached out and hugged him! I remember that as clearly as if it were yesterday! Getting up and leaving Joe's office that day, it seemed the world belonged to me. After all, Joe had seen a number of students, and he knew what it took to be a star, and Joe believed in me. As the semester went on, my schedule got tighter, and I was only able to meet with Joe about every other week. Even though I was meeting with him less frequently, I still felt that these sessions were helpful. But the frustration didn't stop just because I was starting to figure out some of my problems. The anxiety with school, that is. School was still tough. It still required tremendous amounts of time.

I remember one time staying up all night drinking coffee and taking No-Doz, an anti-sleep, over- the-counter medicine, while studying for an exam. Each semester I had at least one really difficult class. Dynamics was the class that was giving me so many sleepless nights this time around. I worked so hard for that exam. I knew the exam would be really difficult. I sat down and felt like I didn't know anything on it, as though I had been studying for a completely different class altogether. I barely answered any of the questions on the exam. As I walked out of the exam, I fought back the tears. Many of the students bounced out of the class as they talked about answers to the problems, and how they were certain they had gotten this one or that one right. I was too embarrassed to stop and converse with them. I went straight to the bus and went home.

After I got home, I changed clothes and went to pick up Annette. I called Mom just before leaving the house and told her I was going to bring Annette over. When we were riding in the car, all I could think about was all my work, all my effort, was wasted because I certainly failed that test. Nothing could be right in that class. It seemed like I was not going to succeed in that particular class no matter what I did. I had to have that class -- it was critical to my major. I remember thinking: maybe, just maybe, I shouldn't be in engineering. How many times do I have to go through this disappointment? Hey, after all, there weren't that many women; there weren't that many Black students. I'm unhappy with this stuff; it's frustrating me. What is it going to take for me to give up on this ridiculous dream to become an engineer?

When I realized I was speaking negatively to myself, I told myself to think positively. Say three positive things. But I couldn't do it. I tried so hard to think. Well, I have my health, I said to myself. But it didn't seem to matter at this point. I was so disappointed with myself and with my performance on that test. I pulled into the circular drive and waved at the daycare worker. She knew I was there to get Annette early and she motioned to me that she'd be back with Annette shortly. I waited for Annette to come out of the daycare center; when she came out, she hopped into the car.

"Hi, Mommy!" she said in her usual cheerful voice. "Here's a picture."

She had made me a picture. I always loved getting her pictures; they seemed to light up my day.

"That's nice, sweetie," I said as I leaned over and kissed

her. "I'm going to take you to Grandma's house, honey."
"Okay!"
"Honey, I have to study a lot this weekend."
"Okay, Momma!"
"You remember, sweetie," I said, "that I'm going to have to study a lot. I'm going to have to work real hard, especially now that final exams are coming up. You remember? I told you what final exams are."

"Yeah, Mama, I remember," she said. "And I remember that you said that if I want to talk to you or I miss you, I can always call you," reciting my comments almost word-for-word. I leaned over, and kissed her cheek. I buckled her seatbelt, and pulled out of the daycare center.

"That's right, sugar, that's what I said."

Each final exam week that I took her up to Mom and Dad's, or as finals approached, I'd always talk to her about how busy I was going to be, but that didn't mean that I didn't love her or didn't want to spend time with her. It just meant that my schedule was busy and crazy. So she'd memorized this line, and she seemed to understand.

As I drove to Oklahoma City, I kept thinking about how hard I'd worked and was working, and how it just seemed that I wasn't getting the results I wanted. I was starting to feel so hopeless about my goals and my life. We stopped at a red light just before turning to get on I-35.

"Mommy," Nettie said. "Would you hand me my coloring book? It's in the back seat." I looked back, but I didn't see the coloring book. It turned out that the coloring book was not in the back seat; it was on the floor behind me.

"I can't reach it, sweetheart," I said. "If you can wait just a minute, I'll pull over into the parking lot and get it, so you can color." After the light turned green, I turned left, and drove into a parking lot where I could stop the car. I reached behind me and grabbed the coloring book and handed it to her. As I started to drive off, she opened to a page and began to scribble.

Then she looked up at me with her big brown eyes and said, "Mommy, you're nice!"

Those three little words, *"Mommy, you're nice,"* melted away all the hurt, all the anger, all of the dismay that I had been feeling. *"Mommy, you're nice."* I'll never forget those three words.

I just smiled back at her, and leaned over and kissed her little forehead and said, "Thank you, sweetheart. You're nice, too." Those three little words became my three positive statements about me. I silently thanked God for my daughter, and the beautiful words she'd just spoken to me. The encouragement that came from my daughter's little voice got me through four days of grueling final exams.

The following summer I worked again, working two or three jobs--waitressing and doing temporary work. I also decided to take one class at Rose State College. This gave me an opportunity to reduce the amount of time I had to put into school, and to spend some more time with Annette.

As the 1986 fall semester started, we got ready for the annual Minority Engineering Program Banquet. This was a big deal for the minority engineering students. We always had people from industry coming and always had a great speaker. That year the speaker was to be Dr. Howard G. Adams.

I'd heard a lot of people talk about Dr. Adams. He was the Executive Director of the GEM program, a program that gave minority students money to go to graduate school in engineering and science. Even though I had no desire, whatsoever, to go to graduate school, I was looking forward to hearing Dr. Adams speak. Everyone said he was a really funny person and a great motivator.

As I sat there waiting to hear Dr. Adams, Marcie and I started to talk. We talked about how the kids were doing. We talked about men and our relationships or lack of relationships. We also talked about how glad we'd be to get our degrees, and to see the University of Oklahoma in our rearview mirrors! It was one our favorite things to talk about. Anyway, as the banquet got started, we saw many of the people who had graduated before us. It was always nice to come to Minority Engineering Program (MEP) banquets for that purpose, too. To see those minority students who had made it, who had gone through the fire, made it, and were out there on jobs being successful. Then they would come back to be the living proof and inspiration that we all so desperately needed.

As Dr. Adams started to talk, he commanded the full attention of the audience. He was so funny, talking about some of his experiences at school. Then he started to talk about graduate school and how graduate school is important. How, when you're in graduate school, nobody cares if you made a "C" in undergraduate physics. How, if you're in graduate school, it can open up a lot more doors for you. He also talked about how much more money we could make with a Master's or Doctorate degree in engineering. Well, at this point, I had only been thinking about a Bachelor's degree in Engineering. How in the world could I possibly even dream of a graduate degree in engineering with all the frustrations I was having with an undergraduate degree? As Dr. Adams continued to talk, I looked over at Marcie.

I said, "Marcie, he's talking about graduate degrees. I'm praying and fasting my way through a B.S. degree in Engineering! And he wants us to consider graduate school?" She let out a restrained laugh, but we immediately re-focused our attention on Dr. Adams.

After Dr. Adams talked, though, whether we wanted to admit it or not, we both were inspired. I don't think we were fully inspired to go to graduate school in engineering, but we knew that he'd touched a very special place in our hearts and minds. We went up to Dr. Adams, and told him how much we appreciated his talk. He was taller than I thought from a distance and nice looking, sort of a Sidney Poitier-styled gentleman. He was also one of the few black men that I'd met with a Ph.D. He was a warm, engaging man, immediately reaching out to shake our hands, telling us he wanted us to think about graduate school. We looked at each other and kind of smiled.

"Now what's that look for?" queried Dr. Adams.

"Well, Doc, I don't think we're the best candidates to talk about graduate school."

"What do you mean, you're not the best candidates?" he asked. He talked so fast and upbeat, and got right to the point. "Now that you're an undergrad, you're in an undergraduate program in Engineering at a good school, a good university. University of Oklahoma's a good school! How can I not be talking to the best candidates?"

"Dr. Adams, we know the University of Oklahoma's a good school; we just think we're not the best candidates, 'cause our grades aren't that good."

"What's your GPA?" he asked.

Marcie and I looked at each other. There was no way we were about to expose our GPA's. At least not to someone we just met.

"Oh, come on now, whisper it in my ear!" Dr. Adams leaned over, I whispered in one ear. He leaned toward Marcie; she whispered in the other ear. "Well, that's okay! You could do better, but you got a couple of more years don't you? You both look very young. What year are you girls?"

I told Doc I had a couple of more years. Marcie told him she had a little more than that.

"Well," he said, "that's plenty of time to turn things around. But I'm going to tell you some things to do and if you do them, you will do considerably better in your studies. I want you to start doing all the homework problems. When the professor assigns the even, do the odd, do them both. Do all of them. When he says his office hours are at 10:00, be there at 10:02. Talk to him; get help. You can go to graduate school if you're interested. It'll make a good future for you. But you need to start working on it now. And don't ever, ever miss a class. Go to class; be on time for class. Be alert in class," he added.

"Wow," I thought, "this man is speaking as if he really cares about us and knows what we're going through. How can he understand so clearly what we're experiencing?"

Marcie and I both reached out and shook Dr. Adams's hand. We promised we'd think about grad school and stay in touch.

Marcie and I both bought into this grad school thing, as much as we were fighting it. Even though we talked to each other later and said – he doesn't know we're mothers – if he did, surely he wouldn't expect us to go to grad school. But the idea of a graduate degree in engineering sounded cool. Dr. Adams also said that scholarships and research assistantships were available for engineering grad school, so we wouldn't have to pay for this degree like we did with our undergraduate degree. The opportunities he talked about in his speech, the doors that graduate school would open, the respect it would offer, and the fact that I could make even more money with a graduate degree in engineering got me interested in the prospect of it all! Then another thing occurred to me. It would give me an opportunity to prove I could be a great engineering student. Not only did I want to prove this to myself, but to all the faculty who didn't have much expectation of me, who really didn't think I was capable of being that student. If I were in graduate school, it could be different. Dr. Adams had planted the seed of graduate school. I had no idea that it would grow like the pea in *Jack and the Beanstalk!*

CHAPTER 7

ADORNING IN DALLAS

After meeting Dr. Adams I continued to be inspired! I continued to work very hard, but started to even incorporate some things that Dr. Adams had talked about in his speech. When the teacher assigned the even problems, I also worked the odd problems. When the teacher had office hours, and I had questions, I went to see him or her immediately. If I had any problems in my homework assignment, I went to the teaching assistant and a tutor on a regular basis. I also went to see them before I had serious problems just to make sure I understood the material.

I also started to work with the students in my class. I'd make the suggestion that we meet weekly to study. Often times, I thought that they didn't want to get together with me, but if I came right out and asked, I thought, how could they turn me down? We'd work long hours. I'd offer for them to come over to my apartment since I had a child. I'd put Annette to sleep, and then we'd study. We'd study until 2:00 or 3:00 a.m. This was really tough because then I'd have to get up early to get Annette off to school, but somehow I managed. I tried really hard not to let the exhaustion get the best of me when I had to do this for three or four days in a row. One day I was so mad and tired, I cursed out loud about every terrible thing I was going through in one of my classes. No one was at home with me to hear this, but I was still fussing and cussing to myself, letting it all out. After I finished cursing, I felt some relief, but I felt more embarrassment. What would my parents think if they heard me talk like that? What would Reverend Parker think? But they hadn't heard me. Then I asked myself, what does God think? He did hear me. I felt so bad, and I was too ashamed to even ask for forgiveness.

Despite my being tired, my new study techniques were working. My grades seemed to improve considerably. I also seemed to be enjoying school a lot more. Although I hung out with many minority students from the MEP office, most of the people in my classes were white males. Some of my white, male classmates were really fun to be around. We'd laugh and we'd joke; we'd make fun of our professors, and talk about how hard it all had been. Surprisingly, some of them were having difficulties, too. I always thought I was the only one having problems, that I was the only one the professor didn't believe in. But it seemed as though many of them had experienced the same things. It was very enlightening to get to know them, to also understand some of their experiences.

I also got more involved in the National Society of Black Engineers (NSBE). Marcie and I both held offices. That spring we were going to the National Conference. Thank God it was in Dallas, Texas, which was the only way we could afford to go. We drove down to the conference with about six or seven other members of University of Oklahoma's chapter of NSBE. That was the first professional conference I had ever attended. It was huge! I was amazed to see so many black engineering students. All that time I thought I was a needle in a haystack, or least one of a few needles at the University of Oklahoma. To see all of these students was so shocking. To see all of these black professional engineers—it was so amazing and so encouraging.

Not only did the conference have workshops, talks, and motivational sessions, there were several employers there. Wow! I thought. They're looking to hire summer interns; that would be so great if I could get a summer internship. I grabbed Marcie by the arm.

"Marcie, let's go in the Career Fair," I said.

"Pamela, I don't know how many resumes I have," she said.

"Oh, come on, Marcie. Even if we don't have that many, we can still get their business cards. We can promise to send a resume. But we need to go talk to them." I grabbed her by the arm, and dragged her into the Career Fair.

The Career Fair was huge. There were dozens and dozens

of companies there to recruit black students. Every now and then, while we were waiting to talk to a company representative, we'd glance down at a resume that had a GPA of oh, say 3.8 or 4.0, for a person who was waiting to talk to a recruiter. "Marcie, look!" I'd point at the person's GPA. "We don't want to talk to the people after they're through talking to the person with that resume and GPA!" We laughed and continued walking to the next booth.

I walked up to the Rockwell International booth, and extended my hand.

"Hi!" I said. "I'm Pamela McCauley. I'm an Industrial Engineering student at the University of Oklahoma, and I'd really like to talk to you about the possibility of a summer internship." I wasn't sure where those words were coming from, but it was what we learned to say to prospective employers in our NSBE meetings at O.U.

"Well," he said, "let's take a look at your resume."

I talked to him extensively about some of my research projects from my classes. See, Dr. Adams had told us in his speech that we could talk to employers about some of our school projects and this would make us sound more experienced and confident. Between NSBE, MEP, and Dr. Adams, we were learning not just about engineering, but how to sell ourselves and how to be impressive.

After I finished giving my spiel, I asked the recruiter if he could offer me any information about Rockwell. He talked for a few moments about some of the opportunities that they had and some of the things that they were doing. I listened intently, letting him know how very interested I was, asking questions that I thought were appropriate. When I finished, I shook his hand firmly, and walked away.

"Thank you," I said in departure. "I look forward to hearing from you." Sure, I thought. He's going to call me. *Right.*

As several students waited behind me, each of them

offering their resumes, I thought, he might find a more qualified candidate, but he certainly won't find any that are more enthusiastic than I am. I went back to the booth to make sure I had a business card from him. I thanked him again, and continued working through the conference.

The conference was a great experience. We laughed and talked; we even saw Dr. Adams there. Later that week we drove back to Norman, talking about our experiences and how awesome it was to see so many black engineers and black engineering students. The NSBE Conference had truly inspired us.

A few weeks later, much to my amazement, I got a call. It was from Bob Lewis, with Rockwell International in Dallas.

"Pamela," he said, "I met you at the National Society of Black Engineers Conference."

"Yes! Yes!" I said. "Mr. Lewis, how are you?" Oh Lord, I thought; I was trying so hard to stay calm.

"Well, we looked over your resume -- and we had several to look at -- and I just wanted to let you know that we're interested in offering you a position with Rockwell International in Dallas, Texas this summer."

I almost dropped the phone as he said those words. Think quickly! I said to myself. How did Dr. Adams say to respond? I wanted to scream and say absolutely, yes! I'll be there tomorrow. Actually, I could be there tonight if you really want me!

Instead, I said, "Yes, I'm very interested in the summer position."

"Well, I know it's late in the year," said Mr. Lewis. "We were wondering if you had already accepted any offers for the summer?"

As I sat down, I thought, how do I respond?

"No, Mr. Lewis, right now I'm still considering my options."

"*Options*," I thought to myself. What stinking options? I

can stay here in Norman or I can pray to God that they give me this job, and I'll take it for half pay! But he didn't need to know all this information just then.

"Okay, then. What time frame are you looking at? How soon do you want to make a decision? Because, as I said, we're interested," said Mr. Lewis. "And if you need an offer letter, I can get that out to you right away."

"That would be great, Mr. Lewis. That would certainly help. If I can get that from you as soon as possible, I'll get back with you right away."

"Okay. I have your mailing address here on your resume. We will get that out to you tomorrow, and again, I enjoyed meeting you at the conference, Pamela."

"Thank you, Mr. Lewis," I said, and I hung up the phone. I screamed at the top of my lungs, and ran and grabbed Annette, saying, "Nettie! We're going to Dallas! We're going to Dallas! They want us to come to Dallas for a job this summer! "

She seemed excited. The only thing that she could relate Dallas to was the amusement park, Six Flags Over Texas.

"Will we go to Six Flags, Mom?"

"We'll go to Six Flags; we'll go everywhere! We'll do everything! We're going to Dallas! We're going to Dallas!"

After jumping up and down with Annette, I immediately called my parents.

"Mom, Dad, I'm going to Dallas! Rockwell International wants me!"

Mom was so excited. She and Dad both yelled congratulations.

"Honey, this is so great! We have to celebrate!""I know! I'm just so happy! Now I have to get a place to live. I've got to do this...."

"Well, honey, that's great! Why don't we have a big dinner this weekend? Daddy will cook some ribs, and we'll celebrate," Mom said.

"Oh, thanks, Mom. I'm so excited. Well, Mom, let me go.

I've got to make some more calls." As I hung up the phone, it made me feel so good to know that my parents were proud of me. It was always such a good feeling when I felt like I was doing what they wanted me to do, making them proud of me, as I so desperately wanted them to be. But what was even a better feeling was that I was proud of myself. I was doing what I dreamed of doing, and it made me feel so good to have this success.

I called my cousin, Stormy. Stormy had moved to Norman a couple of years earlier to attend the University of Oklahoma. I loved Stormy so much. One of the reasons I think I loved her so was somewhat self-fulfilling. It seemed as though she looked up to me since I was the first cousin to go to O.U. Somehow that encouraged me and motivated me. Whether it was self-fulfilling or not, we both seemed to need each other. She would keep Annette for me whenever she could and also be there to encourage me whenever I felt a little down.

I called Stormy and yelled in the phone, "Stormy, I got it! I got the job!"

"Oh, go on, cuzbone! "'Cuzbone,' as we affectionately called each other, "you knew you were gonna get that job!" Stormy had the most wonderful sense of humor, not unlike most of the people in my family. "Well now, Cuzbone, we just need to celebrate!" That's my family; we love to celebrate!

"Okay, Stormy, I just wanted to let you know."

"All right. Congratulations! I'm proud of you, Cuzbone!"

"Thank you, Stormy." As I hung up the phone, I stopped to think about whom else I could call. I went down the list, calling everyone I could think of, my brother, my sister, my cousin, Angel, Sandy, and of course I had to let Dave Scott, my professional friend from the jazz club. I had to let him know that now I was a professional too!

I think the job in Dallas did more than offer financial support. It reinforced my dreams and goals. As I packed my bags a few days later to go to Dallas, Annette and I could hardly see straight, we were so excited.

"Mommy," she asked. "How much stuff should I take?"

"Well, honey," I told her, "it's pretty warm, so we won't need winter clothes."

"Can I take all my dolls?"

"You can take three dolls, Annette," I said. Mom and Dad had bought her a beautiful doll for Christmas, and I had purchased her a pair of Cabbage Patch twins, the popular adoptee dolls from the 1980's.

"Okay, Mommy. I'll take these." She lined her three dolls up on the couch.

I packed my clothes. Fortunately, I had a good eye for bargains, and for the last couple of years when I got my financial aid, I would buy a new suit. As tight as my budget was, I knew if I wanted to succeed, it was important for me to "look the part" or have the successful appearance. I was also lucky enough to have my Aunt Camille, a woman with great taste in clothes, pass several suits down to me. So, thanks to my bargain hunting and Aunt Camille, I had a fairly nice wardrobe.

We loaded up the car. As I finished, I gave Stormy a hug. Stormy had agreed to help me out by taking care of the apartment and the plants while I was gone over the summer. We drove to Oklahoma City to say good-bye to my parents.

Mom and Dad were waiting. They had a big meal ready for us.

"Mom, I don't think we need to eat a big meal," I said. "It's a long drive, and I want to be alert and you know how sleepy I get when I eat a lot."

"Oh, come on, honey. No need for you to go down the highway hungry. If you're not hungry, at least let Annette eat." Annette ran to the door and jumped into my mother's arms. She loved my parents so much.

"Grandma, I'm going to miss you," she said.

"Well, honey, we'll be down there regularly. Pamela, how much are they going to be paying you?"

Somehow I knew Mom would get around to it. She was never once shy about inquiring about my finances. I confided how much they'd be paying.

"Oh, that's very good!" she said. "Honey, we're so proud of you."

"Yeah, I'm real excited about it, and I also think it will give me a chance to save a little money. I can save a little and be ready for the holidays when they come around. And of course, I only have one more year of school. But I still want to try to put back a little bit of money. Mom, I'm so excited, but I'm also a little scared."

Mom looked at me with surprise on her face. As she went in toward the kitchen and Dad was in the dining room, I sat at the kitchen table between them. Daddy heard me talking to Mom about being scared.

"What are you scared about?" Daddy asked.

"Well, Daddy, I want to do a good job."

"Well, you know damn well you'll do a good job!" proclaimed my Daddy.

"I know, Daddy, but I'm just a little bit scared. This is my first professional life position."

"Pamela," Mom interrupted, "you know we've raised you to believe in yourself and to do the best you can. Obviously the people think you're capable, they're hiring you."

"I know, Mom," I said, "but...." I wanted to believe they understood, but somehow I just felt that they didn't. It was no insult to them. They had raised a proud black woman, and as far as they were concerned, I should feel good enough about myself to go anywhere and to do anything with no fear. I sure wish I agreed with them.

This was the biggest opportunity I'd ever had, from a professional standpoint. And I was scared, scared to death. All they wanted to talk about was the confidence they had instilled in me as a child. While I was grateful for their confidence, right now I just wanted someone to understand that I was scared.

"Well, Pamela, you'll be fine. "I just don't understand why you're *scared,*" Mom said, as she sat down at the kitchen table with me. I could tell she was getting irritated with my lack of a sufficient explanation, and I knew Daddy was winding up to tell about a related experience he'd had in the military.

"Well, Pamela," Daddy said as he reached for his coffee, "in all my years in the military, I got several assignments." Here we go I thought! Daddy continued, "And each time they offered a new challenge. It's the challenge that you look for, and you don't say that you're scared. You're ready for this, Roche. I know it's your big job and a big chance for you, but you can handle it." Daddy was right I didn't want to hear this, but I knew he was right.

Well, I thought, that was as close to sympathy as I was going to get! After all, it did make sense. So I was thankful for those words. After eating dinner, Annette and I kissed Mom and Dad. My sister and her daughter had come over to wish us good luck. I loved my niece, LaTisha, so much. I hugged MaRisha, Alex, and my big brother Maurice too. Nettie and I hugged everybody again. I promised all of the kids that they could spend some time with me in Dallas and go to Six Flags.

"Bye, Aunt Rochelle," LaTisha said.

"Bye, Tisha." I love you, sweetheart!"

My brother walked me out on the porch and gave me another hug. "Take care of yourself," he said in his calm but insistent way, as the whole family stood on the porch. They waved good-bye to Annette and me as we backed out of the driveway and drove away.

As I started down Interstate 35, even though I was still scared, I started to thank God. I started thanking Him for blessing me, for giving me the opportunity, for giving me a chance to show that I really, really could do what I'd been trying so long and so hard to convince everybody that I could do. I guess that's what Mom and Dad were trying to say. I asked God to forgive me for being impatient with their lack of understanding. They'd never been in my shoes, but they were right. There's no need to be scared, but God knows, I'm only human. It seemed like I'd taken on so many challenges, so many battles. After all, there were hardly any black women in the College of Engineering and here I was, taking it on. Couldn't they give me a little bit of sympathy? I didn't have time for a pity party, so I said to myself, yes, it's tough but it's about making a dream come true. "Thank You, Lord, thank You for this opportunity," was all that I could utter on my way to this new adventure.

Annette had already leaned her seat back and gone to sleep. I leaned over and touched her face. As I drove down the highway, a tear came to my eye. But this time it wasn't a tear of sadness; it was a tear of joy, of thankfulness. Thank you, Lord, I said, just help me to do the best I can in everything that I do.

The people from Rockwell had been helpful to all new interns. They helped me find an apartment not far from the facility, which was located in Richardson, Texas. The apartment was just about five or six miles from the plant. I also found a good daycare center for Annette. Actually, it was a summer day camp program. She was excited and looked forward to meeting the other kids. I rented furniture and made a trip to K-Mart to stock my new apartment. We were in Dallas, Texas, and it felt so good.

My first day on the job, I sat and waited patiently for Mr. Lewis in the lobby. Before long, he entered through the lobby door and extended his hand. I was so nervous; my hands had been sweaty, so I quickly tried to wipe my hand on my suit. I was wearing my best navy blue suit and a new white blouse, just what they say you should wear when you first enter the corporate world. I kept remembering what Mom and Dad said. I can do this – there is no reason to be scared or nervous. I hoped Mr. Lewis didn't notice that my hands were a little damp or that they were shaking as I entered the Personnel Office to complete all the paperwork. As we went by, he introduced me to several people.

One person I remember vividly is Evelyn Smith. Evelyn had a squeaky voice and a cheerful smile. She extended her hand.

"Welcome to Rockwell," she said. "I'm so glad you're here. I've heard so much about you."

"Well, thank you," I graciously responded.

"Maybe we can have lunch sometime. I would be glad to help you get settled in the area."

"Thank you," I said. "I'd sure like that." What a nice lady, I thought.

Evelyn and I would spend many hours together over the summer, getting to know each other and becoming good friends.

After all the Personnel details, Mr. Lewis took me into the Industrial Engineering Department. As I walked through, I noticed several engineers sitting at desks, working and writing. Then he took me to the manager's office.

I extended my hand to the manager, and told him that I was glad to be there. He assured me that they had many opportunities for me, and hoped that this would be a good experience for me. Wow! I thought. They're concerned that it will be a good experience for me? That certainly wasn't in my mind that they would be concerned about whether or not I enjoyed it. All I could think about was doing a good job.

As I sat down, my new manager told me what my responsibilities would be. His name was Les Smith. I tried to call him Mr. Smith, but he interrupted me.

"Les, just call me Les. These are some of the things that we want you to do. Now, if you feel like there are some other things that maybe you'd like to do, don't be afraid to let us know. We'd be glad to hear suggestions and ideas." Then he called another young engineer into his office.

"This is Leroy Bassett," he said. "Leroy, you'll be working closely with Pamela. I want her to assist you on some of your projects."

I extended my hand and shook Leroy's. Leroy was the only black Engineer I had noticed as I came into the facility. Wow! I thought. They have another black Engineer here! Leroy was friendly and quick to offer suggestions about projects that I could work on as we sat and talked with Les.

Almost immediately we left, and went to my desk. He showed me many of the activities I'd be working on, and started to explain to me some of the things he'd been doing. Leroy was really sharp. He started talking excitedly about the project. As I tried very hard to be attentive, I couldn't help but think, my God, I'm here! I'm actually here working as an Industrial Engineer intern! Thank You, God, thank You. I had to keep focusing back on the things that he was saying. The morning was partially over, and soon Leroy suggested that we take a break and go to lunch.

Over the lunch break, I had an opportunity to meet some of the other Engineers and other people working in the facility. Throughout the entire day I kept thinking, how wonderful it was to be here, and what a great job I was going to do. They won't be sorry they hired me, I told myself. They won't be sorry.

I followed my Dad's rule for punctuality, and made sure I was at work fifteen minutes early every day. To do this I had to put Nettie's and my clothes out at night, sleep with rollers in my hair, and feed her a breakfast snack on the way to the daycare center. But it was all worth it. I wanted to be the perfect intern. Over the next several days I learned more and more about the job I was doing. I also felt that I was doing a fairly good job. Leroy was quick to compliment me on my work. Even though some of it did involve Industrial Engineering, I felt that most of it I could have done a couple of years prior, even before my sophomore year as an Industrial Engineering student. That was a comforting feeling. I was very excited about the opportunity to have the experience.

But going to Dallas was more than just an opportunity to do an internship. It gave me a taste of the success that I knew I had wanted for so long. Being in the environment, doing the things, which I thought mattered, doing the things that I thought would be helpful as an Engineer, meant so much to me. The internship also gave me the necessary resources to do things for my daughter. One of the things I liked most about that summer was going to the grocery store and buying food *with my own money, with my own checkbook,* not with food stamps. I think I went to the store three or four times a week just to have a chance to buy food, without food stamps.

Any time Annette asked me for something, I tried to buy it, even if it was a struggle. I just wanted her to enjoy this summer as much as I did. I thought, these are the fruits of my labor, and I want my daughter to enjoy them! We went to Six Flags. We went skating. We went biking. Everything we could think to do, we did. Needless to say, doing all of these things did not do much for my savings that I'd hoped to acquire over the summer. But somehow it didn't matter that much. I just wanted us both to experience the benefits of my hard work.

On some weekends, Annette would fly home to Mom and Dad. She could fly free since her Grandpa Stokes was retired from American Airlines. So I'd put her on the plane, and forty-five minutes later Mom and Dad would call me from the airport to say she was there.

During those times when Nettie was spending the weekend in Oklahoma City, Evelyn and I would go to one of the local clubs and listen to music or go out dancing. Other times when I just wanted to be alone, I would pull out a good book. One of my favorites was, *You Can If You Think You Can*, by Dr. Norman Vincent Peale. Even though I'd read that book so many times (especially during finals week), every time it seemed as though I grew more from it; I gained more from it; I learned more from it. Today, as an Industrial Engineer Intern, I was seeing that this was really true. I could do these things if I believed in myself, and worked hard. It was really true.

Although I wasn't exactly where I wanted to be, being an

intern in Richardson, Texas, was a far cry from being a fifteen-year-old, teen mom, at Emerson Alternative School!

The summer was going great. I couldn't have imagined a better working experience than Rockwell International. In July, Annette and I decided to go home for the weekend, for the Fourth of July. As usual, Dad had his barrel grill going. We had ribs and potato salad and ate until our stomachs were so full they hurt!

After eating incessantly for two or three days, I decided it was time to get back on the road to Dallas. My brother offered to fill my car up. While he did that, I continued telling Mom and Dad about my experience and what a great time I was having in Dallas. My brother also cleaned my windows; made sure I had a quart of oil; and I was ready to hit the road. After Annette and I did our usual kisses, hugs, and waves, we hopped in the car and headed down the road to Dallas. We were traveling down 44th Street toward I-35. We'd only been on the road for about three minutes, and Annette was already looking for a sleeping position!

All of a sudden, I thought I smelled something burning. I looked out the window to see if something was on fire nearby, but I didn't notice anything. When I looked in my side mirror, I noticed that the paint on the side of my car was bubbling! I pulled over at the next convenience store, and got out to look at the side of the car.

As I got out, I noticed that the paint was still bubbling. I reached back and got my keys out of the ignition. As I opened the trunk, flames leaped up. The entire trunk was engulfed! All of Annette's toys, our clothes, and a vanity that we had just purchased, all were in flames! "Oh my God," I yelled. I grabbed Annette up from her sleeping position, and ran into the store.

"Oh, my God!" I cried. "My car's on fire! My trunk's on fire!" I yelled. "My car's on fire..." Nettie was scared and started crying. "It's okay, honey, it's okay." I picked her up, and turned her head away from the glass door, so she couldn't see our car burning.

The clerk called 9-1-1 and spoke with a dispatcher. As she listened, a look of panic came over her face. She hung up the phone quickly, locked the cash register, and grabbed her keys.

She said, "We've got to get out of here! The fireman says if that car blows up, we may go, too." By now Annette had gotten down from my arms and was looking at the potato chips.

"Nettie," I yelled, "we have to get out of here." I grabbed Annette, and held her hand, eventually picking her up as we ran out of the door and across the street. We ran far enough to be sure we were in a safe location. We stood what appeared to be about a block away; watching as the flames completely engulfed my car. Annette was really crying now.

"Don't cry, sweetheart," I said. "We're okay. We got out of the car, and we're okay. That's all that matters."

"Mommy, I know," she said, "but that's our car!"

"Annette, don't cry," I said. "Everything's going to be okay."

After the Fire Department came and attempted to put out the fire, I called my dad.

"Daddy," I said, "my car caught on fire."

"Your what?!?!" he exclaimed. "Where's Nettie?" I could hear Mom in the background asking him what was going on.

"We're okay," I said.

"Just come up here. I'm up here at the Circle K." It seemed as though before I hung up the phone, he was there. My Dad and my brother-in-law were standing there looking at the car smolder.

After the fire was put out, Daddy said, "Well, I'm glad you're okay, honey."

I was in shock. Just a few minutes before I was driving my car down the street. Now it was just a charred skeleton. All of the toys, the vanity, my clothes, and my car—were completely gone.

My Lord, how am I going to get back to Dallas? When I get back to Dallas, how am I going to get to work? What is going on? What am I going to do? Everything was going so perfectly. Lord what am I going to do?

Daddy drove us back to the house. Immediately, when we entered, Mom grabbed Annette and me both, and hugged us tightly.

"My Lord! You all could have been killed!"

"Mom," I said, "We're okay."

"Pamela, you could have been killed! Suppose the tank had blown?"

"I know, Mom. You're right. I know." I was so confused and shocked that I would have agreed to anything. Mom started walking into the kitchen and thanking God out loud, for Nettie and me being okay.

While I was so busy being ungrateful about not having my car, I forgot to stop and think about how thankful I should have been that we were okay. Mom always had a way of reminding me about my blessings. Seldom did she allow anyone in her presence to feel sorry for him/herself. Well, maybe for five or six minutes she'd allow it, but I'd learned that's a very good rule.

So after my five or six minutes of pity, I started to think about what I could do, how I could manage. I also tried to be thankful. In the back of my mind, though, I still think I was feeling just a little bit sorry for myself. I kept thinking, another setback. Every time I feel like I'm on the road to success, it seems like something happens. But then, thank God, I began to think clearly. Okay, so my car burned up, I told myself. Well, I've had bigger obstacles than this. Of course, the insurance will take care of the cost, but when? Where do we go from here? I know I can handle this too.

As I lay across Mom and Dad's bed, I started to think. Well, maybe I could just go back to Dallas. There is a bus. I've seen a city bus that goes right by my apartment. Also, Annette's daycare center is fairly close by. I can walk her to school, and then come back and catch the bus each morning for work. Yeah, that'll be okay. And there's a grocery store right across the street. Then with my next paycheck, I'll have enough money to make a down payment on a car if the insurance isn't enough to cover all that I need. I can do the bus routine for two weeks; it's not that big of a deal. I went back downstairs.

"Mom, Dad, I have a plan!" They seemed surprised that I appeared to have gotten over the pain and frustration of losing my car so quickly.

"You have a plan? A plan for what?" Daddy asked.

"A plan to get back to Dallas without a car," I said.

"What's your plan, sugar?" Mom asked.

"Well, I want to go on back to Dallas. I don't want to get a car right now, okay? I'll stay until tomorrow, and we can talk to the insurance company and take care of everything. Then, in a couple of weeks, I'll have another paycheck, and maybe by then the insurance will be settled, and I can get another car."

"Well," Mom asked, "how are you going to get to work?"

"There's a city bus that comes right by, and also there's a grocery store nearby. I can walk Nettie to her daycare center; it's not that far."

"Oh, Pamela, that doesn't sound safe walking Annette to her daycare center."

"There are a lot of people out," I said. "There are a lot of people out every morning jogging, walking. It won't be that big of a deal."

"Maurice, what do you think?" Mom asked as she looked at my dad.

"I think it sounds like a good idea," Daddy said.

"Mom, I promise you I'll be okay. If you want me to, I'll call you every morning when I get to work and every night when we get home, just to let you know we're okay. It will only be for two weeks." I waited for her approval. She was not ready to consent.

"Mom," I said, "that's really the only thing I can do right

now. I've got to go back to work. I can call tomorrow and tell them I can't be there, but I really can't miss more than one day."

"All right," she said. "We'll drive you to Dallas tomorrow."

Surprisingly, the plan worked very well. It was terribly inconvenient not having a car, not being able to just jump up and go here and there. Thank goodness I had made friends with Evelyn. Any time we wanted to go to the movies or any recreation over that couple of weeks, Evelyn was always eager to come over. For the next couple of weeks, we spent almost every day together -- me, Annette and Evelyn. She'd bring her clothes to work, and we'd get together, and go right out after work. We would go to dinner or rent a movie. It was amazing to me, and still is, how our attitude and response in a situation can totally change the outcome.

Here I thought I was going to be without any opportunity to finish my internship without a car. Not only was this situation manageable, but also I really enjoyed having an opportunity to spend time with Evelyn. I also enjoyed spending time in the morning with Annette, walking her to the daycare center. Working with the insurance company was a little more challenging. They had so many questions, and I always had to talk to them during the day, which meant everyone in my office could hear the conversation. Somehow we had managed to get through this, just like everything else. It even renewed my strength, my confidence, and my determination. It helped me to see that obstacles, no matter how big or how small, with a little prayer—actually, a lot of prayer—and a whole lot of hard work, and the right attitude, could not keep me down. Nothing in the world was going to keep me down! But I couldn't take credit for all this optimism by myself. I thanked God for the people around me. I thanked God for Evelyn, for my parents, for people like Mr. Lewis, for giving me the chance to work at Rockwell International. Somehow, I was certain, he had talked to and interviewed students with higher grade point averages and more experience. Maybe he'd even talked to students who were more impressive. But for some reason he wanted to give me that opportunity. Over the next couple of weeks, without a car, I had an opportunity to reflect on all of my blessings usually while waiting for a ride. It was a growing and learning experience in the most unexpected place.

About two and a half weeks later, I went back to Oklahoma City. Daddy and I went shopping, and bought me an older car. It was a station wagon. As reliable as it was, and it was the perfect price, I didn't like the idea of having a station wagon! I thought, I'm a mom, but please! I'm also young and cool. Unfortunately, I didn't have time to look for another car, and Daddy was insistent that this was a good deal. So I now owned a station wagon, and I drove my little station wagon back to Dallas.

At this point the summer was just about over. I had a great experience there at Rockwell International, while working, meeting people, enjoying recreation. It was fantastic! As I got toward my last week of employment, they decided to take me to lunch. It was great talking to everyone, visiting with each of them. I hoped so much that I had done a good job, and that they'd want me back the next year. At the end of the summer, when I got my evaluation, they had various glowing comments. As I sat there listening to the comments, all I could think was, I did it! I did a good job! It made me so proud, so very proud!

As I got ready to move back to Oklahoma City, I was sad. Annette seemed sad, too. We'd enjoyed Dallas so completely. We'd made friends; we'd gone places every night. It was like one long vacation! We loaded up the car.

"Honey, don't be sad," I told her.

"Don't you be sad, Mama," she said.

"Oh, I'm not, Annette. It's just that I like it here. You know, honey? But I will come back, either here or some place else. We'll come back. We're going to have a lot of fun! In just nine little months, Mama will be finished with school; we'll have a great life! I'm going to get a job somewhere, whether it's Dallas, Atlanta, I don't know where, babe."

"Well, Mom, I think that's fine. I think we'll have fun. I want to come back here, back to Dallas," she said.

"Well, honey, I'm going to try, I'm really going to try. But if not, wherever we go, we're going to have so much fun, sweetie! So let's just go back to Norman, and Mama's going to go back and finish school. And I'm going to be kind of busy, sweetie, for the next nine months, trying to graduate."

"That's okay, Mommy. If I need you, I'll just let you know."

"That's it, babe." I tickled her, and we ran through our apartment one last time.

We loaded up the car, and drove back to Oklahoma City. As Annette dozed off, I thought again how glad I was to have had an opportunity to prove myself. I showed myself that I could do a good job. And indeed I had. Wow, I thought, "You really can if you think you can."

CHAPTER 8

A WAY OUT OF NO WAY

When we got back to Norman, we unloaded our things and started to get back into our old, familiar routine. Over the next couple of days, I enrolled in school and got ready to reapply for AFDC once again. God, I thought, just a few more months of this, and I'll never need their assistance again! As I went to apply for AFDC, the frustration, desperation, and humiliation just seemed to overcome me. I'd gone from being a proud engineering intern back to being a welfare recipient within 48 hours! My Lord, I thought, how much more? Well, I counted the months; it was already August 1987. It would be nine more months until May rolled around. In May I wouldn't need government assistance any more, I thought. As I pulled into the Cleveland County Welfare office, I went in through those old, familiar doors.

At 8:15, I went up to the counter and said, "I'm here to apply for AFDC."

The clerk gave me the paperwork without even making eye contact. After I completed it, I handed it back, and sat down to wait patiently. I had spoken to Patty Jacobs, my daycare worker before I'd left Oklahoma. She told me to let her know when I got back from Dallas, and I could sign up for daycare assistance. Patty was always so nice and so helpful. I wished she could be my caseworker for everything but that wasn't possible, so I had two caseworkers.

Unfortunately, the caseworker who handled my AFDC and food stamp case, was a little less than pleasant. In fact, I thought she was downright hateful! Ms. Katherine Mann, I thought, "Oh, don't you just look so hoity-toity in your emeralds." She was hateful, but she had great taste in jewelry.

She just seemed to be in a snit, and she always seemed to be looking down on everyone, at least at me and the other AFDC clients that she referred to in the examples that she used. Well, I thought, maybe it's just that she's tired every time I see her. Or maybe she's having a series of bad days or a bad life. I tried very hard not to take it personally. Boy, would I be glad when I didn't have to see her any more! Katherine came to the door.

"Pamela McCauley," she called. As I stood up and walked back to the office, I thought, "Well, I sure hope this is the last time I ever hear her call my name."

"You need to apply for AFDC?" she asked. "Again?"

"Yes," I said. "I didn't receive benefits this summer because I got a summer internship. You know I'm in school. I got a summer internship, so I moved to Dallas, and therefore, I didn't receive any benefits this summer. I need to sign up again. I'll be finishing school in May. And you see, then I'll...."

She interrupted. "You're still in school?"

"Yes," I said. "In just a few more months, I'll be finished. I just need to apply for AFDC for 9 months"

She interrupted again. "Uh, Pamela, you've been receiving AFDC off and on for quite a long time now, in fact, for about five years. I just don't know if we're going to be able to continue giving you AFDC if you're going to be in school."

I was stunned. I sat there for a moment and thought, if I'm still in school, they can't give me AFDC. If I hadn't gotten my summer job and given up my summer benefits, they'd still be giving me AFDC. If I quit school and do nothing, they'll give me AFDC. So, what they're saying is they just want me to do nothing but receive AFDC? All of this must have gone through my head in a matter of seconds.

"You're telling me that you can't give me AFDC because I'm in school?"

"Well you see, Pamela, it's just that...you know. You've been in school for a long time, five years. Why should other people dig ditches to give you this AFDC money when you're going to college to get an Engineering degree?" she questioned. She seemed proud of her logic and her ability to share what she considered useful information with me.

"Well, Ms. Mann," I said, as I leaned over the desk, "in

nine months I will have my college degree, and you will never see me again. But today, I am deciding to get my education. You see, Ms. Mann? I *choose* to get my education. Now, as for those people you said are digging ditches, perhaps they *chose* to dig ditches. I am going to finish my engineering degree." As I spoke, I could feel myself getting emotional. As the tears filled my eyes, I continued. "So, Ms. Mann, whether I get $238 in AFDC and $189 in food stamps, I am going to graduate. I'm sorry to disappoint the system by being a welfare mom with high ambitions."

I got up and walked out of the office. I couldn't fight the tears any more. They started to roll down my face. As I drove home, the anger in me grew even more. I yelled to myself in the car, "Who does she think she is?" I screamed, "This heifer thinks she's been named God over anybody that gets AFDC?!" I was yelling at the top of my lungs. "I don't think so! I don't think so!" I heard a horn blowing behind me and realized that I was sitting at a green light. I hit the gas, hard, hurrying down 12th Street to my apartment so I could call my Mom. Mom is not going to believe this, I thought. When I got home, I was furious. I called my mom.

"Mom," I said, "I just left the welfare office to apply for AFDC. Just for two more semesters until I graduate Mom, and they said that they're not going to give me AFDC because I'm still in school."

"What?!?!" Mom exclaimed. "What in the hell are they talking about? Listen, I don't understand this." Mom didn't curse very often, but when she did, you knew she was upset.

"I know, Mom. I'm going to call back. I was just so upset; I left. I had to get out of there," I continued. "Mom, they don't want me to finish school. They don't want me to be an engineer."

"Pamela, listen. Do not let these people make you think you won't finish school. This is ridiculous. Whether Daddy and I have to help you or you get this assistance, you're going to finish, and get your engineering degree." Mom's tone was serious. She wanted to quickly dispel any power I "thought" these people had over my future. "They cannot stop you from being an engineer whether they help you or not," she said.

"I know, Mom," I said. "But this is not fair. I only need nine months of help."

The last thing I wanted to do was to ask my parents for money. I had worked so hard to be independent, to establish myself. And after a taste of success and freedom this summer in Dallas, the last thing in the world I wanted to do was to depend on them. All I needed was AFDC for about nine more months, and I'd be okay. I'd finally figured this school thing out, and I was getting good grades. I just needed a little more help.

"Who does Ms. Katherine Mann think she is? She's going to tell me it's okay if I do nothing, if I watch soap operas and talk shows all day? Or does she think I should just work at Western Sizzlin' for the rest of my life? But because I want to get my education, they can't help me?" These thoughts burned through my head. The frustration and hurt turned to rage. I reached for the phone, and immediately called the number for the Cleveland County Department of Human Services. I had memorized it over the last four and a half years.

"I need to speak with... well, let me speak with Ms. Mann's supervisor. Yes, Ms. Katherine Mann. Whoever her supervisor is, I need to speak with them." Immediately the operator patched me through. The phone rang and eventually a woman answered the phone.

"Yes?" she asked.

"I have a problem. I have a complaint," I snapped. "I am very upset."

"Yes, ma'am," she said. "What can I help you with?"

"Are you Ms. Mann's supervisor? Ms. Katherine Mann's boss?"

"Yes, I am," she said. "Who might you be?"

"Well, I'm Pamela McCauley. *Ms. McCauley*, okay? I

knew my mom always used Mrs. McCauley when she was commanding respect and that's exactly what I wanted now, respect! Now I was just in there today," I began. I was speaking so quickly that I had to calm myself down. "Well, I was in there today. I was in there to talk to Ms. Mann. You see I'm in Engineering School at O.U."

I always wanted to make an effort to let them know that I was somebody, that I wasn't just someone who wanted Welfare, who wanted a handout. That this help was just temporary, just to help my daughter and until I was at a point of independence. I wanted so much to always make that point.

Fighting the emotions, I continued. "Yes, I am a student here at the University of Oklahoma. I'm going to be graduating in nine months with my Engineering degree. I came in today to apply for AFDC because I had an internship this summer. And when I had the internship, I couldn't receive AFDC. So I came in. And when I spoke to Ms. Mann, she told me she wasn't sure if I could get any help. Don't you understand? This is very important at this time. All I need is this help to get me to where I'm independent, and will never ever need welfare again."

"Calm down, Ms. McCauley, please calm down. I will look at your case right away; I will look at your file. Can you hold on for just a moment?"

"Yes," I said. When she put me on hold, I calmed down a bit, and was able to regain a little composure. She came back to the phone.

"I have your file, Ms. McCauley. Listen, it does appear that we will be able to help you. You need to come back in and finish the application."

"Well, do I need to speak with Ms. Mann again? I'm just so frustrated. I don't think I can do the application with her."

"Yes, you do need to speak with her again, but I will tell her that we've spoken, and I will inform her that you are eligible to receive assistance, based on what you've told me. If there's any problem, let me know. Write down my name and number and feel free to contact me if there's any problem in the future."

Well, I thought, this has been one of the most courteous people I have ever come into contact with in the Department of Human Services. For once, someone other than Kathy Jacobs cared and treated me as though I were a person, and not just some bum on the street. She didn't treat me like someone just looking for a handout, but someone who just needed a little help for a short time.

"Ms. McCauley," she said, "please come back in. We'll be able to help you."

"But I don't understand why Ms. Mann acted that way with me. I mean, she told me I shouldn't be getting an engineering degree, and that other people were digging ditches. She also told me that she couldn't go to medical school because she had health problems, so why should I be allowed to go to Engineering school on this money? I don't understand! I don't understand what that has to do with anything! All I'm asking for is a little help." I said these words quickly, stiff from the frustration. There was a long pause on the phone.

I was very grateful that Ms. Mann's boss had agreed to help me, and that I would get the assistance. But I was still somehow very angry, so very bitter that Ms. Mann felt she had an opportunity or a *right* to trample on people's dreams, to play with people's future, to tell them about what they didn't have a chance to do. So what if she didn't go to medical school? I thought. That's *her* stinking loss. I didn't know her situation, and I thought, "If she had one-eighth of the determination that I've had to have to get through these struggles and frustrations and deal with people like her, then maybe, just maybe, she'd understand that you can do what you want to do, and make your dreams come true. But she sits there all high-falutin' looking over her emerald earrings and necklace, telling me why I shouldn't go to engineering school." All of these thoughts were flying through my head.

The woman on the other end of the phone responded,

"Well," she said, "perhaps, Ms. McCauley, perhaps you intimidate Ms. Mann. Perhaps she is just a little bit bothered by you. Maybe this problem isn't about you at all."

I nearly dropped the phone. Could that be the case? How, I thought, could this emerald-wearing, so-called want to be princess, be intimidated by me, someone applying for AFDC? "Excuse me?" I asked incredulously.

"Well," her supervisor continued, "I'm not sure what the case is. But in any event, Ms. McCauley, we'll help you. There should be no problem in offering you the assistance you need to finish your engineering degree. And by the way, congratulations!"

"Thank you," I said, "thank you very much." I hung up the phone, feeling victorious, but confused.

"Wow!" I thought. I have nothing. All I have is determination and will. I have the determination and the desire to make something of myself, to make a life for myself. How can anyone envy me because of my determination and goals? Maybe the benefit of determination and goals is more than I realized. At that moment, I began to realize just how indispensable determination and desire were in a person's life. It seemed as though no amount of opportunity, no amount of money, and no amount of other people believing in you can take the place of your own sheer determination and will. I swore then that no matter what I desired, I would always believe in my dreams, my goals, and myself and I would rely on them to see me through. Even when I failed, I promised myself I'd still believe and find a better way. Even though Ms. Mann had caused me so much frustration, she also taught me a valuable lesson. And somehow, some way, I was going to share this lesson with other people, so when they run into another Katherine Mann, they won't be discouraged. They, too, will be determined to pursue their dreams and goals, no matter what.

Even though I had gotten the application for AFDC and food stamps worked out, it would be several weeks before I received any money. And to add more difficulties, my student loan was late, once again. In the meantime, since I hadn't saved any money from my summer internship, I had to borrow a few dollars from Mom and Dad. I also borrowed a few dollars from Sandy – Sandy Kay.

Sandy Kay was my best friend, the best friend I thought anyone could have. We had met several semesters ago. She was a Native American Indian, half Cherokee and half Navajo. Sandy was from Tulsa, Oklahoma. She'd come to O.U. about the same time that I did, and we were enrolled in a class together. Sandy would also be the first in her family to get a college degree. We'd sit and talk all the time about finishing school and doing great things for our families and ourselves. Sandy had great parents. They didn't have much money either, but they offered Sandy as much help as they could, and they were so proud of her. Even though she wasn't Black, it seemed as though we had so much in common. The thing I loved about Sandy was her understanding and her patience. I admired her immensely. I admired her character and strength. She had such strong values, and she had committed to staying a virgin until marriage. When Sandy made up her mind about something, she did it! Neither of us usually had any money, but we'd pass $20 back and forth between us, all semester long. If I had it, she had it, and she knew that. And if she had it, I knew I could get it. That semester it seemed like Sandy was passing twenties my way a lot more than I was passing them her way!

"Don't worry about it," she'd say. "Whenever you get it, you can give it back to me." Thank God for Sandy! She never made me feel belittled or bad for needing the help. That semester I also had three night classes. Sandy would come over and watch Nettie for me. I had managed to pick up a used washer and dryer, $50 for the washer and $75 for the dryer! It sure made life a lot easier. Sandy would come over and wash her clothes and do homework while I was in class. Nettie loved Sandy. She'd read stories to her, and, most of the time, she was in bed when I got home. When Sandy was there, I felt like I had family around, and she took care of me as though I was her family.

One evening I remember talking to Sandy about not having my student loan, about how frustrating it was.

"Well," she said, "Pam, if you need some more help.... You know I have an account at the credit union. Maybe I can get a small loan or something for you."

"That's okay, Sandy," I said. I didn't want her to risk her financial future on me.

The next day I went to campus. I went to see Dr. Foote. At that time, he was Interim Chair of our Industrial Engineering Department.

"Dr. Foote, can I talk to you for a minute?"

"Sure, Pam. Come on in."

Dr. Foote was always such a friendly and outgoing person with great stories to tell about O.U. and never a shortage of bad jokes. Even though he was very opinionated and his opinions didn't often agree with mine -- especially with respect to political opinions – I just loved Dr. Foote. He was a Christian, and was always concerned about the students and how we were doing.

"Dr. Foote, things are really getting tight, and I haven't received my student loan." I didn't dare tell him I was also waiting on AFDC and food stamps.

"Well, Pam, I'm sure we can get them to wait to pay your tuition."

"I know, Dr. Foote. Tuition, I know they'll wait. But I'm a single parent. My daughter's father does send some money, and my parents help, but I really do need my financial aid. I have a utility bill to pay, and I also have rent to pay. Things are so tight right now, I can hardly study."

"Well, Pam, let me see what I can do." He picked up the phone and called the financial aid office as I sat there. That was his style. Go right to the source. "Let me speak to the financial aid office. Yes, this is Bob Foote, Chair of Industrial Engineering. Would you please let me speak to the Director? Oh, I see, I see." Dr. Foote hung up the phone. "Well, Pam, she's not in right now. But I'll call her back and see what's going on."

As I got up and started to leave the Industrial Engineering office, I thought, well, it was sure worth a try, but I don't think they're going to be able to do anything.

Much to my surprise, later that afternoon, Dr. Foote called.

"Pam, they say they're doing the best they can. They say that they don't have any way of hurrying up the process. In fact, the student loan is in the lender's hands at this time." Dr. Foote spoke with sort of a Southern drawl, but he managed to speak very clearly and, even, at times, fairly quickly. "Well, Pam, I'll tell you what I can do, as Industrial Engineering Department Chair...."

I listened intently. *Right.* I'm sure he's going to offer to get them to wait for my tuition, maybe even offer to help with my books. Doesn't he understand I have utilities to pay? That I have rent to pay? This is terrible!

"Pam?" he asked.

"Yes, Dr. Foote."

"We can give you a small scholarship here in the Industrial Engineering Department. How much is your electric bill?"

My goodness! I thought. Is he really going to try to help me?

"Hold on just a minute, Dr. Foote." I fumbled through the papers. Normally I kept the bills right beside the phone. "Well, it's for $170 for two months. So I'm a little bit behind."

"Okay. Is that the only thing you have pressing right now, Pam?"

"Yeah, it is. And my rent. See, I don't pay full rent. Part of my rent is due. I pay about $100 a month."

"A hundred dollars a month? Pam, I'll tell you what. I'll have Jane process a check for you for $300 for an immediate scholarship. Will that help you?"

"Yes, Dr. Foote!" I was in shock. "Yes, Dr. Foote. Thank you so much!"

"No problem, Pam. You come up in a couple of days. We should have that check ready for you. It will be an Industrial Engineering scholarship, so you don't have to pay it back."

"Thank you, Dr. Foote." As I hung up the phone, I jumped up and down, and then I started to pray.

"Yes! Lord, You continue to bless me, no matter what obstacle, no matter what frustration, somehow You just direct me exactly where I need to be. Thank You, Lord." I was speaking out loud, talking to the Lord. "Thank You."

Once my financial aid arrived, and I got my Industrial Engineering scholarship, things moved along a lot smoother. School even seemed a lot easier. I was sure that my summer internship at Rockwell had renewed my confidence and faith in myself. I was still thinking about the seed that Dr. Adams had planted, the seed of graduate school. God, I thought, graduate school would be so nice. It would give me an opportunity to prove myself. Knowing how well I had done at my summer internship at Rockwell International, I was confident that I could succeed in graduate school.

In October, I started thinking very seriously about engineering graduate school. Well, I thought, I've got to have some money. I've got to find a scholarship or something. Maybe Dr. Foote will help. Maybe one of my other professors will help. I started talking to faculty, asking them if they knew of any support for graduate school. Though they were very cordial, most of them replied no, they didn't know of any funds that were available. I thought, I'm sure it's probably true, but maybe if they know that I can do a good job, that I'll work hard; maybe they will take me a little more seriously. So I started to put forth as much effort as possible.

I only had three classes that semester. I would make sure that I went to see my professors at least once a week, trying to put forth that extra "umph" in order to help them to understand that I really was graduate school material. Even with my rough start at O.U., I wanted them to know I could still be a good graduate student. Even with all the effort, it seemed to no avail to get them to discuss graduate school or scholarships with me. Then I began looking at scholarship announcements that were outside of O.U.

One day, I was walking down Felger Hall, in the College of Engineering, a place I'd been a thousand times. It seemed like I'd walked down that particular hall ten thousand times! But that day I was alert. I was reading the bulletin boards. On one bulletin board I noticed an announcement from the National Science Foundation about a scholarship. I took it down, and went into the Mechanical Engineering office. I asked the secretary if she would make a copy of the announcement for me, which she did. As I walked back over to the Industrial Engineering Department, I thought about it. Maybe, I can get someone to help me with this.

The announcement said that they wanted a ten-page proposal. My goodness! I had never even spelled the word *proposal*, much less tried to write one, and especially for something scientific! I read on. It said they wanted to make sure that these scholarships went to people who were creative. Creativity scholarships, it said. At the bottom of the page there was something that I'll never forget. It said, "Creativity is not necessarily connected to grade point average." In fact, this scholarship had its primary emphasis on creativity.

"Oh! What an opportunity!" I thought. "This is exactly what I need! I'm creative; I've certainly had to be to get to this point. I don't have the best GPA, but one thing I definitely have been in my seven years of getting this Bachelor's degree is creative and resourceful. I've thought of everything! Oh, man, I thought. This one has my name on it! "Lord, I think you put this here for me. Thank you, Lord. But, Lord, can I compete for a national scholarship? I'm not sure if I can do this!" My thoughts ran wild and were invigorated by the possibilities outlined before me.

Instead of going to the Industrial Engineering office, I turned around and went back to the Minority Engineering Program (MEP) office.

"Wayne," I said, who was the Director of MEP, "Wayne, look at this announcement. This announcement is for a scholarship, a National Science Foundation scholarship!"

"Yeah, Pam, that looks good. They're giving a lot of money away. Whom are you getting that announcement for?" Wayne was a big joker.

Somehow I didn't know if he was joking with me or if he was serious at this point. Even though my grades weren't the best, in fact, they were pretty darn low in some semesters, but if anybody knew about my determination, it was Wayne.

"Well, Pam," he said, "you can apply for it. I don't know if you'll get it. In fact, you ought to plan on finding a job, just in case." He chuckled. I laughed with Wayne, even though I was a little insulted.

"Well, Pam, you know I'm a pessimist. That's just the way I am," he said.

"Yeah, Wayne, I know. You're a pessimist. Unfortunately, you always rain on everybody else's stinking parade." I said. Wayne's favorite word was "stinkin'" and he used it to describe anything he found that was remotely negative, distasteful, or that he disagreed with. So we all borrowed his word "stinkin'" especially if we were in a conversation with him.

"Well, Pam, apply for the stinking scholarship! Go on and do it," he said as he lit a cigarette and laughed. "Go on; you never know." Well, this wasn't exactly the kind of encouragement I'd hoped for, but he didn't completely trample my dreams.

After leaving Wayne's office, I went to the Graduate College. I wanted to know what it took to get into Graduate School. I asked if I could speak to the Associate Dean for the

Graduate College. I sat down and talked to him. He was friendly and cordial. I sat my backpack down, and settled into a chair directly across from his desk.

I said, "I'm thinking about graduate school."

"Well, what's your GPA?" asked the Associate dean. That was a lousy question, I thought! But actually, I knew he needed to know.

"Well, my GPA isn't very good, but my last two years are good, and I'm a very hard worker. I was wondering if you know of any resources that are available. I've learned of an NSF scholarship I'd like to apply for, but just in case that doesn't come through, I'd also like to know if there's anything else available." I was recalling what Dr. Adams had said about graduate school, "How everyone could either get scholarships or research assistantship and that we should talk to our departments and our graduate college."

"Well, Pam," he said. "If your GPA were higher, above 3.5, maybe we could help you. But, no, I don't think that we're going to be able to do anything. After all, you're about to complete a Bachelor's degree. Why don't you just go to work? Don't you want to go out and make around $30,000 a year? That's a great salary!" He stood up, and I knew that was the end of our conversation.

"Yes, Dean. Thank you for your time." As I left the office, I thought, he doesn't think I can do it. He doesn't even think it's realistic. With the kind of grades I have, he thinks I'm just lucky to have gotten through this Engineering program at all. Well he might be right about some people, but he's not right about me.

As I walked to my car, I started to get angry. I thought, well, he has a Ph.D. in Engineering. It's a realistic goal for him. Unfortunately, in his mind, it's not a realistic goal for me. Now whether or not he thinks it's because of my grades, or because I'm Black, or because I'm a woman, that's his fault. He can think whatever he wants to, I will not let him decide what the future holds for me, what the future holds for my daughter, or what my dreams should be. I don't care how unrealistic he thinks they are. After all, isn't a dream supposed to be something you reach for? Isn't a dream supposed to be something you have to work hard and stretch yourself to do? Despite the negativity I had just experienced, I decided I would dream and plan to go to graduate school. My route might be a little different than others, but I'm going!

For the next couple of days I thought about the NSF announcement. I tried to decide who to talk to; I went by another professor's office because the announcement said that I had to have a professor to help me identify my idea and to work with me.

So I stopped by a professor's office that I'd had for a class last semester. "Hey, Doc, I just want to talk to you about this announcement. You know, it's about graduate school." He stood up.

He appeared to be in a hurry to leave. He grabbed a book off his desk.

"Well, Pam, NSF? That's a big scholarship. I don't know if they'll give you any money. But right now, I just don't have time to talk about it."

As he rushed by, somehow I took it personally, despite how hard I had worked not to take things personally. I thought, maybe the word is out that I'm interested in graduate school. They're probably laughing at me. They're probably sitting back in their faculty meetings thinking how very ridiculous it is that someone like me -- a young, Black, woman with a kid and average grades -- is even thinking that she can get into graduate school, much less get a scholarship. I read all of that into his brushing by me! The frustration was starting to get to me. I had really pumped myself up, and told myself that I could accomplish this, but now I was starting to have doubts.

When I went home that evening, I sat down and started to pray. I cried some too, but my praying continued.

"Lord," I said, "maybe this dream is unrealistic. After all, I've managed to get a Bachelor's degree. Or just about, I'll be graduating soon. Thank you Lord. And Lord, I can get a good job. I'm thankful for that. I can have a good future. Why is it I want so much? Am I being realistic? Do I want too much? Am I expecting too much? Is this dream just that -- a dream, something I won't ever be able to accomplish? Please help me understand, Lord." After I finished praying, I lay on the couch and dozed off.

When I woke up, I was refreshed. It was almost 6:00 p.m. I had to hurry to the daycare center and pick Annette up. When I got there, I apologized for being so late.

"Well, honey, let's go home. Let's have dinner," I said to Nettie.

"Mommy, what did you do today?" she asked.

"Well, honey, I'm just trying to finish school. You know I'll be graduating soon."

"Mommy, what are we gonna do when you graduate?"

"Well, sweetie, I'm going to get a great job. I'm going to do some things, and we're going to go places. Remember we talked about this before we moved back home from Dallas?"

"Like Dallas, Mommy? Like Virginia?" she probed.

"Yes and anywhere else you want to go. I love you!" And she looked at me with her big brown eyes.

Somehow it had happened again; all the uncertainty went away. This, I said to myself, is why I have a dream. Because I want to give my daughter so much, I know my dreams can happen. I reached over and kissed her. As we drove home, we sang a song, the theme song from *"Gilligan's Island."*

"Mommy, I don't know all of that song! Sing one I know."

"Come on, honey, just sing what you know. You'll never learn it if we don't sing it."

"Okay." As we sang, we laughed. I began to think, my dreams are worthwhile, difficult – yes, challenging – yes, but very, very attainable. I also decided that my dreams were realistic. They were real to me.

The next day I was all charged up and ready to go. Well, I thought, I'll probably get four or five negative responses, but today somebody's going to talk to me about graduate school. As I went to campus, I thought, who's nice? Dr. Badiru. Everyone likes Dr. Badiru. And, I thought, he's the only Black faculty member in our department, so maybe he'll understand, and try to help me even if he thinks it's crazy.

Dr. Badiru was from Nigeria, always such a friendly and cordial person, and he was so smart! I had not had many dealings with Dr Badiru, but all my interactions with him had been positive, and in fact, I had never heard anyone say anything negative about him. Well, I thought, I'll start with him. I'll ask him about graduate school, and see if he thinks it's a good idea for me. I went to the Industrial Engineering office. Lisa, the secretary, was always friendly.

"Um...Dr. Badiru. Is he available?"

"Yes, he is. He has class in just a few minutes, but you can try to talk to him."

I went to his door. "Dr. Badiru?"

"Yes, Pam?" he asked. "How are you doing?"

"I'm good, Dr. Badiru." I was shocked and pleased that he even knew my name.

"Dr. Badiru, do you have a moment?"

"Sure, come on in. I have just a few. I'm getting ready to go to class," he said in his Nigerian accent.

"Well, Dr. Badiru, I've been thinking about graduate school and uh...um...." I was stuttering over my words. I reached into my backpack and grabbed the announcement. I was shocked that Dr. Badiru was even taking a moment to speak with me. I handed him the announcement.

"I'm thinking about graduate school. Actually, I'm thinking about doing work in Ergonomics." Ergonomics is the study of humans in the workplace. "Okay. Ergonomics is a good field, Pam. You may well get this scholarship. But Ergonomics is not my area. Dr. Purswell can help you with this. Why don't you visit with him about it? And if, for some reason he's unable to help you with this, come back to see me. I'll be glad to help you. Good luck with the scholarship. That could be very nice to have for you and the university."

"Okay, Dr. Badiru. Thank you." I was shocked! I took the paper back as he handed it to me.

I was shocked that he took the time to review the announcement, encourage me, and suggest that I talk to someone, and even if that person didn't help me, he would. I was elated. As I loaded my backpack, I was practically floating! I decided to go immediately down the hall and talk to Dr. Purswell. I knocked on Dr. Purswell's door.

"Dr. Purswell," I said, "I was just talking with Dr. Badiru, and he said you're the Ergonomics expert." Yeah, I'll use the word *expert, I thought,* maybe that will soften him up.

"Well, yeah, that is my field of research," Dr. Purswell said as he looked over his glasses. Dr. Purswell was a tall and slender man, as well as, one of the senior faculty members in the department.

"Well, Dr. Purswell, do you have a moment to talk with me?"

He could barely see over the mountain of work on his desk, and he had a mountain of papers on the credenza behind him.

"Come on in, Pam! Sure, I can talk to you for a few minutes."

"Thanks," I said. I was elated. I entered his office and threw my backpack on the floor, reaching for the announcement for the National Science Foundation.

"You see, Dr. Purswell, here's this announcement. The NSF, the National Science Foundation, that is, they're giving away a scholarship, and I want to apply for it."

He looked closely at the announcement. I sat quietly while he read. "Well, I think it'd be a good idea if you look at some of these books," he said, pointing to his bookshelf.

"Well, do you think that I can get it?" I asked, sitting on the edge of my seat.

"Well, it's going to be very, very competitive. But, perhaps you can win this award. You never know. What are you thinking about doing research in? What area?" he asked.

I shared some ideas with him. I really liked the ergonomics class. I'm really interested in designing things, and I like studying the body, so I think ergonomics would be a good area for me. Or maybe developing mathematical models that can predict if or when people might have an injury at work. He talked to me about the merit of each of those ideas, and handed me a large stack of books.

"Go home and read these," he said. "Read this and look at this and tell me what you think about that idea." He handed books and articles to me, and then he told me to get out a piece of paper and take down a few ideas.

I feverishly searched through my backpack for a notebook and pen. I grabbed the first notebook I saw. Dr. Purswell handed me a pen. Then he started to rattle off topics, and then he outlined two or three of the topics. He was talking quickly because he was on his way to a meeting. He had no idea how much this precious fifteen minutes out of his schedule meant to me. It would change my life forever. I finished writing and gathered my things to leave his office including the books and articles he'd given me.

I was absolutely ecstatic! Although I had about six or seven books in my arms, it felt like I was carrying nothing. I was so thrilled that he had taken time to visit with me. As I left his office, I thought, God bless Dr. Purswell. As I walked out of the Industrial Engineering office, I passed by Dr. Badiru's office. God bless Dr. Badiru, God bless them both. They have helped restore my faith in my dreams.

I went home and read intently. I read everything that Dr. Purswell had given me. Then I read the NSF announcement. I read everything that needed to be done, and followed the instructions to the letter. I prepared a ten-page proposal. Boy, I thought. This is great! Dr. Purswell's going to be impressed with me, that I did this all by myself! I called him for suggestions and input. Then I went back to him and talked to him about the outline of the paper.

"Do this," he said, "then do that. Then get back with me in a couple of days." I wanted to make sure that I got back with him just when he said to. A couple of days later, I got back with him, and showed him the new outline and summary. He gave me new direction and new input. I left and went home, and worked late into the night on my proposal.

About three weeks later, I finally felt like I had the perfect proposal. I took it back to
Dr. Purswell.

"Here, Dr. Purswell," I said, "NSF wants the proposal in just a few days. So, if you'll read over this, I'm sure it's ready to go, and we can mail it."

"Well," he said, "leave it with me overnight. I'll take a look at it and you can pick it up tomorrow."

I thought, "It's got to be perfect." I'm sure he just wants to look at it and make comments and tell me how great it is. I left the proposal with him. The next day I came back.

"Well, Pam, I have a few comments. And I want you to take this proposal and...." he paused. "It looks good in most places. You see; they're going to be giving away a lot of money. They're going to be very particular. You've got to answer a lot more questions than you have here."

All of a sudden, I felt as though I was being insulted. But that was only half of it. When he handed me my paper, it was bleeding to death! I mean, there was red ink from one side of the paper to the other, from the top to the bottom. It even looked like there was red ink on the back! I was crushed!

Dr. Purswell immediately saw the surprise and disappointment on my face. "Now, don't feel bad, Pam! There's just a few things you need to change, a few things you need to work on. But you're off to a good start."

A good start?! I thought. How can I be off to a good start when there's not a square inch of white paper anywhere in these ten pages? He has red ink everywhere! Nonetheless, I took the paper home. Reading through it, I was a bit discouraged, thinking how hard I had worked. But also I started to think about something. I started to think that Dr. Purswell had taken the time to read each line of my paper. He had taken the time to make suggestions and corrections; and he had also taken the time to make sure that my proposal was good. Even though I was frustrated with him, something gave me the maturity to see that he was trying to help me. This also taught me a very, very important lesson: that every time someone says something negative, it may not be to necessarily hurt you. In this instance, although I did not want to hear the negative things Dr. Purswell was saying about my proposal, I did understand that the things he was saying were purely to help me. With that in mind, I got to work making all the corrections he had indicated, addressing each of the red comments, and trying to go above and beyond. I sent it to him for final approval. He approved it, and signed the paper for the application.

We mailed the proposal out early in December 1987. I remember what a feeling of accomplishment it was to put the proposal in the envelope and send it off. At the same time, I started to think about my alternatives. If I didn't get the scholarship, I needed to go to work. I couldn't see putting Annette through two more years of financial hardship for me to get a Master's degree without a good scholarship, even if she didn't know that we had been financially strapped at times. So I decided that I would look for a job just in case.

I started interviewing. Even though I was very embarrased when I went into interviews, and the first thing employers wanted to talk about was how they wanted students with GPA's of 3.5 or better, I went anyway. The standard discussion was how they only wanted the cream of the crop and how they sought the best and the brightest students.

Well, I thought, I've got to find a way to steer them away from this GPA question. So I started to talk about my extracurricular activities. I started to prepare for the interviews, and let them know how much I knew about their organization, how very impressed I was with the things their organization was doing. Yeah, I thought. These things will get them off the GPA track. But inevitably, it always came back to the GPA. Much to my surprise, despite my less-than-glamorous GPA, I started to get calls for interviews. I went to Texas Instruments in Dallas for an interview. Although that sounded like a good opportunity, the interview that impressed me most was when Conoco Oil Company in Houston, Texas called me. I was elated! I had heard that the oil companies had the greatest pay, and that this company had a fast track to management. I was thrilled! When I got the call, they told me that they would be sending me some correspondence about going to Houston for an interview. It seemed like a dream come true.

When I got there, they had a Lincoln Continental town car to meet me at the airport. I thought, "A driver and a Lincoln. Wow, this is first-class!" The interview went exceptionally well. It was a full day of shaking hands and talking, from breakfast in the morning to dinner and dessert at night. I talked about my classes, my interests, and how much I looked forward to an opportunity with Conoco. I managed to keep a smile, shake hands, and be pleasant. I was very excited about the way it all went. I met a black engineer, Dwight Jackson, on the interview. He was very nice and encouraged me to think seriously about a future with Conoco. I wanted to tell him to have Conoco think about a future with me – but I thought it better to limit my joking and sarcasm.

When I returned to Norman, I thought, hey, this could be a great job. It would be wonderful. And after all, I know that the NSF scholarship is a long shot. I ought to start thinking about going to work. And the people at Conoco are great. Nettie and I could have a great life in Houston! I started thinking that maybe my dreams and goals were misdirected. Maybe I just needed to go to work. Hey, after all, they'll help me with graduate school. I can go to graduate school part-time. Yeah, I know. I won't be able to start for a couple of years because I really want to spend some time with Annette, I thought. But hey, one way or another, it'll work out. This job is for me.

Within about three weeks, I received a letter from Conoco. It was a letter telling me that they wanted to offer me a job. As I read the salary, I couldn't believe it—$31,500! My God, that was more money than I had made in the last three or four years combined. I was ecstatic! I called Mom and Dad.

"Mom! Dad! They offered me a job at Conoco!"

"Oh, honey," they said, "we're so proud of you!"

"Well, you know," I said, "maybe this is the thing I should do instead of graduate school. Mom, it's such a great opportunity, I can't believe it! I cannot believe it!"

By this time it was spring semester, and I was starting to get a little antsy about my application for NSF, so the news about the job offer was exactly what I needed to hear. Later that night as I lay in bed, I started thinking about what a great life I could have in Houston. But somehow, my dream came back to me. Lord, what about my dream? This is good. In fact, this could probably be great. But what about my dream to go to graduate school? You know this is what I want to do. Am I just dreaming too much?

Over the next several days, I began to think about life as an employee at Conoco Oil Company. I started to think about the opportunities and what kinds of things I'd be able to do for Annette, what kind of bedroom suite I'd be able to buy her and so on. I thought about the clothes I could buy and the new car I wanted. But most of all, I thought about never, ever needing welfare again.

While I was thinking about all these wonderful thoughts,

graduate school was still in the back of my mind. I thought about other alternatives if I didn't get the National Science Foundation scholarship. But then I thought about winning the scholarship. Then I'd say that's a ridiculous thought. Perish the thought, I'd think. It's just crazy! You are not going to win this scholarship. Just go to work. You don't need to go to graduate school. That's for those stellar people, and those really smart people. Yeah, the ones the professors like and have in their labs, but not me.

One day as I was checking my mail, I noticed a letter from the NSF. It was a thin letter. Well, I thought, this must be my rejection letter. As I opened it, and walked back in the door, it said "Congratulations!" at the top. "Congratulations, Ms. McCauley! You are a finalist!"

I screamed, "Aahh! I'm a finalist!" I was still outside. My neighbors must have thought I was being attacked. A few of them looked out the door as I ran in the house, screaming at the top of my lungs! I picked up the phone and called Dr. Purswell. He had given me his home phone number while I worked on the proposal, and I memorized it. As the phone rang, I was so excited I was almost breathless!

He answered, "Hello?"

Without even identifying myself, I practically yelled into the phone, "Dr. Purswell! I'm a finalist! I'm a finalist in the NSF competition!" I said, "It's me, Pam, "I'm a finalist."

"That's great, Pam! Just great! This is a time to rejoice. This is a time to be happy."

"Oh, Dr. Purswell, I am so happy!" I said. "I am so happy!"

"They said I have to come to Dallas for an interview. We're going to talk about the merit of my idea, and they want to meet me. They want to talk to me about the creative aspect of the idea. I'm so excited, I just don't know what to do!"

"Well, we'll get you prepared. We'll get you ready for it."

The next few days were a whirlwind. I talked to Dr.

Purswell, to everyone I knew about the interview. I was calling friends all over the country, asking them what NSF might ask me. I called Dr. Adams and told him I was a finalist.

"Oh, great!" he said. Dr. Adams was especially encouraging. "You'll do fine. You'll be fine. Just go down there and talk to them and be yourself. Make sure you talk in detail about your research. You'll be fine. Also, talk to your professors; let them help you prepare. This is a great opportunity and I believe that you can win."

It amazed me the confidence he seemed to have in me, particularly with all the doubts I had dealt with and continued to endure from others. It amazed me that some people, a few dear people, could still have confidence in me and never express the doubts that I had. Maybe it was because I put up a good effort, always trying to be optimistic and confident, even when I didn't exactly feel so positive. Or maybe it was because they had seen me work and work so very, very hard. Whatever the reason, I was thankful, so very thankful.

I drove to Dallas for the interview and thought about every piece of advice I had received from every friend, individual, and faculty member that I had talked to. I thought about how I would sit, the words I'd use, how I'd express myself.

When I arrived, there were other people sitting in the hotel lobby waiting for the interview. There was a big sign that said, "NSF Finalists, please wait here." Wow! I thought. I'm an NSF finalist! I looked around and noticed some of the other applicants waiting. Many of them had poster boards, flip charts, had all kinds of things. Oh, my Lord! Was I supposed to bring a presentation? All I have is my ideas, my energy, and myself. I was terrified.

As I entered the room, I sat down, and started to talk to the panelists. There must have been ten or twelve of them. They were all men, and I believe they were all White. God help me. How can they relate to my idea or me? Lord I need your help. I told them about my idea, why I thought it was important, why I thought it was creative. I articulated my thoughts, moved my hands and expressed with as much energy and intelligence as I felt possible, and ended with why I felt I was the person they should fund. Afterwards, I felt good.

I jumped in my car and drove the 180 miles back to Norman. I felt great! Wow! I thought. I talked and I told them why I deserved that money. When I got back, I called my family, and told them how great the interview went. I explained that I thought it went well. When I went to the campus the next day, unfortunately, it seemed like negativity and negative words had beaten me getting there.

When I arrived at Dr. Purswell's office to tell him how great the interview went, he said, "Now, Pam. I don't want you to get your hopes up. There's a distinguished faculty member from here who was on that panel, and he said that, you know, your interview went well. But some of the students had prepared flip charts and presentations, and that some of the students were just really well prepared. So you may not get it." I was crushed. "But you put forth a good effort. I don't want you to be down or frustrated. We are proud of you."

"Yeah. That's great." Well, I'm not going to get it, just like they thought.

As I went through the Minority Engineering office, someone else said, "Well, Pam. Congratulations! We heard your interview was okay, but it could have been better."

Oh, my goodness! How much of this negativity do I have to put up with? I must have shown something in my face to let them know how frustrated I was with that.

"Well, Pam, we just don't want you to be disappointed. We just don't want you to be frustrated by it."

"Let me be disappointed. Let me be frustrated", I thought.

"Well, I appreciate your concern, but, you know, don't worry about it. I'll be okay."

I could do with a little disappointment. I had learned that when you have a dream, disappointment comes with the territory.

I was so very frustrated at how these negative people were responding. Maybe I should just take the job at Conoco and forget about my dreams. Did anyone on that NSF panel think I deserved the scholarship? I replayed the interview over and over in my mind. After all, if this person was on the panel, maybe I really wasn't going to win. I went home from campus frustrated and confused.

The next few days seemed to creep by. I waited and waited to hear from NSF. Never did I get a call; never did I get a letter. Each day seemed longer and longer.

Conoco was getting anxious. Anxious for me to reply about whether I was coming to work for them. Then I started to tell myself, I didn't really want to go to graduate school. Going to work was the best thing. I started to rationalize or lie to myself. After all, hey, I don't need that scholarship. I don't want to be bothered with these people. Nobody at O.U. or NSF believes me anyway. I felt myself slipping into a pity party.

Then one night, a Wednesday before a final exam in Dr. Foote's class, I called my mom.

"Mom, I'm so frustrated. It's finals week, and I can't even study. I'm waiting for NSF, and nobody's called me. Mom, would you just say a prayer with me?"

Mom said, "Sure, honey. I'll pray with you. But one thing I want you to know is that you've done a great job. Don't worry about what other people say; don't worry about your goals. You've managed to accomplish a great deal, Pamela. And no matter what, the Lord will be you." She said a short prayer. I remember feeling at peace.

"Thanks, Mom," I said. As I hung up the phone, I dozed off knowing no matter what, everything was going to be okay.

The next morning I went to the campus. I started to feel frustrated all over again. I was preparing for my test and I thought, "Why don't I just call NSF?" After all, I've got to get back with Conoco in the next couple of days. I'll just call and ask. All they can tell me is no, I haven't won.

I decided that I had nothing to lose. I reached for the phone in the front of the office. I thought it would be better to go to the back, so if they tell me no, and I start crying, I won't be embarrassed. I don't want people asking me what's wrong. "Hey," I thought, "I've given it a great shot. I've gone a lot further than most people expected me to." I went to the back of the office, and picked up the phone and dialed the phone number from the initial announcement.

"National Science Foundation, Engineering," the secretary said as she answered.

"Yes, ma'am. My name is Pamela McCauley, and I am an NSF finalist for the Creativity award."

"Yes?" she said promptly.

"I was wondering. Can you tell me if the winners have been announced for the Creativity Engineering Fellowship?"

"Yes. We have that information. Can you hold just a moment, please?"

"Yes, I can." As she put me on hold, I felt like my heart was beating a hundred miles a minute. My hands were shaking. I couldn't even think straight.

She came back to the phone. "What is your name again?"

"My name is Pamela McCauley."

"Pamela McCauley? University of Oklahoma? You are one of our winners. One of our winners of a $90,000 Creative Fellowship."

"Aaahhh! Yes! I won!" I was screaming at the top of my lungs. Everyone came rushing around the corner.

"Pam, what's wrong?"

"I won! I won the National Science Foundation Creativity award!" The tears were flowing, I was screaming. All my friends ran to hug me.

I called Sandy. I called my Mom and Dad. I called everyone I knew.

I had won! A dream so unlikely had come true. Thank You, Lord!

The next few days were a whirlwind. *The Daily Oklahoma City* newspaper interviewed me, the Norman newspaper interviewed me, television stations wanted to talk to me. Everyone wanted to talk to the young mom who had managed to accomplish so much against great odds. But, I thought, I don't even feel like I accomplished that much. I just refused to take no for an answer. I kept telling the papers that I just continued to believe, and I was always thanking Dr. Purswell and my family for all the things that they had done, and all the other wonderful people at the university who had helped me. I also sent a long thank you letter to Dr. Adams to thank him for planting the graduate school seed so many years ago. Although there were many negative people, many naysayers, I tried not to focus too much on that. I only focused on it when it was important to make the point that believing in your dreams is more powerful than any negative thing people could say.

In May 1988, after graduation, Mom and Dad threw me a party. I remember they bought me a dozen roses and put two crisp hundred dollar bills in a graduation card. Lewis and Annie, Annette's other grandparents, came. They were always there to support me and believe in me. Annette was so proud. Her teachers had given her copies of the articles that had been on the front page of the *Norman Transcript*. She was so proud, showing the paper around to everybody. It was such a beautiful party. I could hear my mom talking to one of my aunts, telling her how I refused to give up, how I kept going to school. I didn't even realize that they'd noticed how hard I worked some days, but I could hear in her voice the pride and that she had, in fact, noticed.

While everyone was busy celebrating and the music was playing, and they were busy taking pictures, I reached for my purse and I snuck away, up to my room. When I reached into my purse, I grabbed my wallet. I pulled out my AFDC card, my Medicaid card, and my food stamp card; I looked at them. I was grateful because these things, in addition to the loving people who were there celebrating with me, had enabled me to get to where I wanted to be. But at this time I was so thankful that I would never have to use any one of these things again. It had been 7 1/2 years in the making for this dream to come true.

I reached in the bathroom drawer and pulled the lighter out that I used to light my candles with when I took a bath. I used the lighter to burn my AFDC card, my Medicaid card, and my food stamp card. I dropped the ashes into the toilet and flushed it. As I did so, I went back downstairs feeling so liberated, so free, so happy, so proud. All of my dreams were coming true. They all lay right there in front of me.

"Thank You. Thank You, Lord," I said. "Thank You."

****

As I share my story and encourage others and try to help them believe in themselves, it's so important to me for them to understand the power that lies within each of us if we are willing to believe, willing to dream, and never give up. It's not that I'm so great or that the things that happened to me were miraculous—even though I am a big believer in miracles. It's that I believed in my dream and never gave up. All of the negative people in my life may have not been negative to me intentionally; all of their frustrations may not have been with me necessarily. There are many positive people who helped me and who encouraged me, and to them I will always be grateful. But for all those negative people that each and every one of us encounters every day, if we continue to believe, if we continue to dream, their narrow mindedness or negative chatter will not matter. After completing my Master's degree in Engineering at the University of Oklahoma, I stayed on to complete my Doctorate degree in Engineering at, you guessed it, the University of Oklahoma. I applied the same "never say quit" attitude in earning both post-graduate degrees. As for those negative people who thought I couldn't do it? Well, it doesn't matter at all, because, today, they call me "Doctor."

Infinite Possibilities Publishing Group, Inc.
P.O. Box 150823
Altamonte Springs, FL 32715-0823
Office: (407) 699-6603
Fax: (407) 331-3926

ORDER FORM

For Office Use Only

ON#
OD
SD
AUTH#
BY:

Bill to:

Name _____

Business Name _____

Street Address (no P.O. Boxes) _____/_____ Apt./Suite

City _____ State _____ Zip

Daytime Phone _____

e-mail Address: _____

Ship to:

Name _____

Business Name _____

Street Address (no P.O. Boxes) _____/_____ Apt./Suite

City _____ State _____ Zip

Daytime Phone _____

Qty	Item#	Title/Description	Item Price	Total
	0-9729912-6-3	Winners Don't Quit... Today They Call Me Doctor! - The Book	16.99	
	09-1263-4	Winners Don't Quit Kit (Workbook, CD, Video + Bonus Resource List)	24.99	
	09-1263-5	Winners Don't Quit Combo (Book & Kit)	34.99	

PAYMENT METHOD:
☐ Visa® ☐ Master Card®
☐ American Express® ☐ Discover®

__/__/__/__/__/__/__/__/__/__/__/__/__/__/__/__/
Card Number

__/__
Exp. Date Signature *(required for credit card payment)*

☐ Check for total amount enclosed

Sub-total _____

Shipping & Handling* 4.95

Sales Tax: (FL Residents Apply 7%) _____

GRAND TOTAL _____

Fax Completed Form to: (407) 331-3926
or Mail Completed Form to: IP Publishing Group, Inc., P.O. Box 150823, Altamonte Springs, FL 32715-0823

NOTE
Returned checks subject to a service charge of $25 or the maximum allowed by law.
All non-Florida residents: you are responsible for the use tax (if applicable in the state in which the book is shipped)

*For orders of 3 or more, please call (407) 699-6603 for shipping costs.

Thank you for your order!